Irish Rebels in English Prisons

IRISH REBELS in ENGLISH PRISONS

O'Donovan Rossa

BRANDON

First published in 1991
by Brandon Book Publishers Ltd
Dingle, Co. Kerry, Ireland

Editing and arrangement © Thomas J. Cox 1991

British Library Cataloguing in Publication Data
O'Donovan Rossa, Jeremiah 1831–1915
Irish Rebels in English Prisons.
1. England. Prisoners, history
I. Title II. Cox, Thomas J.
365.450942

ISNB 0 86322 125 4

Cover design: John Brady
Printed by the Guernsey Press, C.I.

Author's Dedication

FRIENDS, TO YOU and to your memories I dedicate this book. Representing, as you do, the different parts of Ireland – or its exiled children – I hold you as the truest representatives of its people, their aspirations, and their aims. Scattered as you are over the world, sharing what seems to be the common heritage of our race, with some still in the enemy's bonds, and others in the embrace of the grave, I offer you this humble tribute of my esteem and remembrance.

Jeremiah O'Donovan Rossa

Down by the glenside I saw an old woman,
A-plucking young nettles, she ne'er heard me coming.
I listened a while to the song she was humming,
'Glory-o, glory-o, to the bold Fenian men!'

Some died by the glenside, some died 'mid the stranger;
And wise men have told us their cause was a failure.
But they dearly loved Ireland, and ne'er feared the danger.
'Glory-o, glory-o, to the bold Fenian men!'

Peadar O'Cearnaigh, *The Bold Fenian Men*

Contents

Editor's Preface

WHEN THE 1882 edition (updated from '72) of *Irish Rebels* was brought to my attention, I sensed a social, political and historical document of high importance; and a subsequent close reading of it confirmed that impression. The book itself, out of print, was in the public domain, and had already been used by later writers to win attention for the prison experiences of Rossa and his friends and followers. But none of these versions, to my mind, reflected the flavour of the original, and I felt that this quality was eminently worthy of reproduction, not only as a record of the events themselves, but also a revelation of the unique personality of Jeremiah O'Donovan Rossa.

Accordingly, I essayed the task of this edited and annotated rendition. Disciplines on that effort were the necessities of accommodating to current economics of book publishing and distribution; and the compression and editing of material that, again in my opinion, could be accomplished without sacrificing intrinsic values. I saw it as especially important that no material content should be excluded or misrepresented in any way, however well such exclusion or revision might serve the objectives of anyone other than the original writer. I have yet to see, for example, in any updating of the Rossa prison story significant treatment of the tensions that affected the relationship of Rossa and his spouse as a result of their long separation and sometimes emphatically dissimilar views about the necessity for his continuing to endure the ordeal he did endure. Yet, given the supression by the prison authorities of their correspondence over those years, it was highly understandable that moods of defeat, despair and disillusion would overtake Rossa's Mary Jane. Nevertheless, and allowing for the deeply felt differences they sometimes had, it is undeniable that Rossa continued to show his affection for her and his respect for the vows he made to her in marriage; and that her affection for him and for his children survived despite a rare ordeal of loneliness, poverty, and outrageous deprivation of some of the most elemental of human rights.

The original included considerable repetitious matter; and selections from his verses, for example, that were of lesser quality and poetic feeling than others. Editing judgments here were felt to be in order. But there have been no misrepresentations of his views, even if some of these were ones your editor felt were misconceived, or at least merited reconsideration. For the entire he accepts personal responsibility. Its ongoing importance must surely be held to be demonstrated by subsequent events. The treatment of political prisoners male and female in Northern Ireland in the '71-'81 period, culminating in the latter year in the deaths of ten hunger-strikers who resolved to die rather than continue to tolerate such inhumanity, is vivid proof of criminal violations by high authority of generally accepted human-rights conventions and commitments. Such violations, continuing to occur in Ireland both north and south, appear to be inseparable consequences of the exercise of imperial power by direct and proxy administrators. As long as they persist, so long must people of good will everywhere operate under an urgent necessity of seeing to it that they are commensurately publicized.

Acknowledgements

The editor wishes to acknowledge his debt for the support, ecouragement and inspiration of Mairead Farrell (the younger), Laurence McKeown, the Farrell and McKeown families, Fathers Des Wilson and Joe McVeigh, Sean and Michael Grealy, Seamus Leahy, Mary Ward, and his loving life-companion, Vita.

1. An Overview of Ireland

SOME HAVE THE gift of writing agreeably on disagreeable subjects, and it would take one of these to make an interesting and pleasant book out of a very unpleasant subject — prison life in England. I don't presume to think that prison life in England is worse than prison life anywhere else; indeed, the opinion appears to prevail that it is better. Englishmen labour very zealously to put themselves in a favourable light before the world, and if they cannot do so by showing any superior merit in themselves, they will attempt it by pointing out the demerit in others. They pry into nearly all the prisons of the world; opportunities are afforded them for learning how the inmates are treated, and I admit that they have done good in many cases by throwing light upon deeds of darkness. But all this time their own prisons are closed to every curious inquisitor; no foreigner can enter an English prison and ask a convict how he fares. It is here that we see the genius of this people in showing up the barbarity of other peoples and drawing a sanctimonious veil over its own.

As this book may have readers who know little of Ireland and how she was wronged, it may not be amiss to say something of the cause of my imprisonment. To those who know anything of her history, it is known that for seven hundred years Ireland was cursed with as cruel a government as ever cursed the earth. In the twelfth century the Normans succeeded in conquering England, and, coveting Ireland, laid their schemes to conquer that, too. They were intensely Catholic, but, in the pursuit of conquest, they never hesitated in any country to ravage convents and monasteries. In several cases they were religious enough to endow these institutions, and in doing so would further their ends by showing the Church that they were turning the plunder of their neighbours to a holy use.

The English interest was always able to persuade Rome that the Irish were bad Catholics who required 'reformation'. At present, when England is Protestant, it is able to do this, and to get bulls and rescripts denunciatory of my countrymen. Seven hundred years ago, an English king, making such a representation to the Pope of Rome, received from him authority to possess Ireland for the purpose of improving the morals of its people, and over these centuries the Irish people have been waging a fierce fight against the efforts England has made to 'improve' them off the face of the land. England always brought in the justification of religion to aid her in her conquest. At first professing Catholicism, she had her English priests in Ireland proclaiming that it was no sin to kill an Irishman, and one of them went so far as to declare before a council that he would celebrate Mass on a Sunday morning after killing one, without making an act of confession for the deed.

Then came the Reformation, and she commenced to persecute the Irish Catholics and root out the whole race because they would not become Protestant, for she thought that by becoming Protestant they might become less Irish or more English. For a time the terms 'Protestant' and 'English' were synonymous — as were the terms 'Irish' and 'Catholic'; and hence arose that curse of religious antagonism which, for three centuries, has blighted the prospects of our people for independence. The English interest was represented by Protestantism principally, and the interest of nationality by Catholicism — so much so that Catholic Irishmen came to feel that, in fighting against Protestantism they were fighting against England, and in fighting for Catholicism were fighting for Ireland. The priest was the person most sought after, most persecuted by the English, and the most loved, most looked to, and most protected, by the Irish. He became the guide and controller of their actions, and was ever faithful in defending, and leading the people to defend, the interests of the Church. The faith and spirit of liberty in the people were not crushed, and, in the growing enlightenment of the present century, England has

16

thought it expedient to change her policy. She now patronizes the Church, hugs to her bosom its dignitaries, and trusts that they — having influence over the people — will keep them from rebellion. Some of those dignitaries have laboured hard to do this in the movement for which I was imprisoned. It is in times of peace that the Church flourishes; and, in the interests of the Church, many will not blame the clergy.

Few will blame them, too, for opposing a rebellion where the necessary means of success would not be forecalculated. But where I could be at issue with them would be in the matter of their opposition to us when we were providing the means, and few will deny that we had that opposition in Ireland during the past thirteen years. There was no diocese where the men who were organizing means to fight England were not denounced from the altars and sent away from the confessionals unshriven. It must be said, of course, that there was no diocese in which there were not many priests to bless the labourers and wish God-speed to the work. But the tongues and hands of these clergymen were tied by the higher ecclesiastics, while the 'bad' priests (as we called them) were allowed full scope to denounce and brand us as infidels before we were in any way unfaithful.

In making these observations regarding the actions of Catholics toward the independence of Ireland I must not be understood as excluding the efforts of other religious adherents in that context. During the last century many Protestants and Presbyterians were sent to the scaffold and the convict ship for daring to maintain that they, as born Irishmen, should have an independent Ireland; and in the late revolutionary movement we had a blending of all the sects for liberty. This was as disagreeable to the bigots as to the English enemy. A union of creeds does not seem desirable to Church or State, and both united in assailing those who were bringing it about as 'traitorous and disreputable'. The State had some reason to attack them, but the Church had very little; for those who were banded together to fight for civil and religious liberty would be the first to stand in defence of their faith if any foe threatened their altars. The Catholic members of our organization, at the outset, often found themselves denounced by Catholic priests. They considered that in resolving to battle for the rights of their native land they had taken a noble resolution, and, in swearing to do as they did, did not feel, between themselves and their God, that they had committed a sin. But finding themselves condemned – damned even – for this act, afforded them food for reflection, and what wonder if some of them disregarded the denunciations, and laboured on?

I did. I saw that the time was gone when the priest and the people were as one persecuted. I saw that the priest was free and comparatively happy, while the people were enslaved, and decidedly miserable. The tradition that my boyhood had received of fighting for my religion in fighting for my country, and, in fighting for my country, fighting for my religion, was broken; for here, I had sworn to fight for Ireland, yet was set upon as an enemy of Catholicism. The politico-religious faith of my fathers was no longer acceptable to Church and State; and this reality was one that we in the movement could not ignore. I do not put my country before my God; but I put it before the religious ascendancy of any particular denomination. The Church has many defenders. Ireland has few, and I sometimes fear that they will not be able, unless aided more earnestly than they have been, to work out her salvation.

I do not write as a champion of religion, or as one who would assail it. I come before the public merely as an Irishman, wishing to see my country free for all religious denominations. If I speak of the interferences of religious people in its political concerns, it is not from choice, but from necessity. I hold it absolutely impossible for anyone to write truly of the movements of the people toward independence if he or she ignores the religious elements that are set in motion to sway the people to one side or the other. Religion and politics in Ireland are as yet inseparable. I should like to encounter the man who could give the history of the one without touching on the other.

As this professes to be an account of my prison life, I ought, probably, to have you, my readers, already inside the prison walls. But I don't think it improper to exchange views with you beforehand, so that you may understand the cause of my imprisonment, and judge whether or not I was deserving of it. If I was, I suppose I will have very little of your sympathy. But it is not for sympathy I write; and, as to my suffering, it may not be much more in prison than the sufferings of many who were out of prison. In order to achieve anything, men must be prepared for suffering; and, if they are not, they will lag behind. Men must be ready to brave all that they will learn from me, within and without prison, if they mean to free Ireland; and, if my words be of no use to the present generation, they may be to the next or the one after the next.

2. Ireland's Suffering:
The Revolutionary Society

I CANNOT OVEREMPHASIZE the importance of all that Ireland has suffered and all the sacrifices she has made to attain her liberty. I do not attribute the misfortune of our slavery to Providence; as little do I attribute the famine of '47 to that Power. We are bound down by England. She has the strength to rob us of the produce of our soil till we are reduced to a famine diet, and I should be thinking very ill of our people, and very ill of our Creator, if I attributed our state to anything other than a temporal tyranny.

Within the last century our country has striven gallantly in resistance to her oppressor, but we have not managed to successfully resist. In 1798 we had brave fighting; but many acted timidly while a few fought bravely. Had Wexford been successful, the timid would have come in with helping hands and with hurrahs, when neither were wanting; but they didn't, or wouldn't, come in the nick of time, and the Wexford men were overpowered. Had their action been imitated by the men of every other Irish county we would today have a different story to chronicle, and have no need to keep appealing to our people to act in concert and work unitedly.In 1848 there was another uprising, and another failure, in consequence principally of not having arms to put into the hands of the people who sprang forward to use them. It is noteworthy, in view of the enemy's efforts to perpetuate religious dissensions among us, that the men who were most prominent and suffered most in the cause of Irish independence during the periods I write of were Protestants; and it is no more than equal justice to the Catholic element of the community to state that it respected these men and reverenced their memories more than it

21

did men of their own creed. The names of Tone, Fitzgerald, Emmet, Davis, Mitchel and O'Brien will live as long in the future, and be as dear to Irishmen, as any others in their history.

After the English government had crushed the movement in '48, Ireland appeared spiritless and politically dead. Charles Gavan Duffy left the country in '54, saying he left the cause of Irish freedom 'a corpse on the dissecting table'. But, like seed put into the ground, it must only have been rotting in order to produce new life, for, a few years later, we find it in vigorous existence again, and the authorities putting forth all their strength to overcome it. My own experiences now commence.

In the month of May, 1858, a companion called at my home in Skibbereen and asked me to take a walk with him, as he had a matter of importance to communicate to me. We went out, and in the course of our ramble up the Steammill Road he informed me that on the preceding evening he had received a note of introduction from a stranger, given to him by a mutual friend in Bandon. The stranger told him that the Irish in America had resolved to aid us at home in achieving Ireland's independence, and the aid would consist of arms and of men. If we had a number of men sworn to fight, there would be an equal number of arms in Ireland for these men, and an invading support force of from five to ten thousand. The arms were to be in the country before the men would be asked to move; they would not be given into their hands, but would be kept in hiding places until the appointed time, when every 'centre' could take his men to the spot to get the weapons. As soon as we had enrolled the men willing to fight, we were to have military instructors to teach us how to do so as soldiers. I jumped at the proposition of joining and next day inculcated a few others whom I told to go and do likewise. The stranger who had come to town that May evening was Mr Stephens.

We had a society in Skibbereen at this time called The Phoenix National and Literary Society. It was a revolutionary one, though not oath-bound, and we were contemplating affiliations in connection with it in neighbouring towns. We named it 'Phoenix' to signify that the nation was to rise again from its ashes. We had about one hundred members, and before a month had elapsed over ninety of them had enrolled in the new movement.

In October a drillmaster was sent to us from Dublin. He had served in the American army, and well and dedicatedly did he work with us despite police watchings and huntings. One night we were on a mountainside; another, in the depths of a wood; another near a fairy fort, and another in a cellar. We had outposts on every occasion to signal to us of any menace. In Loriga Wood one evening our sentry gave us a signal to scatter, and we ran in a direction opposite to that from which we apprehended the danger. I was the second man. He who was before me climbed up on a bank and made a leap across the wide ditch beyond it, but he slipped and didn't get clear over. As he lay on the other side I leaped on him, the next man leaped on me, and in seconds nine or ten of us were sprawling in that ditch! In those drillings we departed from the programme of instruction, for we brought more men together than ought to have been known to each other, and this we had to do to keep them in good humour, for when it was known that the military instructor was in the district every company would be calling for his attention, and, as he couldn't be everywhere, we had to bring the men to where he was. The first man who learned the art from him, and became his assistant, and successor when he was gone, was Colonel P.J. Downing, now of Washington. It is said that people in America are fast, and the Irish there are not exempted from that expression; but in Ireland, when it was a question of uniting to fight against England, we were too fast for our brothers across the Atlantic, for we had our men ready to fight before they had provided us with the arms to do so.

The government became alarmed, and took measures to have a number of us arrested and thrown into prison. About four o'clock on the morning of 5 December I was aroused, to find my house surrounded by police. I was taken to the station, and there met some twenty others of my acquaintance. Many of them had left my house only hours before, for we were staying up doing honour to one of our company, Dan McCarthy, who was leaving town next morning to discharge the duties of miller in Ballinasloe.

Extra police had been sent from Dublin down to Skibbereen

two months before we were seized. These were on duty every night throughout the town, and though we were on duty, too, they never managed to surprise us. On the night of the arrests the police of surrounding villages had been drafted into the town. The authorities apprehended that we had arms and would resist, though actually we had very few weapons and didn't dream of fighting till we got orders. From Clonakilty to Bandon, each of us was hand-cuffed to two policemen. In the Bandon jail we met some men from Bantry, arrested on the same general charges facing us, and on their way to Cork Jail. At nine in the evening we were huddled into cells flooded with water. Having travelled all day under rain, and having received neither food nor drink, we now would get neither bread nor a bed. Next morning we found ourselves in Cork Jail, awaiting prosecution on charges of conspiracy.

3. A Dubious Prosecution

LODGED IN SEPARATE cells in Cork Jail, we got oakum to pick. We asked were we obliged to work before we were convicted, and were told we should work unless we paid for our maintenance. Some of the detained arranged to get their own food, but the rest of us thought we would inure ourselves to hardship. But we could not eat the fare we got; and this, with the solitary confinement imposed, starved us out of our resolution 'to suffer and be strong'. The bread was made with rye/wheat flour; it had the appearance of brown turf and you could squeeze the water out of it. The porridge, about the same colour, was flavoured with leeks, which made it disgusting, for when you drew your spoon out of the bowl you would draw up one of those foot-long leeks, and unless you had gone through a course of starvation your stomach would refuse to receive the product as food.

After two weeks in this prison we learned the rationale for our arrests. We were led into a room where four gentlemen awaited us. Two were stipendiary magistrates, and the other two (Sir Matthew Barrington and his assistant) were Crown prosecutors. We were told we were being charged with conspiracy, and that one of the conspirators, seeing the wickedness of our activities, and regretting his part in them, had come forward to give evidence. In a word, they had an informer against us. He was brought into the room, and most of us recognized him — Dan Sullivan Goula. He swore that he had seen me drilling three hundred men on a by-road within a mile of Skibbereen one night at ten o'clock, and on another night seen me drilling some twenty men in a room in town. But everything he swore to was false. He never saw me

25

drilling those men, nor did those drillings ever take place; but he saw me in the room with the twenty men, and he swore against every one of the twenty that they were present on the night of the three hundred. Everyone who could prove the falsehood was to be made a defendant; and he was instructed to swear this way by one of the stipendiaries, Fitzmaurice. This gentleman had developed a reputation as a shatterer of what are called 'Ribbon societies' in the north of Ireland, and for placing informers in them; and a few weeks before the arrests in Skibbereen he had been sent to that town on special duty.

We were represented by a clever solicitor, Mr McCarthy Downing, now the member of parliament for Cork; and it is but just to say that throughout those cases he did us invaluable service in defeating the government's attempts to suborn more witnesses against us. He demanded that the representatives of the press be allowed into the prison and be present during the court proceedings; but his demand was refused, while at the same time the slavish writers of the Anglo-Irish journals were obeying the behests of the Crown, and declaring that all manner of evidence was being brought to light concerning our 'horrible conspiracy'.

According to English law, the uncorroborated evidence of an informer was insufficient to detain men in prison, and the meanest manoeuvres were resorted to to get other evidence. The police had been watching us for months, and could adduce nothing illegal against us; but now they were told by this Fitzmaurice that if they did not find information to corroborate Goula's assertions they would lose their jobs. One young 'peeler' swore that he saw Denis Dowling marching through the Skibbereen streets 'in military order'; and when our solicitor, in cross-examination, asked him who was walking with the accused, he answered, 'No one'. Walking through the town with an independent tread was considered by this enforcer of the law to be something that would corroborate the version of the informer in what he swore about the drilling!

All the men arrested were released on bail except for five others and me. We were to remain in prison to await trial at the March assizes. The assizes came, and we were ready; but the government was not. They brought us into court on Patrick's Day, '59, and ordered then that we be sent back to prison again to await trial at the July assizes. Our counsel asked if we could not be admitted to bail, but was told that we could not. Back we went to prison, and remained there until July, and then they threatened us with another postponement until the following March unless we pleaded guilty to the charges made against us, in which event we would get our freedom. We had been refusing to do this since the first assizes, for we knew we could disprove the evidence of the informer. Our prosecutors knew this, too, and though they were eager to achieve our convictions they doubted their success before a public court, even with a packed jury. They had tried Daniel O'Sullivan Agreem with a packed jury in Tralee and sentenced him to ten years; and now, as a last resort, they offered to release Agreem if we would plead guilty; and to this we consented.

We were eight months in prison, and it would ill befit the image of the great nation that we had been subjected to imprisonment for so long, with the Habeas Corpus Act unsuspended, unless it could have been shown that we were criminals; therefore, it was necessary to get our consent to the 'guilty' plea. Possibly we were wrong in relieving the government of this odium; but we relieved ourselves from further imprisonment, and also relieved him who had been committed for ten years. We were to appear for judgment on this plea of 'guilty' if we were ever guilty of a repetition of the charges against us. (I want this to be remembered when I come to write of my trial before Judge Keogh in 1865.) We were released from prison in July, '59, but the authorities kept Agreem in jail till November, though his immediate release had been promised to us.

*   *   *   *   *

I LIVED IN the most southerly town in Ireland, and now, with the assurance given us of a struggle in the immediate future and the general belief that all Ireland was working toward its success, we resolved to work with all our energies to get recruits for the revolutionary army. He who did most in furthering the work throughout our district was a young man named Mortimer Moynahan. He was manager in the office of McCarthy Downing. This attorney used to attend the sessions in every town in the district; did the largest business of any lawyer in the circuit; and used to take Moynahan with him as his assistant. Every client had to approach the 'big man' through Mortimer, who marked out all who had any sort of Irish spirit in them, and swore them into the movement at night when his law business of that day had ended; so that he was working legally by day and illegally by night. When Attorney General Whiteside was prosecuting him a few months later, he, Whiteside, described him to the jury as 'one who was steeped to the lips in treason'.

Before we were six months at work we had the organization started in every corner of South Cork and in a part of Kerry. The man who swore me in was the first appointed 'centre' of a circle comprising 820 men. Then I became experienced enough to be appointed a centre. Then Moynahan and later two others for remoter districts still were appointed. Fenians in America may talk of the aid they have given to 'the men at home'. But I can tell them that the men at home spent out of their own pockets, in working up the organization, more money than the Fenian Brotherhood collected altogether.

The first reversal we encountered was from the Catholic clergy. Our men came to tell us that they had been turned away from the confessionals, and would not be given absolution unless they renounced our movement's membership oath. We asked them if they thought that they had committed a sin in taking an oath to fight for their country's freedom; and when they said they thought they had not, we told them to tell the priests that they had come to confess their sins and not their virtues, and to ask the priests whether, if they had sworn to fight for England against Ireland, would they not get absolution? The priests were getting vexed with us, and we were getting vexed with the priests. The most amusing stories were afloat of how simple country boys had argued with their clergy on the subject of fighting for Ireland. A pastor told his penitent one day that the movement organization was illegal, but the penitent softened his confessor's heart by exclaiming, 'Arra, Father, what do I care about their illegal? I care more about my soul.'

In July 1858 there was a Jubilee in our area. The young men were going to their duty, and the priests were sending them away without the sacraments. One day I found myself some twelve miles from home, and, meeting a priest who knew me, was asked: 'Jerry, did you do the Jubilee?'

'No, Father,' said I. 'No Jubilee for me. I'm beyond the pale of the Church.'

'How is that?' queried he.

I explained.

'Ah, that's no sin,' he observed. 'I'll be in Skibbereen Saturday, assisting the other priests. Come to me, and we'll have no difficulty.'

I did go to him, and he was as good as his word. The Skibbereen priests and the diocesan bishop were still opposing us, and I determined to have a talk with his lordship, whom the newspapers loved to style 'the patriotic Bishop of Ross'. I went to confession to him, and told my sins, after which he asked me if I belonged to an oath-bound society. I said I did.

'Then,' said he, 'I can't give you absolution.'

'My lord,' said I, 'I don't seek absolution for that. I was at confession since I joined the society, and got absolution; the priest told me that my membership was no sin.'

'It was a sin,' said he, 'and that priest participated in it. Go away; and don't come to me any more.'

I went away, but that day week went to him again. When I knelt in the confessional his first words were:

'Didn't I tell you not to come confessing to me?'

'My lord,' said I, 'it is not to you I come but to the confessional. I came to confess my sins to God, through you; you cannot refuse to hear me.'

'You should have more humility in the confessional,' he rebuked.

We got to 'the political question'. I remarked that Dr Doyle had said that if a rebellion raged from Malin Head to Cape Clear, no priest would utter a decree of excommunication against anyone engaged in it.

'I know more about Dr Doyle than you do,' said the bishop hastily. 'Go on with your confession.'

I did as he directed, and we parted amicably. He told me to come again to him in a week's time. But, before the week was out, I was in Cork Jail.

Some of the priests took occasion to denounce our work from their altars. I was at Mass one Sunday when the gospel of the day contained a recommendation 'to give to Caesar what is due to Caesar'. Father Beausang laid hold of it to show that we should give tribute to England; and denounced the 'wicked men' who, in his parish, were administering oaths for the purpose of getting work done in opposition to that text.

England's police system in Ireland is one vast spy system. More than half of the police are Catholics, and some of these have to attend every Mass in their chapels on Sundays. The priest speaks to his parishioners of a secret, oath-bound society; the policeman goes back to his barracks, and his first duty is to make a report of what the priest said and send it off to Dublin Castle. I may confidently record that it was through this channel the authorities had any certainty of the spread of our revolutionary work. Then, the newspapers took up the cry; and by virtue of their giving what information they could glean, some priests were evidently giving private information to the Castle.

I have evidence to convince anyone that one priest gave such information, and will give that evidence. I know that this priest was not condemned by his bishop for writing as he did; but that will not be wondered at when it is known that his lordship is the charitable Kerry personality who said that 'hell was not hot enough nor eternity long enough for those Irishmen' who were giving so much trouble to England.

Father O'Sullivan of Kenmare does not deny this correspondence: indeed, I believe he justifies it. I saw communications between him and Mr O'Sullivan, the editor of the *Dublin Nation*, on the subject of giving information. The priest, I think, was first to do so in private, but the paper was first in public. Both satisfied themselves, no doubt, that they were doing what was most appropriate, but I blame the layman more than the priest, for something more was expected from him. He professed himself a fighting man for Ireland if there were fighting means. We were trying to organize such means, and thought that he should not be the first to undertake to expose us. He considered the movement would destroy or involve Ireland more than it would redeem it; and he must have liberty of opinion.

Here is some of Fr O'Sullivan's correspondence with the Right Honourable Lord Naas MP:

Kenmare, 5 October 1858

My Lord,

Having discovered that an extensive conspiracy imported from Bantry and Skibbereen was being organized in this parish, I deemed it my duty at both Masses on Sunday to denounce in the strongest language the wickedness and immorality of such an activity, and its consequences to society. Before evening I had the satisfaction of coming at a good deal of the workings of the affair, and even got copies of the organization oaths (which I send to you on the opposite side) for the information of the government.

I was led to believe that seven to eight hundred persons had been enrolled here, and some 3,000 in Skibbereen. The first I know to be a gross exaggeration, and I suppose the latter is equally so. Before I come out on these deluded young men (the names of some of whom I have), I advised the magistrates of the facts, and they, too, have probably advised your lordship.

I have the honour to be.
John O'Sullivan

A second, by the same writer to the same addressee, follows:

Kenmare, 11 December 1858

My Lord,

Since I forwarded to you copies of the oaths that were being administered by the misguided young men (some ten or a dozen of whom were arrested here yesterday), I beg to assure you I lost no opportunity of denouncing both in public and in private the folly and wickedness of their proceedings. Nay, more: I refused to hear the confession of, or to admit to communion, any person who had joined the society, until he should come to me 'extra tribunal' as we term it; and there, not only promise to disconnect himself from the society, but also give the name of every person he knew to be a member. It was difficult to accomplish the latter but I did; and having thus come at the names of the deluded young men, I, either with their parents or with themselves, showed them the insanity of the course they had been following. Almost every one of those now under arrest had made his Christmas confession and communion; and though this may be no legal evidence of their being presently innocent, to anyone acquainted with the practice and discipline of our Church it is *prima facie* evidence of their having solemnly pledged to disconnect from the denounced society.

I assure your lordship that since the 3rd of October (the Sunday on which I first denounced this society) not a single person has joined it. And, had the thing taken root or progressed, I would have been as ready to advise you of its progress as I was of its existence. So completely lifeless has it been that more than once I considered writing to you to remove the extra police force, viewing it as unnecessary.

Under such circumstances I make bold to ask your lordship to intercede with his Excellency for the liberation of these foolish boys. They have had a proper fright, and I make no doubt that an act of well-timed clemency will have more effect in rendering them dutiful subjects hereafter than would the measure of justice they certainly deserve.

If they be treated with kindness they will be grateful; and doubly so if the thing be done at once and in a friendly and fatherly spirit. But carry out the law, and you will of course vindicate it, but certainly will have confirmed a set of young rebels in their hostility to Her Majesty's government.

And a follow-up to Lord Naas:

Kenmare, 26 December 1858

My Lord,

Now that an investigation has been had as to the nature
and extent of 'The Phoenix Society', I venture to call your
attention to a letter I took the liberty of writing to you this day
fortnight. I have just read the evidence of informant Sullivan
in the *Cork Examiner*, wherein he states 'he had been to confession with me, and that I advised him to break the oaths'.
The man never confessed to me. I never exchanged a word
with him. He is not a parishioner of mine at all! If all his evidence be as true as this much, it is of little value.

Looking, therefore, at the unsupported evidence of this
fellow, at the youth of the lads led astray by him, and above
all, at the fact of the society having been completely extinguished since I first denounced it on the 3rd of October, I
venture again to ask your lordship to intercede with his
Excellency for a free pardon for these foolish parishioners of
mine. It will be the most effective extinguisher he can possibly
put on it.

If you call them for trial, a large subscription will be promoted to defend them; for their youth, with the innumerable
perjuries of the informant, has created much sympathy for
them, and great excitement will prevail here until the assizes.
If they be acquitted, a regular ovation will be the consequence, while a conviction cannot entail a very heavy sentence
on such striplings. If his Excellency will graciously grant them
a free pardon, he will attach them faithful and beholden to
Her Majesty, and we shall hear no more of this absurd and
wicked society. I am sure also you must already know that it
was my active interference suppressed the society so immediately here; and though I incurred much odium in the affair,
all parties now admit that I was their best friend. This, I
think, entitles my view to some consideration. Be assured if I
had the slightest reason to think that a prosecution would
tend more to the preservation of the peace and dignity of the
constitution than what I now ask, I would be the foremost in

recommending it. I therefore ask a free pardon for all my deluded parishioners because, if the thing be done, it ought to be done in a free and generous spirit, making no distinctions or exceptions. For, without pronouncing on the guilt or innocence of any of the parties, I am convinced not one of them has had the slightest connection with the society from the day I first denounced it.

The information and the oaths that the priest sent to Dublin Castle were obtained under the following circumstances: A young man went to confession to the Rev. O'Sullivan, and the priest, ascertaining that his penitent belonged to the society, asked him out into the chapel yard, where he questioned him again, and extracted from him a copy of the society's oath. This (to use the priest's words) was getting the information 'extra tribunal'; but I doubt that there are many priests or laymen who will approve of the use made of what was so obtained.

When the Castle authorities got the first information in October they set to work to get an informer, and got one in Kenmare. They sent him to Skibbereen to make the acquaintance of men there, and to swear against them. We, in Skibbereen, knew he was coming, and the friends in Kerry told us to be wary of him, that he was a suspect individual gotten into the society by one who did not know him well. The informer went once to a fair in Bantry, some twenty miles from his home. He was sworn in there, much to the annoyance of his neighbours, who never would have trusted him, but, now that he was in, had to make the best of it. When he came to Skibbereen, some of our young men paid him a visit in order to be able to form an opinion as to his honesty or perfidy, and he swore informations against every one to whom he was introduced. But everything he swore was false, and his employers knew it. They did not care how they got us to prison, just so they had us there. They worked hard to get criminatory evidence against us, and failed; hence our release without a trial after eight months.

The Soldier o' Fortune

Friends of the Irish people — you
  Who'd right your country's wrong —
Should hear from me a word or two;
  My tale will not be long.
In old Iov Laoghaire by the hills
  My youthful days passed by.
That Famine then, that filled the cills;
  I saw my father die.
The bailiff with his notice came,
  The bit of ground was gone;
We saw the rooftree in a flame,
  The crowbar work was done.
With neither house, nor bed, nor bread,
  The workhouse was my doom;
And on my jacket soon I read,
  'The Union of Macroom'.
My mother died o' broken heart;
  My uncle from the town
Came for her with a horse-and-cart,
  And buried her in Gleann.
I joined the redcoats then — *mo léir*,
  What would my father say?
And off was sent before a year
  On service to Bombay.
I thought to be a pauper
  Was the greatest human curse;
But fighting in a robber's cause,
  I learned, was something worse.
I helped to murder and to slay
  Whole tribes of India's sons;
Spent many a sultry, evil day
  Blowing Sepoys from our guns.
I told these things to Father Ned —
  The murder and the booty.
'They were no sins of yours,' he said,

'You had to do your duty.'
Then, when that duty there was done,
 A journey home I made;
And, all my friends being dead and gone,
 I joined the Pope's Brigade.
I got some medals on my breast
 For serving that campaign;
And next was found in Connacht's West
 A-soldiering again.
With fearless Captain Billy O'
 I joined the Fenian band,
And swore to strike one day a blow
 To free my native land.
Back in that sinking isle again
 Where landlords drain our blood,
Where friends are scattered, starved and slain,
 I'm told I'm cursed by God.
If I can swear my livelong days
 To fight from pole to pole,
For any power, however base,
 With safety to my soul,
It cannot be by God's decree
 I'm cursed, denounced and banned
Because I swore one day to free
 Am I lost, am I left, in the world alone?
I can't rest, can't eat, can't sleep, can't pray;
 Can do nothing but drink; and I wouldn't much grieve
If death would just come in a natural way,
 But God in His wisdom ordains that I live.
I'm like a wreck on a sea-washed rock
 That every wave heaves to and fro;
I'm like a lightning-riven oak
 With its source of life all charred below.
All mankind should pity, and come to my aid,
 For the race would die if some hadn't spirit
To marry before they had fortunes made,
 And trust to having an heir to inherit.

Will anything alter the state of my mind?
 I find myself tempted to go on a spree,
Or, continue my verses; am strong inclined
 To appeal through the press for sympathy.
My trampled native land.

Printed in *The Irish People*, 1863.

4. Promoting the Cause; Romance, and a Marriage

WHILE I WAS in prison, landlordism played some pranks with my family. The ownership of my residence and place of business was disputed by two parties. The man from whom I had rented the house lost the lawsuit, and the other, getting a court order to take immediate possession, ejected my family. When I was released I found the old home gone and my dear ones relocated. My business had been critically injured, and so I set to work to put the wheels in motion again, but it was a difficult job to bring as much water to my mill as it had had before. Hitherto, landlords and rich people had traded with me; now, the poor and peasantry alone stuck with me. It is said that the lower you descend into the bowels of the earth the hotter you will find it; also, that the lower you go among an oppressed people the warmer you will find them, and the truer and readier they will be to make sacrifices for freedom, friend or fatherland.

I believe this. I know the Irish people now (at least in Ireland, for it is not as easy to know them in America), and would trust my life in anything for Ireland to the poorest of them sooner than I would to the richest. I travelled England, Ireland and Scotland in connection with the revolutionary movement, met the poorest of our people in small villages and in large cities, and whispered 'treason' and 'rebellion' to them night after night for years. I was three months awaiting trial in Dublin prisons; any amount of money would have been given to any one who would come forward to swear that I was seen in such a place on such an occasion; and though I could count by thousands the humble people I had met, not one of them was persuaded to take the

English bribe. I would not want to run the same gauntlet among the rich.

I recommenced my pursuits, political and commercial, shortly after my release, and found success to be much more difficult in the legal than in the illegal one. To transact political business I could meet the people anywhere, but to address commercial matters, customers had to come to my house, which many were afraid to do for a time, fearing that their landlords would be down on them for having associations with such a 'desperate character', for, of course, the stock-in-trade lies were told — we were going to massacre landlords and overturn altars. Some of the men of the cloth did their parts in this campaign. The 'patriotic' Bishop O'Hea challenged a man and his wife in the confessional for frequenting my house. The man told me that he was challenged, and that his wife had told him that she was challenged. Possibly it is a crime to teach the people to be independent of priests in politics. This I did do, and will do, as long as the priests oppose the organization of means to free Ireland of English rule. And I believe that no organization will do it that will not be oath-bound and secret, and ready to avail of any means necessary to accomplish the objective.

One branch of my business was the spirit trade. Licenses for this were renewed each year, and at each renewal the police came forward to have mine denied. They put me to trouble, expense and annoyance. I always appealed to a superior court and, as no charge of keeping an irregular house could be sustained against me, I came away with my licenses.

I owned an Enfield rifle, a bayonet, a sword, and an old 'croppy' pike with a hook-and-hatchet on it, formidable enough to frighten any coward, and these I hung up in a conspicuous part of my store. Yet this would not satisfy some that I could keep these articles, and I had many a wise head giving me advice. For all that, the arms remained in place, and on fair and market days it was amusing to see young peasants bring in their companions to view them. 'Look!...look!' would be the first exclamations on entry into my shop; and never did artist survey a work of art more absorbedly than some of those boys, leaning their elbows on the counter, would admire the weapons they longed to use one day in defence of their motherland's cause.

My pikes, it seemed, were doing great mischief in the community. And rumours were going around that others were getting pikes, too. Tim Duggan was employed in my shop. Tim would always be at some mischief, and, taking down the pikes one day to take some of the rust off them, no place would satisfy him to sit burnishing them but outside the store door. Next day I was sent for by my friend McCarthy Downing, who was chairman of the town commissioners and town magistrate. He told me that the magistrates had had a meeting, and had talked lengthily about what had occurred the day before. A very diligent sergeant of police named Brosnahan represented that not only was Duggan cleaning the pikes, but was showing the people how they could be used — what useful things they were to frighten landlords and other aides of tyranny. Mr Downing asked me whether I would surrender the arms, and I said I would not. He said that the magistrates were about to make a report to Dublin Castle on the matter. I said I did not care what reports they made; the law allowed me to hold such things, and hold them I would until the district was 'proclaimed'.

'For peace sake,' said he, 'I ask you as a personal favour to give them to me. I will keep them for you in my own house; and pledge that when you want them I will give them to you.'

'Well,' said I, 'as you make so serious a matter of it you can have them.'

I went home, put my pike on my shoulder, and gave another to 'Croppy' McCarthy. It was a market day, and both of us walked through the town, showing the people we could carry arms, making our act of surrender as prideful as possible to our cause, and as disagreeable as it could be to the English stipendiaries.

*　*　*　*　*

IN THE SPRING of 1863 the Poles were struggling against their tyranny, and we conceived the idea of having a sympathy meeting for them in Skibbereen. We prepared torchlights and republican banners, and issued secret orders to have some of our best comrades in from the country. The authorities became alarmed and assigned a large force of police to duty in the town on the appointed night. During the daytime the peelers were pouring in, and, as they passed over our several roads, the peasantry crowded after them. The rumour went around that we were to be slaughtered, and country folk came in to see what would chance. The town was full of peelers and peasants, and – to have another stroke at the 'big fellows' – we got handbills struck off, calling on the people not to be offensive to any of the police, that they were Irishmen like ourselves, and only obliged from circumstances to appear to be our enemies. We posted these bills, and employed boys to put them into the hands of the police. There were six magistrates in the town, and Stipendiary O'Connell, a member of 'the Liberator's' family, was in command of the police. They thought to intimidate us from carrying out our programme, and we felt bound to maintain the confidence of our people by proceeding according to our announcement. They saw in our meeting of sympathy for the Poles a meeting of organized hostility against England; they knew that bringing the masses together and allowing them to realize their strength and union would create confidence; and that is what they wanted to kill.

Our officers, by arrangement, moved from the committee rooms. The committee men, armed with wands, marched in front toward the place where the people were forming in procession with torches in their hands.

The wives of the police, and the police themselves, had been sent to the mothers of some of the young men on the committee to tell them that the police had orders to fire on us; and the mothers, on their knees, implored us to abandon our effort. We paid them no heed, but, as we proceeded to move ahead, the magistrates confronted us, with the police behind them, and stopped our march. The Castle agent, O'Connell, addressing himself to Brosnahan, asked:'Who are the leaders of this tumult?'

The police sergeant answered: 'Here they are, sir – Dan McCarthy, Mortimer Moynahan, Jerry Crowley, Con Callaghan, O'Donovan Rossa, James O'Keefe.'

The exchange now continued thus:

O'Connell: 'I order this assembly to disperse.'

Our committee: 'Why?'

O'Connell: 'It is disturbing the peace.'

The committee: 'It is you who are disturbing the peace. We citizens are met here to demonstrate our sympathy for a people struggling against tyranny. Do you say we have no right to do so, or that we must not walk the streets?'

O'Connell: 'You are meeting in an illegal manner. I shall read the Riot Act; and if you do not disperse you will have to take the consequences.'

And he read the Act, after which we asked, 'What do you see illegal in our procession?'

'That red flag,' he said, pointing to a triangular banner.

The committee ordered the flag taken down, and then asked: 'Anything else illegal?'

'Those transparencies with the mottos.'

The transparencies were put away. We asked if there was anything further.

'Those torchlights.'

'Put out the torchlights.' Again we asked: 'Anything else?'

'You had better disperse,' answered O'Connell.

'Do you come here with your authority and armed force to tell us that we must not walk through the Skibbereen streets?'

'I do not,' O'Connell admitted.

The committee ordered the band to play "Garryowen' and to march on. The boys did so; the magistrates moved aside; the police behind them opened way; the procession marched twice through the streets, and the demonstration ended with the reading of an address.

After those occurrences, Stipendiary O'Connell and Potter, the Inspector of Police, told me that if I did not cease to disturb the community I would be called up for sentencing pursuant to the conditions of my earlier plea of guilty. I told them they should first prove me guilty of the practices of drilling and of other things sworn against me at my trial; and that while in their eyes I was acting unlawfully, I did not care about their threats.

Shortly thereafter I received an invitation from James Stephens to come to Dublin to act as manager of *The Irish People* newspaper, which was about to be started. I accepted the position, and we were not a month at work when we experienced a most active opposition (to the sale of the paper) from some of the priests. As its business manager I can safely say that there was not a county in Ireland in which we had not some clergyman denouncing our activities. I travelled the whole country from that little lake near Fair Head in the north, to that deep pool that sleeps in the bosom of the mountains near Loughine in the south; from the Hill of Howth in the east to Croagh Patrick in the west; and north, south, east and west there were ones to assail us as being enemies of our race and name. It was as Michael Doheny said when he was hunted:

Thy faith was tried, alas! And those
  Who perilled all for thee
Were cursed and branded as thy foes,
  A *cushla geal mo croí*.

Our agents were bullied, and when bullying did not work, were threatened with hell and damnation. Where both failed, the man's trade was threatened. I know one district in Waterford where a priest was in league with the magistrates to refuse spirit licenses to publicans who sold *The Irish People*. And the centre for Kilkenny told me that the penance enjoined in confession on some of his acquaintance was that they should not read *The Irish People*.

Possibly some of these people ought not to be blamed for denouncing our paper if they believed the things they said of us. A priest of Ballycastle, a little town on the north coast near Rathlin Island, preaching to his congregation one day in 1864, said, while denouncing our paper and our society, that the opinions some of us had on marriage were that if a man did not like his wife he could put her away and take another, and put the second away and take a third; and that one of us had carried out his impulse so vigorously in the matter that he was at that time taking a trial of his ninth wife!

Many stories came to my ear in Dublin about the efforts some priests were making to arrest the progress of our work. Some of these might be thought unworthy of credence, and I myself pitched upon one which I concluded was a little exaggerated, and that was that certain priests refused to marry men who were connected with the revolutionary movement, unless they gave it up.

I don't know whether a desire to test the truth of this had any-thing to do with getting into my head, about this time, the idea of marrying, but the idea got there. And as it was associated in my mind with the image of a pretty poetess, I could not put it, or her, out of my head. Indeed, to be candid, I did not try to do so, but cultivated her acquaintance up to securing her consent to marry me. She lived in the south of Ireland, and I in Dublin. I needed to take with me a license from the priest of my parish. The Reverend O'Hanlon lived near *The Irish People* offices. I went to see him, and took George Hopper with me. He introduced my business to the clergyman, and the latter, after satisfying himself that I was marriageable, proceeded to write up my license. After a few words, he stopped, and said, 'I must make this "informal".'

'How is that, Father?' I asked.

'Why,' said he, 'you haven't been to confession.'

'But I am ready to go to confession to you.'

'Oh, I could not hear your confession, now that I know you.'

'You couldn't hear a confession of my sins?'

'I could. But as I now know you belong to *The Irish People* I should ask you certain questions, which you should answer, and which would make it impossible for me to give you absolution.'

'And does belonging to *The Irish People* put a man outside the sacraments?'

'Mr O'Donovan — no use our arguing. My hands are tied by instructions from Archbishop Cullen.'

'Well, Father,' said I, 'you had better make out a license as best you can. You can state that I offered to go to confession to you; and that you couldn't hear me.'

'Very well,' said he. And taking the document from him when he had done, I shook hands with him, and bade him goodbye.

1I took the train for the south of Ireland, and began to reflect that I was going into the diocese of the Bishop of Ross, and into the parish of Father Leader, both of whom knew me well, and both of

45

whom, I knew from previous experience, would place every possible obstacle in the way of my making myself happy. I thought I
had better stop in Cork and try to make the matter all right there
before I got to Clonakilty. I did stop, and strolled into a chapel
near the Northgate Bridge. No priest was there, but I learned that
by going up to a convent at the back of the chapel I'd find one. I
went up and was introduced to a Dominican Father. Dressed in
his white robe, he sat down, and I knelt at his feet. I ended,
perhaps not in the proper spirit, saying, 'That is all, Father.'

He immediately asked, 'Do you belong to a secret society?'

'No.'

'Do you belong to any society in which you took an oath?'

'I do.'

'What is the object of it?'

'To free Ireland from English rule.'

'You must give it up.'

'I must not.'

This went on for ten or fifteen minutes. I got up from my knees,
and asked him if he would give me a certificate stating that I had
been to confession to him, but that he could not give me absolution. After much urging he gave me the certificate, and I left the
chapel thinking that I would leave myself and my sins to the mercy
of God in the future, and it would be a long time before I again
would trouble such priests.

I went to Clonakilty and met the little poetess. Her father very
reluctantly consented to our marriage. The lady and I had made
the match without the foreknowledge of her parents; when they
heard of it they decided it was an unwise undertaking. By their
advice she wrote to me, saying the matter was at an end and I
should not write to her any more. But I threatened her with a
breach of promise suit; and that, or the feared visitation of my
ghost, in the event of my dying of a broken heart, frightened her
into again changing her mind.

I warned Mr Irwin of the difficulties that might be put in our
way by Father Leader. He went to the priest, paid him the marriage
fee, but, in view of my advice, did not at first tell him who his
daughter's intended husband was. However, when he called a

second time for the permit to get us married; the curate, on learning that I was the happy man, asked him to go back and bring him my license. It was brought to him, and he immediately pronounced it 'informal' and said I should be sent to the bishop, who lived some twenty miles away. I told my intended father-in-law I had to leave for England the next day, and that unless I could get married without delay I would have to leave Clonakilty without doing so; and simply asked him to get back the marriage fee from the priest, and to bring himself and his daughter to Cork for the ceremony. The priest told him to bring both of us up to him. I told the Irwins that unless they were firm in telling the priest that they would adopt the above course (in view of my need to leave for England the next day), we would not get the better of Father Leader, and both agreed to be firm in the matter.

When we approached the priest he questioned me as to my license and my residence in Dublin and in Skibbereen. He said I had lived all my life in Skibbereen; my family was there now; it was from that parish I should have my license; the one I had was 'informal' and invalid. I should go to the bishop, for, as things stood, it was entirely out of his power to marry me. To this I said that I had lived in Dublin for the most recent eighteen months; it was my recognized residence and if the license was 'informal' it was no fault of mine as I had made every effort to harmonize things with the requirements of the Church. I added that I had no time to go to see the bishop since I was leaving for England the next day; and if he could not marry me I would have to go to Cork to get married.

'What! Do you think Miss Irwin would give such scandal in this parish as to leave it with a strange man without getting married?'

'I am not a strange man in this country. I want no scandal: I want to get married. And if you put difficulties in the way, I hope Miss Irwin will help me to overcome them.'

Said Mr Irwin to the priest, 'If you don't marry Mary Jane, Father, I believe she will go to Cork to get married. I have given my consent to the marriage, and if you will not marry them, I shall allow her to go.'

'That decision rests with Miss Irwin herself,' said Fr Leader.

'And now, Miss Irwin, I ask you — you who have received a convent education — will you cast such a reflection on those holy nuns who instructed you? Will you give such scandal to the girls of this parish as to leave it with a strange man without being married to him?'

Said Miss Irwin: 'I would.'

Whereupon Father Leader, addressing himself to me, said, 'Whatever your hostility to our poor Mother Church that has protected and promises to protect us through all ages; whatever you may do to create disrespect for the ministers of our holy religion, and to corrupt society, do leave us one thing, — the virtue of our women.'

By Jove, didn't I feel this to be hard? But the man who said it was a priest, and there was no strength in my arm. He is dead, and God be good to him. But my wife and her father are alive to bear witness to the truth of what I say. In the event, we got an order to the curate of the parish to marry us, and, 'if we don't live happy, that you may'.

5. The Irish People Seized

ON THE EVENING of 15 September, 1865, as I was talking to some friends at 82 Dame Street, Dublin, Patrick Kearney rushed in and said that *The Irish People* had been seized. He had fight in his eye, and I saw that the most welcome words to him would be instructions to resist the police. But, with very few arms, I knew we could not fight that night; and I told Kearney, who had a number of men at his command, that there was nothing for it but to keep quiet, and that I would go up to the office. I was expecting the swoop to be made, and, taking precautions to have no papers about me, searched my pockets and gave a few business receipts and a small pistol to Mike Moynahan. I lived across the street, and when I left my residence had left my wife there packing. I was under orders from Mr Stephens to go to America, and was taking her to the south of Ireland next morning. I had always given her instructions to destroy any papers connected with the organization that she might find about the house, but there was one document I had told her to preserve, and this she had sewed into the leather lining of her handbag. The thought struck me that it would be better to destroy that, too. I told the boys with me that I would run over to speak to my wife and then go to *The Irish People* office. But as I was crossing the street two detectives pounced on me.

One of them stuck his hand into the side-pocket of my coat but pulled out nothing; the other searched another pocket; and they then conducted me through the Lower Castle Yard to Chancery Lane Police Station. I was the first in. They took me to the searcher, turned my pockets inside out, and found nothing but my money, which they returned to me. By and by, others were brought in, and by twelve o'clock we were a company of about twenty, among whom was Captain Murphy, who kept up our spirits by proclaiming himself 'a citizen of Boston' and protesting against his 'illegal' arrest. George Hopper, John O'Clohissy, I and a fourth party were huddled into a privy and kept there till twelve o'clock the next day. The compartment was about seven feet square – a receiving-cell for a drunken man or woman. The lid was broken off the closet; we had no bed, no room to stretch in or to walk about, so that our first night's imprisonment was not very encouraging.

When my captors had secured me they made for my residence, and turned everything upside down in search of papers. They seized a lot of old Irish manuscripts belonging to Nicholas O'Kearney, a Gaelic scholar lately deceased. These they took away, and I've never seen them since. I had a revolver, and they took it away, too, though at the time it was perfectly legitimate property. James O'Callaghan was in the house when the detectives arrived. He had come to tell my wife that I had been arrested. He asked her whether there were any dangerous papers around and she said no, except for one that she had in a safe place. He told her that however safe the place was, it was safer to put it in the fire, so she ripped open the handbag and burned the treasure. It was a letter from James Stephens.

I had had many letters from him over the four or five most recent years; but this was the only one that had given me a disturbing thought and made me fear I might lose his friendship. Someone might ask why I should fear to lose the friendship of such a man, and I say for the simple reason that I liked him, believed he was going the right way to free Ireland, and saw him working in that direction through all kinds of difficulties and under circumstances that would paralyze the spirit of an ordinary man. I worked with him, or under him if people will have it so. I believe I have since been regarded by some of my friends as being too friendly to him, and, particularly since his failure, this prejudice follows me. I am told by friends that I had a religious belief in him, and did everything he wished to have done. It is true I was obedient, but this never degenerated into subserviency. I did do everything I was told, but Stephens never told me to do anything that my heart was not in and that my own judgment did not tell me was promotive of Irish independence. I did many things without his instructions; but, with them or without them, was not ashamed of anything I did in connection with the revolutionary movement.

The nature of the document my wife had hidden was this. In the first week of September the races of Ballybar were to come off near Carlow. The men in the organization availed of gatherings of this kind to meet and discuss questions affecting their interests. At previous races I had been with Stephens himself at Ballybar, and now the Carlow men wrote to Dublin asking that someone be sent down there, and that Rossa was the person they wished to meet. On this occasion I planned to ask to be relieved if delegated to go, for I had attended the Navan and Trim races, was tired of running around, and my wife was beginning to look even blacker than she does look at my being out nearly every night. I received a letter in *The Irish People* office; and, it being my duty to forward it to 'the Boss', I did so. That same evening I got a note asking me why those Carlow men were attempting to dictate to him the proper party to be sent down. They should be taught that they could not do that; it was for him to determine the appropriate party to meet them. I could not go. He bade me write them to tell them so, and told me to be ready to start for America the following Friday.

If he had learned that I had written the Carlow men asking them to write for me, he might have been justified in sending me such a letter. I had been to America in July; was asked to go again in August; but, by permission, had delegated the duty to another. I was a newly married man, and wished to show my wife I had something to me besides those rambling propensities that the exigencies created, and to which, from memories of those times, she still imagines I am too strongly inclined. In deference to my own wishes and hers I did not go in August, but now I saw that there was nothing I could do but follow orders. I took the letter to her, and told her that she could see that my sphere of usefulness was closed in Ireland. My easily earned popularity was getting me into difficulties. I fancied Mr Stephens showed signs of a little jealousy,

51

and, having something perhaps of woman's nature in me, felt hurt at seeing this emotion aroused in my partner, for whom I had not a disloyal thought.

About noon of the day after our arrests we were taken out of our 'privy', were locked into one of the black vans, and were conducted to a police station. Vast numbers of people were in the streets, and the detectives in the crowd that surrounded the van found many whom they suspected of some connection with us, and arrested them. About thirty of us were in custody, and I saw around me the proprietor, the editor and sub-editors, and printers, porters and reporters of The Irish People. The authorities had broken into the premises, had seized all papers and materials, had carted them off to the Castle; and had taken possession of the establishment and left police in charge of it. The police tore up the boards, arrested every man who came to inquire after anything about the concern, and refused our wives admittance. They seized Mr O'Leary's bank book, laid an embargo on our account, and refused to allow him to draw on it until his counsel made a motion in court for its release.

Prosecutor Barry appeared in court, and, addressing the stipendiary magistrate, charged the prisoners in the dock with conspiracy, made remarks about our fell designs against Church and State and priests and landlords, and wound up by saying that the ends of justice demanded that, without disclosing their evidence against us, we be held for a week, as other parties were implicated also who were not then in custody. The evidence was so voluminous it would require time to marshal it. The magistrate granted his request.

The prosecutor left the court. We were detained in the dock for about an hour, and here something occurred that set me thinking about Nagle, who was also a prisoner. Detectives were all around us – I knew some of them – and asked them if they would not allow my wife in. I was told it couldn't be done. I heard Nagle make a similar request, and the detectives went out and brought in Mrs Nagle, who remained talking over the railings to her husband for some minutes. A bad thought came into my head, not about the woman but the man; but I banished it promptly, and set the favour down to the detective's personal friendship for him.

Into the black van again, amid huzzas of the crowd, and up toward Richmond Prison. The big gates opened, and the cars rumbled over the cobbles. We were taken out, and found ourselves inside and locked in. We were taken into a large hall, registered as inmates, and all went smoothly until we came to the 'religious' part of the business. Mr O'Leary, Mr Luby and I were there together. I was asked what my religion was, and I told them I was an Irish Catholic. They had no such denomination on their books, so I must register as a Roman Catholic. I was Irish, not Roman, but this would not do: the printed heading 'Roman Catholic' was on the register, and I should sign my name under that. I offered to go to the chapel, but they would not let me go to church or chapel unless I signed the register, and this I refused to do. Mr O'Leary took a similar stance and, I think, so did Mr Luby. We were left in our cells while the others were at prayers, and then it was industriously circulated to our prejudice that we refused to be of any religion, which consequently gave plausibility to slanders that were being uttered against us and will ever be uttered against every people who dare to oppose an established tyranny.

They stripped me naked, took my clothes, and turned their pockets inside out. An inventory of my possessions was taken. My pocketbook, pencil and knife would not be returned to me. I was shown into a flagged cell, seven feet by six, which contained no furniture but a stool, and a board attached to one of the walls to serve me as a table. I was told I would be allowed to pay for my board, but if I did not pay I should work. Mr O'Leary occupied the cell next to mine. The jailer communicated between us and we agreed to pay for our subsistence. No wine, porter, or spirituous liquor of any kind would be allowed us; nor tobacco nor snuff. We got an hour's exercise every day in the open air, and the most rigid precautions were taken lest we should carry on any kind of conversation during this hour. We were made to walk six paces apart, and ordered to always keep our faces to the front. This was treating us to convict life before we had been convicted. I often thought to kick against it, but did not like to make myself exceptional in company or set a bad example.

The remand time elapsed, and we were due to appear in court; but the court visited us (in the person of a magistrate who informed us that we were remanded for another week), and when that week had passed we were taken to the Lower Castle Yard to be confronted by our accusers.

My wife was allowed to see me in the presence of the prison governor, and during our vocal interchanges we were required to speak loudly enough for him to hear whatever we said. She told me of the terrible things the papers were saying. Archbishop Cullen had come out in a pastoral against us and aided the Crown's work by abusing the prisoners. Our natural enemies were bad enough; but when the sanctity of the Church corroborated the slanders of the English enemy, we were pretty badly off.

This is a paragraph from his pastoral, and not the worst one:

> If the charges against the originators of the movement had been made known, every one would have been filled with alarm, for they are said to have proposed nothing less than to destroy the faith of our people by circulating works like those of the impious Voltaire, to preach Socialism, to seize the property of those who have any, and to exterminate both the gentry and the Catholic clergy. Whatever is to be said of such fearful accusations — which we hope are only founded on report — it is certain that the managers of the Fenian paper, *The Irish People*, made it a vehicle of scandal, and circulated in its columns the most pernicious and poisonous maxims. Hence, it must be declared that, for suppressing that paper, the public authorities deserve the thanks of all who love Ireland, its peace and its religion.

The cry of 'mad dog' was being raised against us with a vengeance; and what wonder that, after this, the pious Catholic and Crown Prosecutor Barry would add to the slander? Here are some of his words, as then reported:

> The design in their writings both public and private, as will

be proved by evidence at the trial, took the form, not as on earlier occasions of a similar character, of a mere revolutionary scheme of regeneration by substituting one government for another, but of Socialism in its most pernicious and wicked guise. The lower classes were taught to believe that they might expect a redistribution of the property, real and personal, of the country; to believe that the laws by which any man possessed more property than another were unjust and wicked; and the plan of operation was horrible to conceive. This revolution, so-called, was to be commenced by an indiscriminate massacre — the assassination of all other than the lower classes, including the Roman Catholic clergy, against whom their animosity appears, from their writings, to be especially directed, by reason of the opposition which those clergymen felt it right, as Christian ministers, as Irishmen, and as men of peace and honour, to give to the projects in question.

The Lower Castle Yard was one of England's strongholds in Dublin. With all their power, they were afraid to take us into one of their ordinary courthouses, and went through the farce of trying us behind closed doors, refusing to admit our wives and sisters. The press reporters, however, were admitted for the express purpose of giving publicity to the calumnies with which Prosecutor Barry assailed us, but which he was never able to establish. It was necessary to paint us black in order to justify the illegality of the arrests, the illegal seizure of *The Irish People*, and the tyranny and despotism that characterized every act of the executive regarding us. When England was fighting in India, English papers, in order to justify the atrocities, attributed all kinds of demon tricks to the barbarous Sepoys. Women were assertedly sawn across deal boards, who afterwards were seen in England without sign of a saw's tooth on them. When it was thought that the Irish were going to fight, Hugh Rose, who had operated in India, was sent to Ireland; and, to pave the way for his process of pacifying Ireland, it was necessary to incite hates of the 'bloodthirsty Irish'. Barry denounced men who meditated 'imbruing their hands in the blood of pious priests and lenient landlords'; but the men so denounced could not open their lips because they were represented by counsel; and counsel were bound, under penalty of severe reprimand, to act with decorum and not interrupt counsel for the Crown when he was making a statement.

This was the first time Nagle came forward to swear against us. He had been employed folding papers in *The Irish People* office, and had, he said, engaged with the detectives eighteen months previously to give information.

Not one of us would be allowed to communicate with the other before those preliminary hearings. My deeds were evidence against John O'Leary and Thomas Clarke Luby. But Luby or O'Leary would not be allowed to speak to me about means of defence, which anomaly went to account for passages such as the following in the reports of our trials:

O'Donovan Rossa, addressing the Court, declared:
'Yesterday, we wanted to have an hour's conversation in the presence of an officer of the prison, and sent this message to the governor':

Richmond Prison, 1 October 1865
Sir,
In taking measures to prevent us from speaking or communicating with each other, the government, we consider, is precluding us from any means of defence. We were before the prosecutors yesterday, and many things came under our notice that demand our consideration before we are taken before them again tomorrow. We ask that we be allowed to confer for an hour or so.
John O'Leary
O'Donovan Rossa
T.C. Luby
James O'Connor
George Hopper

The governor sent back a message saying he could not grant our request himself but would send a copy of our communication to the authorities, and, if they gave him permission, would give us the opportunity we asked. Under these circumstances, I think we were treated very harshly. Not allowed to consult with each other, we and were taken before magistrate Stronge, who had his instructions on how to dispose of us. He and the counsel on all sides were very anxious that the prisoners should keep silent, but the prisoners were not inclined to do so, as the following extracts from newspaper reports of the trials confirm:

Mr Stronge: 'I consider it my duty to commit the five prisoners — Jeremiah O'Donovan Rossa, C. Manus O'Keefe, Thomas Clarke Luby, John O'Leary, and James O'Connor — for trial on a charge of high treason. It is my duty to ask them if they wish to say anything in reference to the charge. They are not obliged to do so unless they so desire. Whatever they do say will be taken down in writing, and may be used in evidence against them. I may remind them that they are represented by very able counsel, and it is for them to consider whether it would be wise for them to say anything.'

Mr O'Leary asked permission to make a statement.

Mr Sidney, QC: 'It is right to say that any statement he makes is not made with my concurrence.'

O'Leary: 'Certainly. When first we appeared before this court, Prosecutor Barry said the government was not proceeding against us from any fear of so-called Fenians; but, as well as I could understand him, because certain weak-minded persons — I suppose including my Lords Bandon and Fermoy — were afraid. Now I do not care to go into detail as to how the government has treated us since our arrest; but I may say that a government that has been so spiteful must be somewhat afraid.'

O'Donovan Rossa said he supposed there was no use applying to be admitted to bail. Regarding *The Irish People* office, which had been seized, he understood that guards who had been sent to that office had intercepted all its letters and had transmitted them to the government.

Mr Stronge said that they were charged with high treason; and the newspaper and everything connected with the conspiracy was seized by the government. They were charged with conspiring to upset and overthrow the government, and it was not likely that the government would allow them to avail of the means by which they sought to accomplish that. He was really surprised that O'Donovan complained of being deprived of said means.

Mr Luby said that not since 1803 had any government adopted such harsh measures except where martial law had been proclaimed.

Mr Stronge: 'You are now committed on the informations presented to me.'

O'Donovan Rossa: 'We have not seen the informations.'

Stronge: 'You cannot refer to them. They were not resorted to here. They are not essential.'

Rossa: 'I understand you got information from the American government.'

Stronge:'I cannot discuss that question with you.'

Rossa:'I think I can speak with reference to Mr Barry's speech

Stronge: 'Do you deny this charge?'

Rossa: 'I beg your pardon, sir; I want to make an observation with regard to Mr Barry's opening statement. He charged the parties here with holding the opinion that no man had a right to hold more property than another. I deny that he could prove what he charged from any article in the paper. He brings matters forward that he has obtained since we were arrested, and says: "Under these circumstances, it was impossible for the government to forbear"etc. That is, impossible for the government to forbear making the seizure after getting evidence which they did not get until *after* they had made that seizure.'

Stronge: 'Is this by way of a defence?

Rossa: 'It is.'

The paid officials attempted to silence me, but I persisted in my right to defend myself. Before we were brought to this court session, it had, of course, been decided by the authorities that we would be sent back to prison again; and back we were sent, to await trial on a later date.

One day the County Sheriff came to the prison, and I and some others were brought before him. He unfolded a parchment, and told us that the charge of 'treason felony' had been withdrawn, and that we were to be tried on 29 November for 'high treason'. I swiftly had that ugly sensation that men who are fond of the world are supposed to experience when, in health, they are told that they must die. I hanged myself that day, and what harm if I say that I did not like the operation and felt a bit of cowardice? I went through the whole ceremony thereafter in imagination, and survived it; and if the reality of the ordeal had had to be gone through, I believe I would have endured it well, even though it should actually have resulted in my real death. The scare was past: I had died, and felt able to go through the rest without breaking.

Day by day, for two months in Richmond Prison we were put through the routine of solitary confinement and an hour's exercise in the open air, except that instead of being exercised with my companions, I was put into a separate yard and exercised by myself.

During the first fortnight an attorney named Ennis had attended on us. He had a large business in the police courts, and feared that this would be injured by his continuing to act as our solicitor. While with us, he did the best he could, but if the magistrates in the courts he appeared in took it into their heads to be adverse to the success of his suits they could ruin him and his reputation in short order, and we thought it only reasonable to allow him to withdraw from our case. He informed us of the best attorneys we could employ, and we were about writing to some of them when I heard from Counsellor P.J. Smyth (now member of parliament for Westmeath) offering us his assistance. On this particular subject, our jailers gave me permission to consult John O'Leary in their presence, and he decided I might write to Mr Smyth accepting his offer. I wrote, and in a few days had a reply from him stating that he had called to see us and was refused admission to the prison. I asked the governor for an explanation, and was told that the authorities would not allow Mr Smyth to have any communication with us. He was a 'suspicious character', not considered very favourable to the maintenance of English rule in Ireland, I suppose. He sent word saying that as he was denied permission to assist us himself, he would recommend a Mr John Lawless, an attorney on whom we could rely. I wrote our acceptance, and Lawless was introduced to us.

The plans for Stephens's escape from prison were being advanced. It has been stated in *A Life of James Stephens*, published in America by someone who was intimately acquainted with him, that the basis of his escape was an agreement with a jailer to effect it for a sum of £300. I do not believe a word of this. But I do believe that the men who effected his escape, and who could as easily have effected ours as well, were men who would not have moved one inch in the matter for mercenary motives. And I am able to state that they got no money, or made no money bargain, for his release.

Our attorney, Mr Lawless, visited, and, as trial time was approaching, it was deemed necessary that Stephens and Duffy should meet O'Leary, Luby and me. The solicitor made the application to the prison governor, and the governor allowed Duffy to be brought to our 'consulting room', which was Luby's cell. But Stephens would not be allowed to approach us. We remained in conversation for half-an-hour. Duffy whispered to me that Stephens was going out that night. I whispered it to John O'Leary; and, as we were parting, Lawless said he would renew his application for an interview between Stephens and the rest of us next morning. We said that the meeting was absolutely necessary, inasmuch as our trials were calendared for the following Monday.

We shook hands and parted. In my cell I could not help dwelling on the projected escape. I thought I could stay awake all night and keep my ears open for the least noise. But sleep stole a march on me till the jailers came to my cell about three in the morning, awakening me by the noise they made in opening my door. The alarm had been given, and the question with me now was — had he escaped or had he been caught in the attempt?

The noise, bustle, and running of jailers about the wards unnerved us all, and, knocking violently on my gate, I told the officer who was passing by that the noise was preventing me from sleeping and that I would report it to the governor in the morning. One word led to another; my keeper's comments told me that something extraordinary had happened; and I concluded that 'the bird' had flown.

At eight next morning, Lawless visited, and informed us of the 'terrible news' of Mr Stephens' escape. We talked of the coming trial, and of the propriety of having no counsel listed to defend us, in case the Crown packed the juries and persisted in pursuing toward us a course against which our counsel would have to battle. O'Leary, Luby and I agreed to this. The programme was to be that counsel would throw in their briefs if certain just things were not allowed by the judges; but this the attorneys could not agree to do if things came to crisis, and the projected strategy of 'no defence' was abandoned.

Luby was the first man tried — or rather convicted; O'Leary was next. Putting them through the portals of twenty years penal servitude occupied four days for each. I was called up after them, and, as I was placed in the dock the usual question was put: was I ready for trial? My counsel answered, 'Yes.'

'I beg your pardon, gentlemen,' I said, at which the counsel started, turned their heads, and adjusted their spectacles. 'My lords,' I continued, and here the gentlemen of the long robes looked at me forbiddingly, as if I should not have spoken — 'I had papers connected with my defence prepared for my counsel; and these were seized by Governor Price of Kilmainham, and they have not been returned to me. It is reasonable to suppose that there are channels of communication between Kilmainham Prison and Dublin Castle, and I surmise that these papers have been put into the hands of the Crown prosecutors. I now ask for them, and am not prepared to go forward with my trial until I get them.'

There was a murmur in the court. Judge Keogh asked where was the governor of Kilmainham, and, as he was not present, it was ordered he be sent for. Prosecutors and judges looked at each other, and a question was heard, 'What are we to do, my Lord?'

Keogh decided that prisoner Rossa must be put back and another prisoner be brought forward. The Attorney General, the Solicitor General, and the host of assistant generals who were around, held a consultation, and then addressed the court to the effect that as the case of Michael Moore was a short one, they would put him on trial. But he had not been brought down to court that day, and the van would have to be sent for him.

I was taken back to the waiting-room, and there told my story to Charles Kickham, Charles O'Connell and James O'Connor, who, with me, had been selected as the most deserving victims after Luby and O'Leary. I told them I had other plans that would keep them from being convicted at this Commission anyway. Moore was sentenced to ten years the next day; and I was again brought forward.

I got my papers (from Governor Price) in open court. Judge Keogh rebuked him, and told him it was quite improper for him to make use of the papers of any prisoner; but this impropriety afterwards appeared to have been legalized, if we may judge from the number of times during the following trials that Price seized on manuscripts of prisoners to have their handwriting identified and sworn to — on many occasions, I believe, before Judge Keogh himself.

When I was brought forward a second time, and asked if I was now ready, I stated that it was necessary for me to have witnesses who were mentioned in these papers of mine that had been seized. Price had had them in his possession for a week, and during that week I had been able to do nothing about preparing my defence. The judges and prosecutors could not get over the reasonableness of my demand. The black van was again put into requisition; I was put back; there was a repetition of the recess; and another short case was put in — that of John Haltigan, the printer of *The Irish People*. It was now Friday evening, and I thought I'd be able to keep the court engaged until Thursday, when the judges were scheduled to open in Cork City. Kickham, O'Connell, O'Connor and I were brought into court on Saturday morning. Haltigan was sentenced to seven years, and for a third time I was put into the dock. The High Sheriff came by during the forenoon and in the blandest of tones wished to know if I was ready for trial that day. I knew he had been sent by the big wigs to 'worm' me; but while I was very civil in answering his questions, I conveyed as little as possible with my answers, and kept my mind to myself.

The judges asked me if I was now ready for trial, and when I said 'Yes,' there was a rustling of papers and a pleasant appearance of business on every face.

An official proceeded to call the jury panel, and one by one, as names were called whose owners could not be relied on to bring in a verdict of guilty, those individuals were told to stand aside. My counsel were challenging on my behalf, and I was twenty times at the point of telling them to desist. I was most anxious to assert the right of every man who was called there to act there — in a word, was resolved to have something to say to this jury packing when I myself was to be packed off by it. But my tongue was tied by my having counsel to act for me, and this was making me feel most uncomfortable.

The jury being duly packed, the first witness was called and put through; the second witness was examined and cross-examined; my discontent was increasing; and before the close of the day's work, when I attempted to say something and was silenced, I determined to dispense with counsel and on Monday to commence my own defence.

Again when I stood before the judges, and when they and the lawyers were proceeding in the usual form to 'try' my case, I handed in a paper requesting that my counsel withdraw. The news report of the trial said:

> The prisoner interrupted the proceedings by saying he wished to address the court. Judge Keogh said that the interruption could not be permitted. If the prisoner had anything to say, he should communicate it through his counsel. Mr Dowse (one of these) said he understood that the prisoner wished to inform the court that he did not desire to be defended by counsel.
>
> The Prisoner: 'I have seen the Crown in action. I heard the jury being called, and heard the words "stand by" directed to

thirty or forty gentlemen. What did that mean? It meant that the Crown was determined ...'

Judge Keogh: 'We cannot permit this.'

The Prisoner: 'I believe this trial to be a legal farce, and won't be a party to that farce by being represented by counsel.'

Mr Dowse said that he and his colleague were quite ready to conduct the prisoner's defence, but, under the circumstances, would withdraw.

Judge Keogh: 'I have to express my regret that the prisoner has not left himself in the hands of able counsel.

The Prisoner: 'I fully concur with your lordship with regard to the ability of counsel. I want to know what papers and documents the Crown will rely on for my conviction.'

Judge Keogh suggested that Mr Lawless should take a seat near the prisoner, so as to be able to assist him with documents.

The Prisoner: 'I don't want Mr Lawless's assistance. I want only the documents.'

But if I did not want the assistance of counsel, Judge Keogh wanted I should have it; for, in having it, I was precluded from being anything in the play but a silent spectator. He now ordered Mr Lawless to sit by my side to instruct me. I said I didn't want his instruction, but it was of no use. Lawless took his indicated place, and I commenced to cross-examine Nagle.

All the records of *The Irish People* had been seized. The government selected as many as would tell against us. But there were others that would explain and clear away many things, and these I wanted to have for my defence, but could not get them. I contended I should have for my use as many of the documents as did not contain matter that the Crown could urge as criminatory against us. The judge said that 'all the documents required by the prisoner should be forthcoming at the proper time'. But though the prisoner was four days on trial he never got them.

Nagle at one time had been discharged from *The Irish People* by James O'Connor. He applied to Mr Luby to be taken back, and

Luby had him reinstated. And as I was cross-examining the informant as to the state of his conscience in swearing away Luby's liberty, he felt a bit puzzled:

> The Prisoner: 'Do you believe that in swearing against Mr Luby, who treated you so kindly, you did anything you must answer for to Almighty God some day?'
> The witness hesitated.
> A voice in the gallery called: 'Answer!'
> Judge Keogh: 'Who spoke?'
> The Crier: 'This gentleman, my lord.'
> Judge Keogh: 'Let that person be removed from the court instantly, and do not allow him in again.'

Judge Keogh, again interposing, told the prisoner he thought that the line of cross-examination he was following was not calculated to serve him, but he had been reluctant to interrupt because he desired to afford the prisoner every opportunity of cross-examining the witness.

The prisoner continued to cross-examine.

> Judge Keogh: 'I have allowed the greatest latitude – an extravagant latitude – to the examination. Only a part of this book has been put in evidence by the Crown. You have gone through a large number of entries in it, merely asking the witness questions as to the handwriting of these entries. The Court thinks you have gone far enough in this line of cross-examination, and I cannot allow the public's time to be wasted further with it.'
> The Prisoner: 'Once a book or a writing has been put in evidence, I believe that the whole of the book or writing can be examined.'
> Judge Keogh: 'If at any time during the trial you wish to put any relevant question with regard to this book you can have the witness recalled. But I again tell you I will not allow the public's time to be wasted by irrelevant questions.'

The Prisoner: 'The public's time is mine as well as yours, my lord.' To the witness: 'Look at that writing.'

Judge Keogh, to the witness: 'Don't look at that writing!'

The Prisoner: 'Do you see that entry about the Midland Railway?'

Judge Keogh: 'State to the Court, and not to the witness, the question you wish to put.'

The Prisoner: 'I am bound to examine the witness myself.'

Judge Fitzgerald: 'I beg your pardon. My brother Justice and I are both satisfied that this is a new attempt to waste the public's time, and we cannot permit it to continue.'

The Prisoner: 'Well, I am not satisfied. Twenty years is a long time; and I want to use these few days as best I can. I want to have the court's ruling in writing.'

JudgeKeogh: 'You have already heard the ruling of the court; and we will not allow you to carry on a moment longer.'

The prisoner again essayed to put to the witness several questions in reference to entries in the book, when Judge Keogh interposed by saying that if the prisoner did not put relevant questions, the witness would be directed to retire.

At another stage of the proceedings it was necessary for me to have those papers which Keogh, days previously, had said I should have; but, on my applying for them I found I could not get them. The judge got out of this part of the business by saying that he had made the order, and that is all he could do. 'You must go on with the cross-examination of the witness, or he will be allowed to retire,' he demanded.

And here is another excerpt showing how I was shut up:

The prisoner then examined the witness at considerable length as to the interview he had had with Nagle, until Judge Keogh again interposed, stating that it was 'trifling with justice' to be occupying the time of the court in that manner.'

After the examination of many witnesses, the papers reported:

The prisoner then proceeded to address the jury. He said that no overt act had been charged, and no criminal act had been proved, against him. When he heard the Attorney General tell thirty gentlemen last Saturday to 'stand aside', he considered that he (the Attorney General) looked upon them as persons who would not bring in a verdict of 'guilty'; and he also took it for granted that when the jury was sworn, the Attorney General looked upon those sworn as men who would bring in such a verdict. That observation was not complimentary to the jury, but he could not help that. It might be the jury's duty to give a verdict of guilty, but it was also their duty to protect a prisoner from tyranny. The executive was taking harsh measures against the prisoners. As they (the executive) had outraged all law, and had had recourse to dark courses of despotism, the jury should protect the prisoners, and not condemn men to penal servitude when nothing that was wrong was proved to have been done. If a man should say that Ireland, Hungary or Poland should be free – would he be guilty of 'treason felony'? A judge might feel it his duty to tell them that if a man said so he should be found guilty; but in that case, trial by jury was a bulwark of tyranny instead of a safeguard of liberty.

The great crimes brought against him, he said, were the words 'Jerry' and 'Rossa'; and his having known Stephens, O'Mahony, O'Leary and Luby, whom he felt it to be an honour to know.

He now cited an extract from a speech of Mr Potter on the subject of the 'Jamaican massacres' and the execution of Mr Gordon. The prisoner read the passage, which was to the effect that, in order to justify a massacre of the black population in Jamaica, calumnies were published of them, representing them as contemplating hideous crimes. The same course was adopted during the Indian Mutiny. The soldiers were worked up to the perpetration of acts of cruel barbarity by accounts of insurgent crimes; but it turned out that many of the accounts were false; and he (Mr Potter) took it that the same was the case now in Jamaica. He (Rossa) told

the jury that the same was the case with regard to the statements made about Fenianism in Ireland.

On this subject he read an article from *The Irish People*. In
the article it was stated that conquest was always accompanied
by calumny. The English denied the claim of the Irish to
humanity, the better to reduce them to the condition of
beasts. Forty of the Cromwellian soldiers actually swore that a
number of the Irish killed at Cashel were found to have
'tails'. The jury were sitting there for no other purpose than
to have the Attorney General point out to them prisoners
who also had 'tails'. *The Irish People* had striven to put an end
to religious differences, and to unite all the religions against
England. The policy of the English government had been to
use religion for the purpose of conquest. It was amusing to
see how the government could get Dr Cullen and all the
other 'Doctors' to abuse the Fenians.'

Again, a newspaper report:

He (Rossa) wrote a letter to Sir Robert Peel last week about
procuring him proper facilities for a trial, and suggested to
him that he should resign his position if he had not the
power to correct these things – and by and by, Peel did
resign. The prisoner then proceeded to read the following
extracts from his letter:

'I am keeping you too long, Sir Robert – but, have a look
at the piece that has been prepared for "the end of the play".
Judge Keogh is to try us. Well, you know – or if you don't
you will – that *The Irish People*, since its commencement, has
been writing down agitation, and has been writing up Judge
Keogh, as the symbol of the benefits derived by the Irish
people from tenant leagues and parliamentary agitation.

'The two points I present for your executive consideration
are – the restrictions here, and our right to bail, on either of
which or both, I should be most happy to hear from you;
and remain, your obedient servant.'

Of the many reported allusions to Judge Keogh's actions

made by Rossa in the course of his trial, here are specimens:

'Justice Keogh speaks of cowardly men who, in their privacy wrote violent and inflammatory stuff that led others to acts such as were the subjects of these investigations, but who themselves shrank from joining in the dangerous practices they led others into.

'It must have been refreshing for the learned judge's audience to hear him coming out in the character of *censor morum*. But has the high-flying moralist never heard of men who spoke violent and inflammatory stuff, and swore rhetorical oaths that they never kept? Has he never heard of men in high places who were once, if not the accomplices, at least the intimate associates of forgers and swindlers? But it is a waste of time to bandy words with Justice Keogh. To be sure, he is a judge — but so were Jeffreys, Macclesfield and Norbury!

'Judge Keogh is not an angel, much less a saint. Indeed, he has as little chance of canonization as you or I have. The judge is a human being like we are, subject to all the little irritations that afflict human beings, and subject to being affected with dislike of those who treat him with contempt. Selecting him as the judge to try the persons connected with *The Irish People* may be in accord with the rest of these proceedings, but it cannot impress people with feelings of respect for the administration of justice.'

The prisoner went on to read additional extracts from articles that had appeared in several newspapers, and which, he alleged, had been published to prejudice the jurors. The reading of these extracts occupied more than an hour-and-three-quarters. Having concluded, the prisoner said that if there was any gentleman connected with the Continental press in court, he begged that he would take down the words from the London *Times* of the 14th of November last, to wit: 'Treason is a serious thing; and these men are undoubtedly guilty of it'. He thought that the publication of that comment in Dublin sufficient to justify any court in removing the trials from Dublin. He would now read the affidavit that had been made for the purpose of a motion [to that effect].

Judge Keogh: 'I cannot allow it to be read. We have given you very considerable latitude. Everything you have read is irrelevant to the case, and wholly beyond the bounds of evidence. But, as you are undefended, we have given you every latitude. If counsel appeared for you here, and attempted to do what you have done, we would not permit it for one moment. You have occupied two hours with reading those articles, and we cannot now allow you to read the affidavit, which would only be a repetition of everything you have gone over. Proceed to address the jury.'

The Prisoner: 'I ask no concession from your lordships but what the law allows me. Give me the pamphlet of the Chicago Convention.'

Judge Keogh: 'Certainly.' To an attendant: 'Give him the pamphlet.'

The Prisoner: 'Give me whatever other books have been given in evidence.'

Judge Keogh: 'Anything material to the issue you are entitled to read; but you may as well understand once and for all that you will not be allowed to fritter away the time of the court, jury, and public, to make a defence when you are not making any.'

The Prisoner: 'The time of the public has been given to try me.'

The prisoner then proceeded to read the pamphlet. When he had gone through about twenty pages, the jury foreman said: 'I am requested by the jury to state that if the prisoner would mark any portions of the pamphlet that he thought bore on the case for his defence, the jury would give them the same consideration as if he had read them.'

A Second Juror: 'What he is doing now is greatly against him.'

The Prisoner: 'I am reading the pamphlet to show that it has nothing to do with me.'

A Third Juror: 'We are quite willing to sit here as long as may be necessary to fully and fairly hear the case; but we can consider this pamphlet in our room.'

A Fourth Juror: 'Occupying so much time in reading what does not concern the case is enough to stir up an armed insurrection among the persons in court.' [Here laughter erupted.]

The Prisoner: 'I don't see how the book can be considered in connection with me at all. You can only blame the Crown for putting in such books against me; but, as they are in, I shall read them.'

The Jury Foreman: 'We are only making a suggestion...'

The Prisoner: 'Do you think the book has anything to do with me?'

Keogh: 'You cannot question the jury. I may tell you in point of strict law that you are entitled to read it – every line of it – if you choose.'

The Prisoner: 'If the Crown will withdraw the pamphlet I will give it up.'

The prisoner then proceeded to read through the pamphlet, which consisted of about eighty octavo pages of small print and contained all the proceedings of the Chicago Convention, the Constitution of the Fenian organization, and the statutes by which its members were bound. Having concluded, he said, 'Now gentlemen, I will not further occupy your time, but ...'

Judge Keogh: 'Before you go further, it is scarcely necessary for me to warn the press of the grave responsibility that would attach to the publication of that document which the prisoner has just read under the pretext that it would form a necessary part of his defence.'

The Prisoner: 'I have used the document to show that there was nothing in it that could concern me. Are there other pamphlets received in evidence?'

Judge Keogh: 'No.'

The Prisoner: 'Two volumes of The Irish People were produced.'

Judge Keogh: 'The volumes have not been given in evidence; but certain articles in them have been proved, the particulars of which were furnished to your solicitor.'

The Prisoner: 'I understand that all the articles were put in. The Crown counsel having quoted in a garbled manner several articles, I think that I am entitled to read them all to the jury.'

The judge said that the prisoner was entitled to read all the articles that had been read in evidence; and also all articles that tended to explain or qualify them.

The Prisoner: 'I submit that, as I am charged with publishing this paper, I have a right to show all the articles to the jury, so that they may judge from all its issues what sort of a paper it is. I don't of course, mean to read the advertisements [laughter]; just to read what is necessary for my defence.'

Judge Keogh: 'You will proceed with your address to the jury, but will understand that it shall not degenerate into absolute abuse.'

The prisoner said that, in opening the case, the Attorney General had referred to a copy of the first publication of *The Irish People* to show that he was the manager of it. In that issue was an article headlined 'Isle, Race, and Doom'. Was he to be precluded from reading that article?

Judge Keogh: 'It is quite competent for the Attorney General to show that you were the manager of the paper, without permitting you to read all the articles published.'

The Prisoner: 'The jury cannot tell what kind of paper it is unless they hear it read.'

Judge Keogh: 'Well, sir, proceed at once. You have been addressing the court for four-and-a-half hours, and you shall have every opportunity, but there is a limit to all things.'

The court then adjourned; and, on resuming, the prisoner repeated his request to be allowed to read all of the articles that had appeared in *The Irish People*. Judge Keogh said he could not allow any such thing. The prisoner might read articles that had been used against him, and other portions of those publications that might go to explain the articles relied on by the Crown. The prisoner then asked the Crown to withdraw the charge of assassination made against him by Mr

Barry; in which case he would content himself with alluding to the articles put in evidence.

Judge Keogh: 'Proceed with your address, sir.'

The prisoner said he would show that the charge [of assassination] was false; and that the charges made against them by the Dublin press (which, he said, had prejudiced the public against them) were also false.

He then proceed to read an article which, he said, was written in reply to English articles abusing Ireland. In replying to these, the editors were to be excused for getting up a little spirit. They (the jury) would say the same things themselves. If their country were run down by Englishmen, they might possibly say things that the judge, perhaps, might say amounted to 'treason felony'. He would now read an article headlined 'Tall Talk' in the issue of 28 November.

Judge Keogh: 'We have looked carefully over the article, and find it has no relevance to the case.'

The Prisoner: 'Then you will not allow me to read it?'

Judge Keogh: 'No.'

The prisoner said he would read the article headlined 'Bane and Antidote'. Judge Keogh said it was not mentioned in the indictment. The prisoner said he wished to read it for the purpose of showing that it was not appropriate for him to be tried before his lordship.

Judge Keogh: 'That at once settles the question. You cannot read it.'

The Prisoner: 'Well, I'll read this article of December 5th.'

Judge Keogh: 'We cannot allow you to read it.'

The prisoner then referred to an article entitled 'National Self-Reliance', which, he said, ridiculed the idea of inviting foreigners to come in and invade the country. That was one of the charges against him. The article stated that if fifty-thousand French or Irish-American soldiers landed in Ireland, and the people were not prepared for them, they would be swept into the sea by British troops in less than three months. Judge Fitzgerald said that he had read an article headed 'A Retrospect'. He should tell him that they would not allow the court to be the means of spreading articles that were treasonable, and certainly seditious.

The Prisoner: 'The jurors who are here for my protection.' Judge Fitzgerald said that the article could not be read. The prisoner said he could not consider it right to have a 'packed bench' trying him. The Attorney General then protested against the court being made a medium for the dissemination of treasonable doctrines. It should not be allowed in a court of justice.

Judge Keogh: 'The prisoner is entitled to make any observation on them he pleases; he is merely reading them.'

The prisoner then read an article entitled 'The Approaching Crisis', observing, *en passant*, that tomorrow he would read articles which would explain those he was now reading. After reading some others, he proposed reading from *The Irish People* John O'Mahony's 'Letter to Bishop Duggan'. Their lordships ruled that this could not be read, as it was not in evidence.

The Prisoner: 'Am I not charged in connection with O'Mahony?'

Judge Keogh: 'You have heard the ruling of the court.'

The Prisoner: 'Very well; we will return to it again.'

The prisoner, having read the article 'Priests in Politics', expressed a wish to read the letter signed 'A Munster Priest'. Judge Keogh asked him for what purpose he proposed to read the letter. The prisoner said he wished the jury to understand the article. Judge Keogh said he might read the letter in point. The prisoner proceeded to read it, when he was interrupted by the judge.

Judge Keogh: 'You have read enough of that letter, purporting to have been written by a priest, to show the nature of it; but we really think that to allow you to continue would be propagating the worst kind of treason. I will act upon my own responsibility, and will not allow the further reading of that letter.'

The Prisoner: 'What use is it, then, for me to try to explain these articles?'

Judge Keogh: 'There has not been the slightest attempt, from the beginning to the end of your address, now of seven-and-a-half hours duration, to qualify, pare down, or soften a single published article; on the contrary, everything that has been read to the jury has been read in order to exaggerate them.'

The Prisoner: 'I say it is my right.'

Judge Keogh: 'The ruling of the court is that it shall not be read.'

The Prisoner: 'But you gave me permission to read the letter.'

Judge Keogh: 'I gave you permission to read it in order to explain the article. But I now perceive that it is quite inadmissible.'

The Prisoner: 'You change about; rule one thing now and another thing later.'

Judge Keogh: 'If you don't proceed, I shall terminate your right to address the jury; and that, peremptorily.'

The prisoner proceeded to refer to an article headed 'The Regeneration Scheme' and said that before he read the article it would be appropriate for him to first read the letter by Dr Moriarty.

Judge Keogh: 'We will not allow any such thing to be done.'

The Prisoner: 'But the Attorney General charges in his speech ...'

Judge Keogh: 'Proceed. We won't allow it to be read.'

The Prisoner: 'Very well. I shall go on, but reserve my right to read these things before I am done.'

The prisoner then read an article headed 'Peace in America'. At its conclusion, he said, 'It is now six o'clock, my lord, and I suggest that we close for the evening.'

Judge Keogh: 'Oh, certainly not. The court will continue.'

The Prisoner: 'I am now speaking for eight hours, my lord; and the court closed every other evening at six.'

Some of the jurymen intimated a desire to proceed.

The Prisoner: 'Why, it is a '98 trial. A regular "Norbury" case!'

Judge Keogh: 'Proceed, sir.'

The prisoner then proceeded to read other articles, and, on coming to one in which allusion was made to 'the advancement of Keoghs, Monahans, and Sadlier's said:

'And now, gentlemen,.a few words. I say that that indictment has been brought against me; and that man (pointing to Judge Keogh) has been placed on that bench to try me; and if there is one among you with a spark of honesty in his breast, he will resent such injustice. The article has been brought against me in the indictment; and do you all believe that that man on the bench is a proper man to try me? He has been placed there to convict me. There, let the law take its dirty course.' And he flung on the table the large volume of *The Irish People* from which he had been reading.

Prosecuting counsel were quite unprepared for my sudden stop, and when I declined to take further part in the proceedings, they and the judges decided that they would adjourn the court until next day.

My last court day was Wednesday, 13 December. The judges were scheduled to open their circuit court in Cork on the 14th, and I felt satisfied at having occupied them the time I had intended. As the *Evening Mail* commented, 'the Crown's game was a fast one; but the defendant's was a slow one, and he had the right to play it as it pleased him'. This was part of the closing continuity:

His lordship next called the attention of the jury to an *Irish People* document that had some reference to Paris. Now he had a notion that conspiracies of this kind would be dealt with in a very different way in that capital. The Frenchman would clutch at once with a strong hand all those who dared to interfere with his authority.

The Prisoner: 'That is a nice address by a judge to a jury!'

Judge Keogh then proceeded to speak of Robespierre and the revolution of his day. He was glad to see the spirit of the real public journalism of this city which did not report the articles the prisoner read here yesterday in the expectation that they would be published; and did not allow them to be distributed to contaminate this country's moral atmosphere. Then, ultimately:

'Gentlemen: I send these papers to your box. If you believe that that wild confederacy existed, and that the prisoner at the bar was a member of that confederacy, you ought unhesitatingly to find him guilty. Let no words be bandied about "assassination" or "massacre'. I leave this case to your arbitration, and believe that whoever reads these trials in a calm and tranquil way will say that if we here have erred at all it has been on the side of indulgence to the accused.'

The Prisoner: 'You have told them to convict me.'

The Crown Clerk: 'Remove the prisoner.'

The jury retired at half-past one. At thirty-five minutes past two it returned to court, and the prisoner was brought in.

Crown Clerk Geale, reading from the foreman's note: 'Your verdict is that he is guilty on all counts!'

The Attorney General: 'I have now to ask your lordships to pronounce judgment on the prisoner; and, in doing so, to refer you to an entry on the calendar, by which it appears that this prisoner was arraigned and pleaded guilty in July 1859, at the Cork assizes, to an indictment similar to the present one of treason felony. He at first pleaded not guilty, but afterwards withdrew it, and was released on condition that he would appear when called on to receive sentence. Having regard to the lapse of time, I thought it fairer and more constitutional not to call for sentence to be passed without a trial, but to allow the present case to take its course. I think it right to now call attention to the record, by the Clerk of the Crown for Cork, of the earlier conviction.'

Judge Keogh: 'Has the prisoner anything to say? You pleaded guilty to a similar indictment at the '59 assizes.'

The Prisoner: 'My lord, that is a small matter. I was arrested in '59 and charged with an offence; but everything that was sworn against me was false. I believe Mr Whiteside was Attorney General under the Derby government. Through our attorney we were told that if we pleaded guilty, Dan O'Sullivan Agreem, who had been transported, would be released. We would not do so until there was a change of government, and on the second day of the Assizes we were discharged.'

Clerk Geale: 'Jeremiah O'Donovan Rossa, you have been indicted and found guilty of compelling Her Majesty to change her measures; and of stirring up and inciting foreigners to invade this country. What have you to say as to why sentence should not be passed on you?'

The Prisoner: 'The fact that the government seized papers connected with my defence and withheld them; the fact that the government stated that they would convict; the fact that they sent Judge Keogh, a second "Norbury"' to try me. With these facts before me, it would be useless for me to say anything.'

The observations of the prisoner created a profound sensation, to which audible expression was given in court. The judges retired and, after a short absence, came back into court.

Judge Keogh: 'Jeremiah O'Donovan Rossa, you have, after a most patient trial, been found guilty by a jury of your countrymen of the offence charged against you in this indictment. You have now twice been found guilty of the same offence — once on your confession six years ago; and now by a verdict of your countrymen. We have considered the details of the evidence in your case, and have contrasted them with the degrees of guilt of your co-conspirators. We have considered whether there could be a distinction drawn between your case and those of the others who have been tried, but, the more we have done so, the more we come to the conclusion that you entertained those criminal designs at a period long antecedent to *them*. On the occasion on which you pleaded guilty, you must have entertained those designs as far back as 1859. You may have entertained them again immediately after your liberation from custody — there is no evidence of that — but you certainly, on the clearest evidence, have been connected with these transactions as far back as the year 1863.'

The Prisoner: 'Ah, I am an Irishman since I was born.'

Judge Keogh: 'We have on the clearest evidence that as far back as 1863 you were the most trusted of the friends in this conspiracy of James Stephens and John O'Mahony. No unprejudiced man who has listened to these proceedings can arrive at any other conclusion than that the jury were imperatively coerced to find the verdict they have reached. I shall not now waste words by trying to bring to your mind any sense of the crime of which you have been found guilty.'

The Prisoner: 'You need not. It would be useless for you to try.'

Judge Keogh: 'But it is our duty — and the public interest requires it — that a man who has once experienced the clemency of the Crown, and who afterwards violated good faith and proceeds again to conspire against the institutions of his country, shall not again have the opportunity presented to him of entertaining such designs and projects. We could have drawn no distinction favourable to you as between your case and that of the prisoners Luby and O'Leary, who have been convicted of similar offences; and, our attention having been drawn by Her Majesty's Attorney General to this plea of guilt entered at Cork in the year 1859, we have no discretion left but to sentence you to penal servitude for the term of your natural life.'

The Prisoner: 'All right, my lord.'

Clerk Geale: 'Put him back!'

The custodians, assisted by a large force of police, pressed the prisoner from the front of the dock. As he turned around, he saluted friends in the gallery, and, with a smile, proceeded from the court by its underground passage.

6. Mountjoy Jail, Ireland; Pentonville Prison, England

FIVE MINUTES AFTER the sentencing I was ushered to the black van. In fact, it had been awaiting me for two hours, the horses harnessed, and the soldiers equipped, to escort me to Mountjoy. Before I entered I shook hands with the police who had been keeping watch over me in court for the previous fifteen days. They looked as if they were sorry for me. The van rattled through the streets, the soldiers galloped at each side of it with sabres drawn, and in less than half-an-hour the outer world closed upon me. The soldiers scattered about Mountjoy's entrance-yard ran to the structure's steps as our cortege approached. I got out and, with as kind a look as I could give and light a step as I could take, passed through them.

I was ushered into a room; my clothes had been prepared for me; I was divested of everything I wore belonging to a free man; and, after an examination of my naked body, got my outfit. It consisted of a shirt, a flannel drawers, a waistcoat, a grey vest, jacket and trousers, a pair of stockings, a pair of shoes, and a cap.

After dressing I was taken to the registry office. My height, I believe, was five feet nine-and-a-half; my hair was fair, my eyes were blue. They wound up describing my features as 'average', and sent me from their department to the next custodian. He escorted me to my cell. One of two others held a candle; and the other, a razor. The first gentleman, drawing a scissors out of his pouch, commenced clipping away at my beard. Whenever he had occasion to say 'Hold up your head,' 'turn this way,' or 'that way,' he said it in as gruff a tone as he could command, and I obeyed in silence. While using the scissors on my face he scarred me a little. The man with the razor came on, and, as he worked, my eyes fell on the face of the man who was holding the candle, and they began to swim in their sockets. It was the first time I would feel soft during my imprisonment; but when I saw the tears on the cheeks of that Irish-hearted jailer who was holding the candle, I could not restrain my own from starting.

After being shaved I was led to have my picture taken. The photographer had a large black-painted pasteboard prepared, with my name painted across it in white, and, pinning it to my breast, he sat me in position. I remained sitting, and looking according to his instructions. The rules were read to me, and I saw that one of them said that I could write a letter on reception into prison. I ask for pen, ink and paper, and am told I cannot have the benefit of that rule; there are instructions in my case, and I cannot write until there are special orders. On the first day of my imprisonment there were these instructions to treat us exceptionally. I would not have grumbled or wondered if, as political prisoners, it had been exceptionally better; but, no, it was worse than if we had been the worst criminals in society. I respectfully demanded that I be allowed to write to a member of parliament about the illegal conduct of the judges at my trial. No, I could not,and might as well put the thought of doing so out of my head.

I had determined to bear all things patiently; and to obey in everything, conceiving that the dignity of liberty's cause required that men should suffer calmly and strongly for it; but the more obedient and humble we were, the more our masters showed a disposition to trample on us, and the more they badgered us with humiliating annoyances.

My cell was about ten feet by seven. It contained a water-closet, a table, a stool, a hammock-bed made like a coffin and about two feet broad at its top, a salt-box, a tin box, a tin pint, and a spoon. I got a pound weight of oakum to pick the first day, and picked about two ounces of it. I went to bed at eight o'clock, and immediately thereafter was roused up and ordered to put my clothes out through the trapdoor. This was something not required of ordinary prisoners; but, in consequence of the flight of James Stephens, they were afraid that the fairies would fly away with us.

Every fifteen minutes of the night the trapdoor of my cell was opened by officers. One of them held a bull's-eye lantern toward my head, and, if he did not see my face, would keep calling me until I put in an appearance. Then there were two soldiers outside my cell window who kept calling 'All right!' to each other every half-hour. This continued night after night. For the ten nights I was there I never got an hour's quiet sleep.

My breakfast was gruel and milk; my dinner and supper, bread and milk; and two days a week we got meat for dinner. I got an hour's exercise in the open air each day, and in this matter was treated exceptionally also. The other prisoners were exercised in squads, but I was exercised alone.

The second day of my residence in Mountjoy my cell door opened, and who came in but a priest. I well recollect how delighted I was to see anyone, and that one a priest, for perhaps the dormant tradition of my younger days had revived. It was in periods of darkness and difficulty that the Irish people clung to the Irish priest; and I felt as if I could forget the past, if the pastor could do so also.

I knew that 'Pagan' O'Leary, Mr Luby, John O'Leary, Haltigan and Moore had preceded me to Mountjoy, but I never could get a sight of them. I was taken to chapel on Sunday, but was put into a compartment that permitted only a forward view. I could only see the backs of the others, but I believe that my companions were placed in boxes similar to mine. These compartments were arranged for very refractory characters, and before we had had time to acquire any prison reputation at all we were ushered into them.

On Christmas Eve, the eleventh day of my conviction, at four in the morning, the bull's-eye patrol ordered me to get out of bed. He threw my clothes in through the trapdoor, and told me to dress in a hurry. He gave me a piece of bread and a pint of milk, and told me to waste no time eating my breakfast. While I was carrying out that part of the order that related to my breakfast, the door was opened, and some men came into my cell. One of them felt my pulse and pronounced me fit for a journey. A few minutes later I was brought into one of the large halls and placed alongside five other men. I could not take a good look at them as I was adhering to the orders to look to my front and never turn my head sideways. I thought that I would become a splendid prisoner and get a most excellent 'character' by obeying the rules. When I was a young man, a girl once flattered me by saying I had the happy gift of making myself amiable in every gathering in which I mixed. That memory followed me into prison, and did not forsake me for years. Not until I had been worn down to a skeleton, the old flesh off my bones and the old thoughts out of my mind, did I come to learn that sometimes not all the arts of my nature could make me agreeable company.

When ranged alongside the other prisoners, I took advantage of the officers' eyes being off me to whisper to the man beside me, 'Where are we going?' He replied, 'I don't know.' I knew his whisper, and blurted out, 'Luby!' He responded 'Rossa,' and we shook hands. The officer frowned at us, but I got up courage, espied O'Leary, 'the Pagan' and others, and gave them nods of recognition. The handcuffs came. Luby was next to me; they were fitted on him first; and I was cuffed to him. His hand was very small and I told the jailer that the irons were too small for my hand, but he could get no others, so I had to suffer my wrist being bound in a restraint that caused me considerable pain.

The order came for us to move, and we were conducted to a black van. Six warders were put in with us. We were all locked in; the wheels rumbled over the Dublin pavements; the cavalry galloped alongside; and on we went for an hour or more, not knowing to what quarter of the world we were bound. The irons were tormenting me, and when the horses stopped I remarked that it was not at all necessary for safety to bind me so tightly. One officer turned the bull's-eye of his lantern to look at my hand; and as the light fell on the face of another jailer beside me, I saw tears streaming down his cheeks. I knew his name, and had memorized the name of the other man whose sympathy had shown while I was being shorn.

I was taken out of the black van; looked around me to see where I was; and saw the pier of old Dun Laoghaire. The steamer was in front of us, and between us and the steamer were two rows of soldiers, between whom my companions and I trudged to the ship. It was a dark morning, but the appearance of the redcoats through the mist told us it was an occasion of high importance. At the gangplank I had the honour to be helped on board by the Dublin detectives who had arrested us. They were there to see us off.

The ship sailed. Dawn was breaking as we parted from the land whose soil we were to tread no more, unless it would be against the will and power of those whose rule has been a curse to it for centuries. We were about an hour at sea when I thought it time to make a little noise about the irons that were crushing my hands. My wrist was quite swollen. I showed it to the jailers, and asked if I could not have some relief. The deputy governor of Millbank Prison had come with six of his aides to take charge of us; and I asked if I could not talk to the officer in command, in order that, as we were now bound for a free country, I might be supplied with freer irons.

One of my companions observed that it was a most unsuitable time for a display of wit. This put a damper on me and may have made me seasick, for I began discharging the contents of my stomach. But it may have put some manhood in me also, for I demanded to see the superior officer immediately, or would try my best to break the irons. Captain Wallack came, examined my hands, said that the handcuffs were 'a little tight', had me untied, and chained to Michael Moore; and, having released 'Pagan' O'Leary from Moore, had him tied to my partner, Mr Luby.

I have previously mentioned the O'Leary name, but one should understand that there were two individuals of that name who were confused with each other. 'Pagan' O'Leary is not John O'Leary. It would not be easy to find two men more unlike each other, or any man readier than either, each in his own way, to risk life in an honest endeavour for Irish independence. John O'Leary was editor of The Irish People. The 'Pagan' is a soldier, and I'm not sure he aspires to be anything else.

The telegraph must have carried the news that we were bound for England because, as the ship approached Holyhead, the pier was crowded with spectators. The company of soldiers who had accompanied us from Ireland was drawn up on the quay, and we ran the gauntlet between them to the railway carriage that awaited us. A few hours later we arrived at Chester. One of our keepers was called out by the officer in command, and, coming back, brought a meat pie and divided it between us. My hands were bound to prisoners on each side of me. We would not be unbound while we were eating, and whenever I put my hand to my mouth the hand of one of my companions had to accompany it. Nor would they loosen our hands for any other reason. It is some hundreds of miles from Holyhead to London, and our journey would take until eight in the evening. One might have thought that, once we were in England, our masters would have had no further fears about our security; but no, the scare never left them, and they never left us to the normal vigilance to which other convicts were left. When we went to the water-closet on the steamboat, the sentry kept opening the door every half-minute lest we should attempt an escape through the pipes or the portholes, and they would not for any consideration allow us off the railway-car during the journey from Holyhead to London.

It was Christmas Eve, and at every station we could see the filled hampers that were being taken to homes by the merry people of 'merry England'. How could it be helped that we had sad thoughts at the reflection that those near and dear to us were to be having a poor time of it?

In the evening our train arrived at London's Euston Station, and a little army of jailers and police awaited us. Outside they had two vans used for transferring criminals from the courts to the prisons, and we were put into these. So close a place of confinement I was never before in. The compartments were about two feet square; and, after having been unbound from the others and getting a pair of handcuffs all to myself, I was locked into one. The horses galloped through the city streets, and I got no glimpse of light again until I was within Pentonville's gates.

The prison governor viewed us as we stood in one of the large halls, and, having examined the papers that had been brought with us, gave us over to the petty officers to be processed and located. We were ordered to strip, and I threw off my shoes, jacket, trousers and vest. Thinking so much was enough, I stopped; but one of the warders cried out, 'Why don't you strip?' I asked him had I not taken off as much as was necessary, to which he said, 'No; take off those stockings and that shirt.' And quickly the six of us stood naked on the flagstones.

Then commenced that examination of us that cannot well be described but left an impression in our minds never to be effaced. The English people speak of their sense of decency; have laws in the interests of morality that punish wanton exposure of the person; but such ruffianism as attended our entrance into residence in the City of London is something that should be put an end to, even in a convict prison.

I had assumed that upon our removal from Ireland, the fears of our masters would be dispelled, and I could have the opportunity to write to my family. I gave the English credit for a desire to treat us fairly, but if I live to be as old as Methuselah they'll never have such credit from me again. The first experience I had in England of their disposition was in the dressing of us. They took our Irish clothes away, and opposite to where we stood were six little parcels that turned out to be our sets of clothing. I looked for my flannels, but sought them in vain. I asked where the inner clothing was, but was told there was none. I remarked that I had received flannels in Ireland; had just taken them off; and asked that, if new ones were not to be given to me, I might be given the old ones. To no avail. Our reception had been prepared, and the prison doctor had decided we were to have no flannels after reception. It was midwinter, one should remember, and snow was covering the ground. To give any idea by words of the cold I felt is something I cannot do; and when hunger came with cold it was surprising that so many of us managed to survive.

When we six were 'dressed' we were led to our cells, no two of us being placed in the same block. I proceeded to make up my bed. That consisted of a board, seven feet by three, with other boards about eight inches wide nailed on the head, by way of a pillow; a mattress about half-an-inch thick, not quite as hard as the board; two sheets, a blanket, and a rug. I took off my clothes, and folded them according to instructions, so as to have them ready to put outside the door when the officer came. The table, the pint, the plate, the spoon, the salt-cellar, the towel, the soap, the stool, and the Bible, were the only moveable articles in my cell, and these I had arranged to put outside the door when the orders came. I put out article after article, and everything I put out was counted and noted by the keepers. My light was put out, my door was locked. I lay down, and tried to warm myself by wrapping the clothes tightly about me, but all to no purpose. I shivered the whole night through.

Six in the morning came. My door was opened and I got a lamp to light my gas; I took in my clothes and furniture; and commenced my day. But, except for eating and dressing, no work was to be done, for it was Sunday. I got my breakfast, which consisted of a pint of cocoa and eight ounces of bread. The drink I swallowed greedily, but I could not eat the bread. Dinner came at twelve. I got eight ounces of bread and four ounces of cheese, but my stomach refused to receive either. Supper came at five and for it we had six ounces of bread and a pint of porridge. And that was our Sunday fare at Pentonville as long as we remained there. At half-seven the bell rang to prepare for bed. The previous night's operation was re-enacted — my cell stripped of its contents, my body-clothes laid outside, and I, left with nothing but that comfortless bed-and-board. To sleep here was almost as impossible as in Dublin. I was weary, and wanted to sleep, but the intense cold left me shivering and shaking. However, if the cold was bad when you first went to bed and tried to sleep, it was worse when, after hours of uneasy slumber, you awoke to shiver and shake, with the prospect of hours more of that before the time came to rise and get back your clothes. For sheer physical discomfort, I do not think I ever experienced anything worse than those early morning hours in Pentonville.

My second day was Christmas Day. My breakfast was eight ounces of bread and three-quarters of a pint of cocoa. My dinner, four ounces of meat, five ounces of bread, and a pound of potatoes; and my supper seven ounces of bread and a pint of porridge. Dinner came on a tin having two compartments, in one of which was meat, and in the other the potatoes. The porridge and the cocoa were measured into my 'pint', which, with everything else I used, was to be brightened after each meal. I was allowed a knife, a plate, and a spoon. The knife was a bit of tin about four inches long and an inch-and-a-half wide. The spoon was a wooden one, substantial enough to fill my mouth, and the plate was wooden also. I had a comb, and a brush about two inches long and one in width. I had two leather knee-caps to wear when I was required to polish the floor, and these, with my stool and my table, constituted my household furniture.

In one corner of the cell was an open cupboard in which my bedclothes were to be placed nicely folded. My towel was also to be folded with my bit of soap in the middle of it, and open to the view of the 'principal' who came in every morning to see that everything was in order. If the clothes were not folded so as to please him, he would pull them off the shelf and throw them on the floor, ordering me to go at them again.

My gas-burner had a little brass tip, and this was to be kept brightly burnished. The water pipe, turned one way, flowed into my washbasin (which was also of brass); and, turned another, flowed into a closet that was set in my narrow and badly ventilated cell. All the brasses connected with closet, tap and washing apparatus had to be polished; and the wooden cover of the closet-bowl, the table, the stool, the plate and the spoon, were required to be spotlessly clean. At night my ribs and hips felt the proximity of the hard board of my bed, so much so that in time the skin on those parts of my body on which I was accustomed to lay became quite rough, and I learned to roll from side to side every fifteen minutes or so without waking.

Tuesday morning, 26 December, dawned; the 'up-out-of-bed' bell rang; the cell trapdoor was opened; a little lamp was handed to me to light my gas jet with, and my breakfast followed. There was an air of business I had not noticed on either of the two preceding days. It was the first working day since we had come, and getting us started made for a busy time. At nine I was conducted to the centre of the prison's large hall. Deputy Governor Farquharson made his appearance with a copy of the rules-and-regulations in his hand. I saw John O'Leary, and one after another of my companions appeared from different parts of the prison till we six stood in line. John whispered to me, 'This is hell.' 'Yes,' said I, 'hell.'

When the rules had been read to us, we were measured and weighed. I had lost some twenty pounds since I had left the world. Back to our cells again, every warder taking his own prisoner with him. My door was locked on me, but no sooner locked than opened again, with an order to strip off everything but my trousers and shoes. A bell sounded, and, pointing to me with his club to go before him, my warder urged me through corridors and around corners until, opposite a cell that contained a loom and an individual dressed in civilian clothes, he cried 'Halt!' I was motioned to go in, and the civilian felt my pulse and examined my chest. I asked if I might put a question to him, and he said, 'Yes.'

'Well, Doctor,' said I, 'when I arrived here, I was stripped of the flannels I had, and got none in exchange. I asked for some, and was told you had ordered none for us. I feel intense cold, and make application to you for more clothing.'

'I cannot give you any more than you have,' said he.

In minutes I was locked in my cell, where I dressed myself. Shortly, the door was again opened, and the order was given me: 'Prepare for exercise.' I stepped outside, was told to open my jacket and waistcoat, take off my shoes and cap, unbutton my braces, extend my hands, and keep my feet apart. I did each in turn, and the warder, as the prison phraseology went, 'rubbed me down' — that is, put his hands to the back of my neck and felt the collar all around; slipped them inside my unbuttoned braces till his fingers met behind my back; explored every inch of my body front and rear; seized one arm and felt it down to the tips of my fingers; did the same to the other; then, laid hold of a leg and searched along till he came to the big toe; and after repeating the process on the second leg, finished by rubbing his palms over my cropped skull.

The convicts were exercised or 'aired' in a large yard. There were three circles, one within the other, the arc of each being a flagging about eighteen inches wide. The convicts walked on these flagstones, and between each circle there were raised pathways on which the officers walked and had a view of the whole. The prisoners walked about four paces apart, and if one of them was detected attempting to whisper or make a sign of recognition to another, he was immediately sent back to his cell and put 'under report' (for punishment). I didn't get my 'airing' in this yard; the place I was taken to was one especially set aside for the taming of 'refractory characters', and they treated me as such. A man's clothes or cell furniture are not taken from him at night unless he has attempted to escape or to break his prison. A man is not sent to the 'coach wheel' for his 'airing' unless he has been sent from another prison for solitary confinement at all hours; but none of these preliminaries to such punishment seemed to be required in our cases.

To thoroughly understand what 'the coach wheel' was, you may imagine a large wheel, some hundred feet or more in diameter, on the ground. It had fifty spokes, and on every spoke was a wall ten feet high. Between every two of these walls one of us was confined for an hour each day. The rim of the wheel was an iron grating, around which the governor walked occasionally, requiring us to give him a military salute. Toward the centre of the wheel a door opened from every compartment, and within the hub of the wheel was a room in which the officer kept watch on the convicts.

If the law's victim stops to pick up a pretty pebble, or to scratch a word on one of the bricks, he is immediately challenged; and it was surprising the number of inmates who had risked the challenges, if one could judge from the number of scratches on the brick wall, which was covered with notations of all kinds. One stone bore the record of the conviction of 'Stepney Joe' and the unmentionable offense for which he had been convicted. Another told how 'the Pig' was sent back to Portland, and the crime he had committed. A third informed how 'Prince's gal', after 'Prince' was 'lagged', went to live with 'Crow'. A fourth told the reader that the governor was a brute. And so on in a variety of comment on things in general. 'Twas a recreation to read the evidence of living beings having been around, even though you hadn't seen them. It was the dead wall speaking to you, and though the language had not the chastity of death about it, it brought you more cheer than if there had been no trace of life. I read 'Cheer up!' so often that I felt myself in sympathy with those writers. During my time in prison, my masters sought to punish me by putting me in close association with them, and I as often kicked against it. But let me here declare that I would choose their society before my own solitude; and if I often spurned it and went back to the loneliness of my cell and the poverty of bread and water, I did it more in opposition to the authority that would degrade an Irish rebel than from any choice I had in the matter. If you who shudder at the thought of contact with the vilest of human beings come to test the strength of your horror and sense of contamination by two or three years of solitary confinement, you may change. The sight of a face, however deformed, and the sound of a voice, however vile, is a gladsome thing for me if I am any considerable length of time out of reach of either.

When exercise was over in the refractory yard I was ordered to my cell, with every precaution being taken that I should not see anyone else on my way to it. A 'schoolmaster' calls, and says it is necessary to classify me in order to give me suitable reading matter. He tells me to read a little for him; puts me down as a 'number 3'; and leaves me a book about birds' nests. I thought I should be getting something to feed my mind on, but what he gave me was of little use. 'Class 3' was one of very moderate attainment, and he must have thought there would be no use giving me heavy matter to read. I was supplied with a set of religious books, consisting of *Garden of the Soul*, a *Think Well On It*, a *Poor Man's Catechism*, and a *New Testament*. He also gave me a grammar and an arithmetic, which, with the religious books, I could always keep; and told me that the other books could be changed once each fortnight. He left me a slate-and-pencil, and said I would get one hour's schooling every week, and he would call back to see what progress I was making. After the schoolmaster left, a most important individual visited me, a prison director. He was accompanied by the governor and three of the warders, and the moment the cell door turned on its hinges, the sub-officers cried out, one after another, 'Attention!' I rose. My cap was on my head when the key had turned in the door, and I left it on. I was ordered to take it off; and did. The governor told me I should never wear my cap while in my cell, should always keep it hanging on the bell-handle, and that it was only given to me to be worn out of doors. I said that my head was shaven so close, and my clothing was so light, that I felt intense cold, and was more comfortable with my cap on. The director said I had as much clothing as the regulations allowed; if more was necessary the doctor would order it for me, but the discipline of the prison must be maintained before anything else. The director's name was Gambier, and he and I afterwards became very well acquainted with each other. No social acquaintance, discipline merely. It was his duty to order infliction of punishment. He was a tall, smooth-tongued old gentleman of about seventy, with very white hair, a glass eye, and a red, jolly looking nose, which I could never look at without thinking of good old times and Irish whisky-punch. He could order you fifty lashes on the bare back and twenty-eight days on bread and water in the most sorrowful tones of regret that your bad behaviour and the necessities of maintaining discipline called for. And you'd think that his glass eye, as well as his unglazed one, was swimming tears over your misery.

Shortly after this group left, an officer brought me needle-and-thread and scissors and a thimble, and told me to practice stitching on a piece of jacket fabric he left on the table. 'Sew it all around, and when you have made one circle of stitches, make another an inch further in, and so on till you have the whole piece sewn. When you've had practice enough to enable you to stitch well I will give you a jacket to make.'

My appetite had not yet returned. I had accumulated seven or eight small loaves of bread in my cupboard. The officer told me that that was against regulations, and I should either eat them or have them removed, as the rules did not allow more than one day's bread to remain in any prisoner's cell. I told him I could not eat it; and on his asking me if I would permit him to take it away, I replied, 'Of course.'

The rising at six was the same every day; the breakfast of bread and cocoa; the polishing of the floor; the making up of your bed; the search before getting your hour's 'airing', with an additional hour every second day; the same search upon returning to your cell. And the eternal stitch, stitch, stitch, with the block spy stealing around in soft slippers, looking occasionally to see if he could catch you idling and report you; the supper of bread and porridge at six; the hour-and-a-half's work afterwards; and the preparation for bed and putting your furniture outside.

You were supposed to be at work from breakfast until half-seven in the evening, except that you had one hour for dinner. And if you were minded to read, this left you fifty-five minutes for it, for, with the ravenous appetite you developed if you were not in a dying state, you could devour all the food you'd get in less than five minutes. After the first three days my appetite returned, and my craving for food became intense. It was the greatest imaginable pleasure to have enough to eat. Many a time I regretted having allowed my warder to take away those accumulated little loaves. For years this feeling of hunger never left me, and I could have eaten rats and mice if they had come my way, but there wasn't a spare crumb in any of those cells to induce a rat or a mouse to visit it. I used to creep on my hands and knees from corner to corner of my cell sometimes to see if I could find the smallest crumb that might have fallen when I was eating my previous meal. When I had salt in my cell I would eat that to help me to drink water to fill my stomach.

My whole prison life was one of dreams, and the night portion of them was not the pleasantest. Some of them would be tolerable enough until awakening brought me back to bitter reality. The platefuls of bread-and-butter that I ate in dreams some nights would be alarming to any physician were he to have seen me eating them. My mind must also have received impressions of punch and mulled porter, for I envisioned myself indulging in one or the other till the sound of a bell, or the jingling of a key, would dash the pewter or tumbler image out of my mind.

Hunger, in fact, had brought me to view things in such a philosophic manner that if, when eating my ration of bread I found a beetle or a *ciaróg* cracking between my teeth, instead of spitting out in disgust what I had just chewed, I would grind away, telling myself that nature had provided for the excretion of anything that was foul and the retention of what was nutritious. Again and again I found myself regretting that I had not eaten more of the good things of the world when I was in society, and my mouth would water at the recollection of some long-since-devoured leg of lamb.

* * * * *

ON THE WEDNESDAY after my arrival I was in regular working order. The master tailor who examined my stitching thought I did it very well, and brought me a waistcoat to make. The 'principal' of the block brought me a button and told me to sew it on the breast of my jacket; and when this was done he handed me a little board on which was painted the number 26. A leather strap was nailed to it, and he told me to attach it to the button and never take it off. This was the number of my cell, and would be my name in prison. 'Rossa' would be heard no more. The governor and the deputy governor visited 26 every day, and the number was ordered to stand to attention. The jailer who accompanied the deputy governor told 26 several times that besides standing to attention he should salute the superior officers by raising his hand to his uncovered head. Twenty-six listened patiently, but always seemed to forget those instructions, for when the orders were given to so stand, he stood with his hands rigidly at his sides. For this he was often reprimanded.

A bell rang at eight one morning, and I heard the whole prison astir, but did not surmise what was up. I eventually was told that the prisoners were 'going to prayers'. 'And cannot you take me to prayers?' I asked. 'No,' he answered, 'there is no service in this prison for Catholics. Millbank is the place for that.' When the governor came around I begged leave to ask a question, and he gave me permission.

'I understand, Governor,' I said, 'that the prison rules accord religious services to all convicts. How then is it that I am kept from chapel.'

'We have no Roman Catholic services here,' he told me, 'but I understand the directors are taking measures to have a priest visit you.'

Friday came, and I got my dinner of four ounces of mutton. I asked if I could not have a fish dinner, or some dinner other than a meat one on Friday; but was told I couldn't. 'You'll be very glad before long to have that on a Friday,' said the officer; and he spoke truly. But I didn't eat it that day, and when he came around for my tins after dinner, I put the meat and soup outside the door. 'Can't you keep that meat?' he queried, 'and eat it tomorrow.'

'No,' I said, 'I would eat it today if I kept it.' And, smiling at me, he shut the door more gently than usual.

I was shaved three times a week by one of the warders. The ordinary prisoner, I learned afterwards, was allowed to shave himself, but the razor was never entrusted to me in that prison. It was a most unwelcome task for the warder also; one or two of them would do it smoothly, but others would give me an awful scraping. Occasionally, convicts released themselves from prison by cutting their throats; and so many of them had cheated the government in this manner that the authorities decided to abolish the use of razors altogether. Now, prisoners' beards were clipped monthly with a scissors.

I got a bath once a week. The water was warm, but very dirty. The bath was a long trough over which covers were erected to prevent the prisoners from communicating; but there was nothing to stop the water, in which the prisoners on each side were washing, from flowing in on me. Our legs could touch each other under the sheet-iron that kept us apart and I hardly ever took a bath that I hadn't some unfortunate thrusting his leg into my compartment in order to pick up, or rather kick up, an acquaintance. 1One day I chanced to be next to Charles Kickham in one of these places. I had seen him as I was passing the door of his crib, so I stripped in haste, jumped into the trough, and stuck one of my legs as far as I could into his compartment, poking about until I touched him. I spoke to him as intelligibly as I could with my big toe; and he seemed to understand me, for he gave it a 'shake hands'. To do this he must have dived down a bit, so I drew back my foot, and, taking another dive, thrust my hand in and caught his; but he gave it such a squeeze that I would have screamed had I not feared to attract the officer's attention. The next day I bathed, I thought Kickham was again in the same place, and endeavoured to renew the acquaintance. I dressed in a hurry, and, as the officer had his back turned, I got out and cried 'Ready!' but simultaneously snatched at the hand of the other man who was dressing. He grasped mine affectionately, but as our eyes met I saw that it was not Kickham, but some poor fellow who was blind in one eye and in possession of a most pugnacious looking face. Next period, when I was getting my hour's 'airing', the new acquaintance never lost sight of me. It amused me, when passing him, to see how amiably he would try to look at me, and what an expression of friendship would beam from that one eye of his. I reciprocated the look as well as I could. I suppose he was an offender of some kind, but, no matter — he was a human and a prisoner, and here we stood on equal terms.

I took advantage of one of the governor's visits to repeat my application to be allowed to write, but was told he wasn't authorized to permit me. I asked him could I write to the Secretary for Home Affairs, and he said that that was a matter I could bring before the directors. I wanted to know how, and was informed that they met in the prison once a week, and any prisoner, on application to the governor, could have his name taken down to see them. 'Then, Governor,' I said, 'please take my name.' But the governor told me that I should tell my officer; and my officer would take me before him the next day and would make the order to have me see the directors if my business was legitimate. I gave my name to the officer. He took me to the governor; the governor put my name down; and when the directors came I was conducted into their presence. They gazed steadfastly at me and, in obedience to the order to stand to attention, I took position in front of a large table. The officer who conducted me in announced, 'Treason felony convict 26, Jeremiah O'Donovan Rossa; servitude for life.' Captain Gambier (the old gentleman) was chairman. 'What do you want?' he asked bluntly.

'To write a letter to Mr Stansfield, member of parliament.'

'We cannot permit it. Anything else?'

'To write a letter to the Secretary of State.'

'Granted. Anything else?'

'Can you give me any information regarding the religious services which the rules say all prisoners must attend, for I can see nothing of the kind in this establishment?'

'We have made arrangements to have a priest visit you, and he will give you whatever information you may need on the matter. Anything else?'

'No, thank you.'

A few days later, the door of my cell was thrown open, and in came a priest. I was very glad to see him. 'Twas a sight for sore eyes to see any one or any thing that had not the colour of the prison on it, and as the holy father closed the door behind him, I felt joy that at last I had someone I could talk to. But I was soon chilled by the icy words of this personality. My readers may guess that I would soon ask him something about Ireland, but as soon as I did he told me I was not to ask him anything that did not appertain to his prison duties. The conversation turned back to religion, and again I offended by asking some irrelevant or irreverent question. Fr Zanetti stamped his foot, and told me his honour was at stake, and not to be trespassing on it. A third time I offended by asking him could he tell me anything he might have seen in print about my wife and children, and a third time he told me I must not ask him questions about the outside world or anything in it. I turned the conversation to the state of my library, asking him what he could do for me in the way of books. He would see about that, and tell his man in Millbank to make out a list of books from the Catholic library so they might be forwarded to Pentonville for us. He would try to have each of us get one every fortnight, in addition to the one we were getting; and I was elated at this, for the little book I had was worthless.

The next week came, and with it his reverence, bringing a double-columned volume of Lingard's *History of England*. I hugged it to my chest on seeing the large amount of reading it would make possible. I parodied for it the old Irish song in praise of whisky, where the lover of it, embracing the bottle, exclaims:

'*Mo bhean agus mo leanb thú*
Mo mháthair agus m'athair thú,
Mo chóta mór is mo 'rappar' thú
Is ní scarra mé go brágh leat.'

'My woman and my child are you,
My mother and my father, too:

My greatcoat and my wrapper new;
And I will never abandon you.'

Fr Zanetti told me he had made arrangements (with Canon Oakley) to say Mass for us every Wednesday and Sunday; and, as he would come by every Thursday to visit us, the week would be pretty well broken up. If anyone notices that I refer frequently to priests or ministers, let them understand that they were the only Christians I met in my prison life, and the only ones to break its monotony. I could see no other man who did not have the prison livery on him, and as for seeing a woman – Lord bless you! – I was for two years without setting eyes on the face of an angel, and nearly three years without hearing the voice of one.

The day the priest brought me the *History* I had a long talk with him about my religious duties. He counselled me, seeing that I was imprisoned for life and could do nothing in the outside world, to give up my movement oath and become a good Catholic. 'And, Father,' I asked, 'can I not be a good Catholic unless I give up that oath?'

'No.'

'Then I fear I'll never again be a good Catholic.'

'If you were on your dying bed, wouldn't you give it up?'

'I would not.'

'And would damn your soul for eternity?'

'I don't believe God would damn my soul for that. If all my other sins were forgiven but that of swearing to fight for the liberty of my country, I would face my Creator with a light heart.'

'Well,' said he, 'I'm sorry for you. Your heart is better than your head. I will pray for you; and, as a special request, ask you to pray for me.'

He told me that in the prisons they did not alter the fare on Fridays for Catholics, but that the Church had given us permission to eat meat on those days, and that no fasts need be observed. I did not tell him that I had been 'a Friday dog' for two weeks now. Hunger, and reflection in solitary confinement, had got the better of my scruples in complying with the abstinence practice. The first Friday I put out my meat. The second Friday I kept it in my cell and ate it on Saturday. I did not feel there was much merit in doing this, and the third Friday I broke the pledge quite deliberately by eating my four ounces of mutton.

One Sunday morning my door was opened, and the officer told me to prepare for chapel. I told him I was prepared, and he ordered me to bring my prayer book and my stool. I was marched through halls, around corners, down stairs, and along dark passages, till I was halted outside a little chapel. It was in the basement of the building where the 'dark cells' were located. Two dykes had been dug along the sides of the hall for the purpose of laying pipe in them, and the prisoners sat, each on his own stool, a yard apart between the mounds of earth that had been thrown up. A warder with club in hand stood in the door of each of the 'dark cells', and if a side-squint was noticed from any one of us, the warder shook his stick at the offender.

My eyes were fixed on the prayer book, according to discipline, but my mind was elsewhere, and I was rambling through graveyards and abbeys of the old land, till the warder prodded me in the side with his club to make me aware that I should not be kneeling when the others were standing and the priest was reading the Gospel. I was the last man taken into the cave, and, when Mass was over, the first to be taken out. The officer made a motion toward the rear with his club. And I took up my stool and marched away without having seen the face of one of my companions.

While I was taking my 'airing' one day, someone came into my cell and took away one of my library books. I made a noise about it, but was told it had been taken away by order, for the rules did not allow a prisoner to have more than one library book, and as the priest had given me one a few days before (contrary to regulations), the matter must now be corrected by taking it away.

Twice a week the searching officers came into my cell and turned everything upside down and inside out, looking for something but finding nothing. I had to strip to the buff in their presence; and when they had examined me quite naked, they'd leave me to dress again.

I managed to keep in my cell two little bits of slate, each about an inch square, but it wouldn't be nice to tell where I hid them. I kept them for communicating with my friends. We were exercised in that yard I've called the 'coach wheel' and, by throwing pebbles over the wall and getting pebbles thrown back in return, could learn if there was someone in the 'spoke' adjoining. I'd throw over a bit of slate with a few words scratched on it. At first throw it would have my name on it, and the words, 'Who are you?' And if he was anyone I knew, we'd keep throwing our pieces to and fro while the hour lasted. I watched to see when the officer's eyes would be off me, to write a few words; and I suppose the same instinct that guided me would guide my correspondent. 'The Pagan' was the person I fell in with most often, and he was at a disadvantage, since he could not read well without his spectacles. Sometimes he would take my bit of slate to his cell, and it might be days before I could contact him again and have a reply. In taking in my tablet and bringing it out, I hid it in my necktie, just opposite the apple of the throat. This was the only spot that used to escape the fingers of the jailer who searched me. If he found my treasure, I don't know how many days bread and water it would have earned me.

The prisoners got a 'school hour' every week. During this interval the cell door was left open, and the 'schoolmasters' perambulated the wards, calling at each cell to see how their scholars were progressing. (This schooling was not conceded to us until we were a month in the prison.) My door was unlocked, thrown wide open, and left open without anyone entering my cell. This, for me, was an extraordinary development. What did it mean, I wondered. Soon, a respectable old man came in. He asked me, 'How are you for books?'

'Badly. I get but very poor books from the librarian; things that are not worth reading, and which I can read in one day.'

'What class are you in?'

'Third.'

'Well, I'll put you in a better one,' he promised, 'and the officer will have to give you better books.'

I thanked him. We had a few more words; then the bell rang and the hour was up. He bade me a good evening; and when the librarian came around the next day, he looked at my new card and gave me a better book than the ones I had been getting.

Some days afterwards my cell door was again thrown open, and another strange gentleman entered, announced himself as the prison chaplain, and, after asking me if I had a wife and children, where they were, how they were situated, and how I felt about them, opened a book and showed me a letter lying in it.

'That's my wife's writing!' I exclaimed.

'Yes, it is. It's for you. And you're to get a sheet of paper to write to her.'

I thanked him as forthrightly as a happy convict could, and, hoping I'd get along well, he bade me adieu. I have that letter before me now, and, to put a little variety into this memoir of mine, will let you read it.

> 17 Middle Mountjoy Street,
> Wednesday night.

My love, my darling husband,

I could not write to you earlier, my mind was so unsettled by disappointments, and it would have been bad to vex you with a despondent letter. Indeed, Cariss, my conscience accuses me of having indulged privately in very unhappy feelings. I wish you could look into my heart and give me absolution.

Now about the children. The last, I suppose, I may put first, the wee one. That makes me sigh for you every time I sense its presence. I don't know whether I'm most happy or most miserable about it. 'Tis all I have of you, and if things turn out badly, will be the only thing I'll care to hold my life for. The others are well. I spent an unhappy Christmas at Mr Hopper's in Kingstown, and dined here in my lodgings later that day. I thought of you all night, and cried myself to sleep near morning. Two years ago, I sat in a circle of father, mother, brothers, sisters, and friends, and did not dream of you. One year ago, I sat with you, and forgot home and family in your smiles. But this year, I sat alone and heart-weary, with strange faces instead of those I loved; and wondered what the next year would bring.

I was dreaming a few nights ago that you had come out of prison; and imagination painted you without that beard I was so fond of. I dropped a few tears especially for that, the night you were convicted. Goodbye, my own. I don't know whether this letter will reach you, or I'd write more. All our friends send love.

Fondly, your wife,
Mollie J.

I read that letter twice, three times, four times; and had not done reading it when the cell door opened and two officers entered. One of them held in his hand a leaf of paper, and the other had pen-and-ink. 'Here,' said the man who had the paper, 'is material for you to write a reply to that letter you've received; but I am instructed to tell you that if you write anything about the way you are situated, the work you are at, or about the prison officers, your letter will be suppressed.'

I wrote my letter and it was sent to the governor for transmission. Four days later he sent for me, and told me there were two passages in it that had to be expunged. In one, I had asked my wife to try to get me permission to write to an English member of parliament about the manner in which I had been tried; in another I had told her to write me a reply as soon as she could. I told the governor he might void both passages, and he said that that would make the matter all right. We also discussed the question of my asking a reply to the letter. I argued that the rules gave me the right to receive an answer to every letter I wrote; but he told me I should take the letter I had just received as the answer to the letter I was now sending.

* * * * *

ONE SUNDAY AT MASS I noticed that we had a larger congregation than usual. I was in my regular position, but found a man on each side of me, and others behind me. I side-glanced, and recognized the man on my right as being James O'Connor. I had heard there were new militants from Ireland, and was itching to know who they were. When the priest prayed aloud, I pretended to be responding to him, but, instead of uttering prayers, I muttered to James, 'Where is Stephens? Are they going to have a fight? How many of ye came? And who are those behind me?' James kept answering my 'prayers' till the officer beside him laid hold of him by the shoulder and conducted him to the rear of the congregation.

I'd learned from O'Connor that Stephens had remained in Dublin for some time after he was taken out of Richmond; that a fight was expected; that fourteen or fifteen had landed in Pentonville; that the men behind me were Kickham, Brophy, Mulcahy, Keneally, Roantree, Carey, Brian Dillon, John Lynch, Charlie O'Connell, John Duggan, Jerry O'Donovan of Blarney (the 'Galtee Boy'), and some others.

As I returned to my cell a prisoner impeded my passage at the foot of the stairway. His jacket, waistcoat and braces were loose, and his arms were extended. The officer was searching him before his entry into the cell, for we were all put through this search going to and coming from chapel – in fact, every time we left our cell or entered it. Looking at the prisoner, I saw it was Kickham, and had I acted on first impulse, I would have rushed to embrace him before the officers could have restrained me. I did not do so, and when I entered my cell, felt sick. I had checked my instinctive urge, and felt most uncomfortable until I found relief by bursting into tears. They flowed, and I let them flow. Some verses of Kickham's came into my head as I paced my cell, thinking of the unnatural events that had sent men like him to penal servitude. An Irish Catholic; yes, as true a one as any priest or bishop who had ever denounced the cause for which he was now suffering. As full of faith, as pious, and as moral, too. I should liked to have had Kickham's mind and faith, but fear I can never have either.

When I went to chapel the next Sunday, I had a position more favourable for observation. I was placed under the stairs and the officers could not see my head; when their eyes were off me I managed a glance or two at inmates who were nearby. I could not make out who Denis Dowling Mulcahy and Hugh Brophy were, though I had been intimately acquainted with both in Dublin. The clipping of their hair and beards had made such a change in their appearance that I could not recognize them until I managed to whisper to Hugh, and to be in the compartment next to John Keneally in the exercise yard, when he told me who Denis was by throwing his bit of slate over the wall that separated us. By and by I discovered that Mulcahy had been trying to convey news to us by scratching on the walls. A few words had been written on one brick which, by themselves, were unhelpful; but on other bricks I found words that made additional connections. In this way I learned that there had been no fight in Ireland, nor was one likely to come.

The letter I had received from my wife was a sort of burden for me, as I could not communicate its news to anyone else. Sorrows, it is said, are halved, and pleasures doubled, by sharing them with others; and I intensely wished to share my letter with my companions. I took it to 'exercise' with me every day for a week without success. But at last I discovered that 'the Pagan' was alongside, and, tying a bit of slate to the missive, threw it over the wall. I got the slate back again with the words 'All right,' written on it, and felt pleased that I had managed to give him a peep at the outside world. We ran heavy risks trying to communicate in this manner, but the relief we felt in doing so always had a greater effect on us than the fear of any punishment.

It was a week or more before 'the Pagan' could throw back my letter, and during that time I had contacted Keneally, Dillon and Lynch, and had some interchanges with them over the walls. When I had gotten the latest news they had brought from Ireland, our 'telegraphs' focused on our cold and hunger. We felt both constantly, and when the doctor visited, I thought there could be no crueler mockery of my state than his asking me if I ate all my food.

One morning about the first of March I awoke to find myself utterly sick. For three days I was laid up with a dysentery attack. The doctor ordered medicine for me, which the pharmacist brought me three times a day. Orders were issued that I be kept in my cell; I was to get no 'airing' or exercise, but must not stay in bed or refrain from work. An ordinary prisoner, I have since learned, would have been sent to hospital under similar circumstances, but there would be no hospital then or thereafter for me. The doctor ordered a flannel waistcoat for me when he saw how I was affected.

Another morning, when ordered out for exercise, instead of being sent to the 'refractory yard' I found myself in the area where the criminals were all tramping around in concentric circles. The variety of human I now confronted made things most interesting. I had had no society before, but now, found myself in a new situation; and the question was — whether to accept it, or kick against it. I thought that if I were to be separated from my companions and be associated regularly with these hard characters, I would rebel. Later, however, I did see Kickham, Lynch, Dillon, 'the Pagan', Moore, Duggan and others; but no two of our men were allowed near each other; four or five of the criminals would always be between them.

I saw Kickham pulled up once for having his hands behind his back with one stuck into the sleeve of the other to protect them from the cold. This was forbidden; one should always walk with one's hands by one's side. And on frosty mornings you'd see every man on the yard with his shoulders and his hands tightened up in the effort to make the sleeves of his jacket cover his fingertips. Dillon made signs to me one day that filled me with concern. Whenever I passed him, he'd point to the ground; and the inference I drew was that he was sinking into his grave.

John Lynch whispered to me one day, 'Rossa, the cold is killing me.' And it did kill the poor fellow. I missed him from the exercise ground shortly thereafter. He sank under the treatment ordered for us by the State authority, was sent to Woking Hospital, and from there, a few months later, went to the prison graveyard.

Some two months after I wrote my petition to the Home Secretary, asking for permission to write to an English member of parliament, the governor sent for me, and told me that my application has been refused. I wish I had a copy of this petition to put before my reader. I dare say it was not considered humble enough.

Coming from Mass one Wednesday morning, I encountered Charles Underwood O'Connell. We were ordered out of the chapel one by one, and had to keep twelve paces apart while walking along the corridors. Each of us carried his stool. Charlie turned a corner, and, seeing no one in sight, faced around to me and whispered, 'I was dreaming about you these past two nights, and you'll shortly hear some important news.'

In my cell I commenced stitching away. Charlie's dream coincided so closely with my own that I could not help but dwell on what he had told me. Pondering it further, I was startled by the turning of the key in the cell lock. My keeper entered, and told me to come. Off I marched till I was ordered to halt opposite the door of the governor's office. The door was opened from the inside, and my guard, in a voice that was almost a shout, roared, 'Forward!' I stood before the governor. Behind his desk he held a letter in his hand. My guard hollered: 'Number 34; 11-A; 227. Convict Jeremiah O'Donovan Rossa: life.'

The governor, addressing me, said, 'I've received a letter from your wife; but inasmuch as no letter is due you, I cannot give it to you. Yet, as the news it contains is of a family nature, and as the rules give us discretion to communicate to prisoners information similar to what this one contains, I'm able to inform you that on the 30th of April your wife was delivered of a son. She is not yet strong enough to be out of bed; the child is to be christened James Maxwell, after the names of her father and her brother.' Addressing my keeper then, he said, 'That will do.' The guard ordered me to 'right about face' and, as I raised my hand to signify that I wished to speak to the governor, he raised his club and ordered me to keep my hands by my side.

The governor asked what I wanted; and I asked him if he'd allow me to read the letter. He could not give me possession of it, but, on my asking him to read it, he did, and I thanked him. I then inquired if I would be allowed to write to my wife, and was told I would not; that the rules allowed a prisoner only one letter every six months. I said I had written only one letter since my conviction, was about five months a convict, and, under the circumstances of my wife just having been delivered, might I be allowed to write my second letter a month in advance? He informed me that that could not be; I should wait until six months from the date of my previous letter. Minutes later, I was again locked in, to wonder whether or not this event — the birth of a sixth son, which should have made any father rejoice — was a matter of grief rather than of joy to me. I paced the cell, unmindful of rules that forbade me to do so during working hours, but was soon brought to task for my lack of heed by a voice from beyond my door: 'What are you doing there? Stop that pacing, and start work!'

I sat down on my stool. The Bible, the prayer book, and the other religious book lay on the little table before me; and, instead of praying as a good man should have done, I dwelt on the hypocrisy of those people who supplied me with such books and trampled under foot all the principles of religion they contained. Here was my wife delivered of a child seven months after I had been taken from her, and they would not allow me to write her a line!

Fr Zanetti came by a day or two after I was given the news of my wee son, and I spoke of the heartlessness of my jailers. But patience, obedience, and resignation were his panaceas for the ills of life, and he enjoined me to cultivate them as diligently as I could. He put several questions to me that he hadn't previously touched on, asking if I didn't feel my chest sinking, my breath getting shorter, and my legs getting weak. I said, 'Yes.' After he had gone, I began to brood on what those questions might have meant, and concluded that there was something in the wind that indicated a possible change of climate. The following Sunday, Canon Oakley, in preaching his sermon to us, also touched on something similar; and when he had ended, I darted a look at a companion sitting next to me. An officer saw my glance, raised his stick, and threatened that if he again caught me turning my head aside, it would be worse for me.

Another Sunday in Pentonville, however, never came, for, on Wednesday morning at six o'clock we were taken out of our cells and marshalled into line on the same spot as on the night we had arrived. The scales were there before us, and, one by one, as we stepped on and off, records were taken of our weights. I had lost eight pounds since I had come to London, but others had fared worse. Cornelius Kane, Michael O'Regan and a few more had each lost as much as thirty pounds. Chains and handcuffs were brought into requisition. I found myself linked into a chain that bound eight of us together. It ran through the handcuffs, and a locked link attached each of us to a particular part of the chain, so that no one could slip away from his position. We were escorted to a van that awaited us in the courtyard; eight more were put into a second one, the remainder into a third. The gates opened, and we had a drive through the London streets.

At the station of the railway that would take us to our next prison, detectives and police were on hand to conduct us to our carriage. The three chainfuls of us were directed into it, and our jailers took seats in our midst. One old fellow, in charge of the escort, held the papers connected with us, but was as grim as a statue, and we couldn't get a word out of him. The train moved off. Addressing the 'commander in chief', I said, 'Governor, where can we be going?' He shook his head; another officer commanded 'Hush!' One of the other prisoners observed that we certainly ought to be allowed to exchange a few words now; a second seconded the suggestion; and Mulcahy debated the issue with the jailers, who were now threatening to report us when we arrived at our destination. At length it was settled that we might talk a little while the train was in motion, but were to keep silence during times when it laid over at stations on route. Our guards carried canvas bags with them, and the contents of these turned out to be bread-and-cheese for our dinners. Orders had been given that we were not to be let out of the cars until we reached the end of our journey at three in the afternoon.

Vans were awaiting us at the Portland Station, accompanied by the necessary number of guards. Twenty minutes later we were in Portland Prison.

7. In Portland:
The First Visit from My Wife

INSIDE THE ESTABLISHMENT'S gates we stood side by side in a waiting-room. Our chains were unloosed; our names were called; and as we answered we were told to strip, and were marched into a bathroom. After going through our ablutions we found new clothes set out for us, and having dressed, were directed back to the hall from which we had come. The old clothes had vanished. If we had had anything concealed in them, these were the precautions taken to deprive us of the contraband items. Our names were again called, and as we answered, each of us got three religious books and a library book. This latter was to be changed once a fortnight, but the religious ones would be 'permanent stock'. Two schoolbooks, also given us, could be changed every three months.

We were lodged in basement cells that had never previously been occupied. They were seven by three-and-a-half feet and separated from one another by corrugated-iron walls. The flooring was of stone, and the ventilators and windows of cast iron. When it rained the water poured into those cells, so much so that I often had to leave my hammock at night and huddle into a dry corner. I have before me as I write the report of five commissioners who inquired (in the summer of 1870) into our treatment, and take from it a few questions and answers in corroboration of what I say about this 'rain down'.

Dr Lyons: 'Is it possible that rain could have got in and flooded these cells, and wetted the bedclothes and beds?'
Prison Governor Clifton: 'It is quite possible, in the extraordinary gales we have here, and, the building being of

wood, that a man's blankets may get damp in the night, or slightly wet in those cells exposed to west and south winds. And when the treason felony prisoners complained to me that those cells were flooded, I visited the cells, and there were signs of moisture and wet, and the blankets were slightly wet.'

Dr Lyons: 'While the cells were in that condition, did you direct that the prisoners should be removed to other cells?'

Prison Governor Clifton: 'I had no other cells to send them to unless I located them with the other prisoners, which I knew would be distasteful to them.'

To me, who knew how little those jailers accommodated matters to our tastes or distastes, it was amusing to learn of the governor speaking as he did. It may be interesting to record the instructions that followed us to Portland, and to observe that these were written by an Irishman and a Catholic, the son of a man who was a champion of Catholic emancipation and an associate of Daniel O'Connell — William Fagan, member of parliament for Cork. Men like him got an emancipation that left us enslaved. It freed them from the disabilities that prevented them from filling government positions; withdrew their support from the cause of nationality (of the people at large), and opened a way for the Keoghs and O'Hagans to become the oppressors of their own race.

Governor Clifton was questioned by Lord Devon as to the instructions he received regarding us.

The Governor's Office, Portland Prison,
15 May, 1866

To Wm. Fagan, Esq.

Sir,

I have the honour to acquaint you that pursuant to warrant dated 5th inst., I received twenty- four treason felony convicts from Pentonville, but have not yet been furnished with the instructions (as to their treatment) referred to in the circular letter of the 9th. The Secretary of the Board of Prison Directors intimated that they were coming, and merely stated that instructions would be forwarded. Pending orders respecting them, I have employed them in the washhouse.

Your obedient servant,

George Clifton.

A few days later Clifton reported that he received the letter back with this memorandum:

Mr Clifton,

I regret that my absence at Chatham prevented my issuing instructions to you on the subject. They are to be located in the last lot of new cells passed by me at my last visit as fit for occupation. Those are the cells in 'D' Hall that we visited. They were then completed. The prisoners are to be worked in a separate party at labour equal to their ability, and are to be kept and exercised by themselves on all occasions. Full marks are to be awarded to them for their labour, except in cases of proved misconduct; and they are to be worked by Protestant officers (English, in whom you have full confidence), and not employed in prison domestic duties except as to their own cells or halls. You must therefore locate them on the works in a secure position where too much attention will not be drawn to their isolation; at the same time, in a position where their safe custody, or the officer's honesty, will not be compromised. Due provision will be made for the attendance of a Roman Catholic priest, but, until one is nominated, there will be no objection to one of these prisoners being designated to read prayers to the others.

William T. Fagan

There was a works prison in Portsmouth where there was a resident Catholic chaplain, but that would not do for us. Portland was a place where a priest's foot had never polluted the soil, and there could be no sympathetic influence there to imperil our safekeeping. These people, as can be seen from the instructions from a Catholic director, would not trust an Irish Protestant near us. No, he had to have the English brand on his Protestantism to make it acceptable when the guardianship of Irishmen was in question. Mr Fagan would possibly be a good Irishman and good Catholic if an Irish Catholic government were paying him the same salary he is now getting. He is paid to work for the English, and is doing it faithfully, like many other pious, 'patriotic' Irishmen.

The day after our arrival we were taken to be fitted with shoes and boots. The shoes for Sunday and cell wear; the boots for the prison works. But weren't they boots! Fully fourteen pounds in weight, those that my youthful mind had imaged in reading of the 'seven league' boots of Jack the Giant Killer were nothing to them. The felon's broad arrow was impressed on the soil at your every step. It was not enough to have it branded on your cap, your shirt and vest, your stockings, jacket-and-trousers, but the nails in your boot or shoe soles were hammered in so that whatever ground you trod left traces that 'government property' had travelled over it. The handle of the cat-o'-nine-tails that opens the convict's back is marked with it, as is the Bible that the minister reads to soothe him when he is groaning in his cell after a scourging. You see it on your comb, your tin pint, your knife; and if it does not enter your soul, it does find its way into your mouth branded on the bowl of your wooden spoon.

It took about two hours to fit us with the boots and shoes, and during this time we were walked about the yard and allowed to speak to each other two by two. This was the first sunny glimpse we had had of prison life. To be allowed to walk about and hear each others' voices; and to have the news that O'Connor, Carey, Mulcahy and others had brought (who were in the outside world three months later than some of us), were things the value of which a free man could not appreciate. O'Leary said it would be grand if this kind of prison life continued. We did not know what disposition would be made of us, of course, but the question was soon answered. When we had all been foot-fitted, orders were given us to draw up in a double line. The governor appeared and, to the cry of 'Hats off!' we uncovered.

He made a short address, trusting we would be of good conduct, as he intended to maintain with utmost strictness the discipline of the prison. He could be mild or severe as might be necessary. I asked the governor if I could write a letter to my family, as the prison rules stated that every convict could write one on reception. He informed me that that was a privilege not permitted in our cases — we could not write until special permission had been received from the authorities; and here again, in this matter, we were being treated worse than the English thieves and throttlers.

Next day we were taken to the washhouse, and the labour of our life in Portland commenced. There were tubs full of suds and dirty clothes, and, feeling that I would rather have a hand in anything but them, I looked around to see if something better would turn up. I laid hold of the handle of a pump, and commenced pumping away. A large water-trough had to be filled. I kept at my task for half an hour, by which time the tank was full, and, as I turned about, wiping the sweat from my face with a kerchief, I saw that I had gained my point. All the tubs were now manned, and I was detailed to fill the tank whenever it was empty. This done, my duty was to sort the linens. Broken garments were to be picked out from the unbroken sets and sent to the menders, and the good articles were to be made up into kits, each consisting of a shirt, a handkerchief, a pair of stockings, a flannel drawers, and a waist-coat. Every Saturday night each prisoner got his bundle, and every second week the bundle would be minus the flannels, the prisoner only getting changes of these once a fortnight. Occasionally I had half-an-hour or so of taking clothes into the drying-room and bringing them out; so my labour in the washhouse was somewhat diversified — just what suited me, for of all things in prison life or in any life I cannot bear, it is to be kept from morning till night at one occupation.

Sunday came; the bells rang for religious service; we heard the assemblies and trampings to chapel; but there were no devotions for us unless we chose to be devout in our cells. We had come to Portland bringing with us our registrations of 'Roman Catholic'; but, because no priest was assigned to the prison, the governor informed us that one of us would be allowed to officiate on Sundays until a clergyman was assigned. The prisoner chosen suggested that we might read prayers or a passage from the Bible in the hall outside our cells. Denis Mulcahy was our chaplain. He knelt at the end of the hall on a stool, with his books on a table beside him, and repeated aloud for us the morning and evening prayers, a litany, and a chapter from the Bible. In the latter devotion he selected those parts of the Holy Book that harmonized best with our feelings. It was pleasing to hear him reading of denunciations of tyrants and oppressors, and sympathy for their victims, with curses and punishments for the liars and perjurers, and blessings for all who had suffered persecution for justice's sake. It was the most treasonable preaching I had ever heard.

AFTER A WEEK, an order came down to put us to work in the

*   *   *   *   *

quarries. And in obedience to the mandate of Mr Fagan — 'locate them on the works in a secure position, where too much attention will not be drawn to their isolation' — we were placed in a little valley in view of the governor's office. He had his spyglass on us whenever it pleased him, and all diligence was shown in carrying out the instruction to place the Irish convicts 'in a position where their safe custody, or the officers' honesty, would not be compromised.'

The valley was within three hundred yards of the main prison. It opened towards the building, which was the only view we had, as on all other sides it was surrounded by high ground on which trolley-ways had been constructed. We dared not ascend any of this ground to take a view of the sea, or the island, or the other prisoners working in the distance. We had, however, opportunity now and then to see some of these as they were being taken to hospital or to 'the dead house' on stretchers after being maimed or killed, or having committed suicide, on the works.

Our first day in the quarries we occupied ourselves erecting blocks on which we were to dress stones. The blocks were three yards apart, and I found Luby, O'Leary and myself on the points of one triangle. When I turned around, I was on the apex of another triangle having Denis Mulcahy and James O'Connor for its base; and so with each of the others. At this time it was about the middle of May, and we were obliged to work with our jackets off. Some cold days came, and the sea-wind seemed to cut clear through me; yet the prison rules decreed that it was 'summer' season, so we had to work as all the others worked. Our first task was to make 'nobblers', a 'nobbler' being a stone with five sides dressed and one rough side. When the worker had his rough stone chipped down to a nobbler, he laid it by his block, called a companion, and, both taking the handbarrow, went to the quarry for another rough stone.

We got up at five in the morning, had our breakfast at half-five, and were in the quarries at six. 'Twas a long day, and I always had a splendid appetite for my meals. When you came to dinner you entered your cell and shut the door. The orderlies for that day were called out, and placed at your door a canteen containing the dinner. The orderlies were then sent in, and the warder opened door after door, each prisoner taking in his dinner, the officer taking care not to open one door till the others were shut. Opening mine one day to pick up my tray, I heard, 'Leave that there, and turn your face to the wall.' I obeyed. I was taken before the governor. He had a large book in front of him, and said: 'Rossa, you are charged with speaking to the prisoner occupying the cell adjacent to you.'

'When, Governor?'

'Yesterday evening, at seven o'clock. Do you deny it?'

'I only ask, who makes the charge? In England you certainly are not going to convict a man without someone giving evidence.'

The governor addressed me: 'The patrol that was on duty outside your window yesterday heard you. Do you deny the charge?'

'I admit or deny nothing,' I said.

The governor continued: 'As this is your first offence, I will not punish you severely, but the discipline of the prison must not be despised. I order you to be degraded; and fine you eighty-four marks. You must not speak or make noises in your cell while in this prison.'

'But can I speak at all?'

'Yes: you can speak to your companions while at labour; but must speak loudly enough that the officer in charge can hear you, lest you should be planning anything.'

I was marched back to my cell again and the door was locked. By and by it was reopened and I was handed my dinner. But I had to eat it without knife, plate or table, for this was one of the prison's punishment cells.

The bell rang at one and I was told to dress and get ready for labour. I had one piece of pleasant news to communicate when we arrived at 'pleasant valley', and that was that the governor had told me that we could speak while at work We availed of that privilege, much to the mortification of the officers in charge, for a great part of their recreation consisted in catching any of us who seemed inclined to carry on a conversation with his neighbour. But now they were curbed themselves, and appeared to regard that as a curtailment of their authority. As we were at the height of our glee at this change in our affairs, Gunning, our supervisor, cried out, 'Two of you men come and clean out the privy here.' In obedience to his command, the two who were first on his list went at the work. Once every three weeks this unpleasant duty was performed by us. Gunning, talking to me later, told me I was one of two who should empty the closet next. When I went to cell that evening, I called my officer and told him to put my name down to see the governor; and next day was taken before him. 'Governor,' I said, 'the officer told me I was one of two expected to clean that privy next; and I wish to know if that work is expected of me.' He said that it was and I answered, 'All right,' and turned away; but was simultaneously nursing a determination to refuse point blank to do such work when the time came. I told my companions I would refuse, and some of them remonstrated with me. Luby observed that obedience and subordination were more than anything else in accord with the dignity of the national cause; and in this I agreed with him. John Mitchel submitted to the prison discipline, he said, and did his work like any other convict. But I could never imagine Mitchel shoveling dung out of a privy; and I know I never did it myself without wishing that the English Prime Minister and the Secretary for Home Affairs were within reach of my shovel. Luby's argument at length persuaded me to rethink my resolve, for some of our own party had cleaned out that closet earlier, and my refusing to do it would appear to be a reflection on their spirit, or some presumption of my superiority.

*   *   *   *   *

THE PARTITIONS BETWEEN our cells were of corrugated-iron, and in the one adjacent to mine was a slit through which you might have passed a shilling. We occasionally had whispers through this, and the spy outside our cells must have heard me through the venti-lator on the occasion for which I was fined eighty-four marks. When a convict is sentenced, every day of his term is put down against him as six 'marks'. He is then told that if he is obedient and works hard, he can earn eight marks a day. Thus, if his term be twenty days, he can work out his 120 marks in fifteen days. But he may work for fourteen days, earning eight marks a day, and his officer may report him for looking at another prisoner, or for some other offence, so he may be fined as many marks as would put him back to his original sentence.

A fortnight after we had gotten permission to talk to one another, the governor stood over us on the trolley-way, and, in our presence, brought the officers to account for permitting us to talk loudly. The annoyances then commenced in earnest. If we talked softly we subjected ourselves to a report; and so worried was I at length that, on Gunning scolding me one day, I said to him, 'Officer, I have had warnings, threats and admonitions enough from you. I know the rules and regulations. You know them, too; and when you see me infringe them, just report me to the gov-ernor. Let him punish me; but let you keep your tongue off me.' Next day I was reported, and got my twenty-four hours on bread and water; that is, eight ounces of bread at half-five in the morning, with a pint of water, and eight at half-five in the evening with water. No dinner, no bed at night, no open-air exercise; no stool or other seat in your cell; and, of course, solitary con-finement.

Repeatedly I was reported for speaking too loudly while at work, and bread and water followed each report, till at length orders came down that we were not to speak loudly or softly. When that order was issued, Gunning had us remove our blocks two yards further apart than they had been previously; and, thinking that I was too comfortably situated with Hugh Brophy, he took me away from the quarrying and placed me in an isolated position with O'Keefe and Luby. O'Keefe had just been sent to Portland. He had as great a desire for speech as anyone else, and would often try to reach me with a whisper. I could not hear, and occasionally alarmed him by asking, in an ordinary tone, what he was saying or trying to say. O'Keefe was a good Irish scholar, and I would try to draw him out by giving him a phrase or two in Gaelic, which was high treason to the jailers. They forbade us to use our mother tongue even on the days when we were allowed to talk. They called the Irish language 'slang'. Thomas Duggan of Ballincollig was severely reprimanded once for speaking Irish, and was threatened with punishment if he repeated the offense.

At this time, Kickham was in a very poor state of health. Five days after he came to the prison he was sent to the hospital. Two weeks later, he was sent to the quarries in weak condition with running sores on his neck. So weak was he that he could hardly stand. We were required to march to the quarry in military step, with one officer walking to our front and another at our rear. I was behind Kickham. Suddenly I saw Gunning rush at him and stagger him four or five paces out of the ranks. He then laid hold of him and dragged him to the rear. The reason for all this, I suppose, was that Kickham was not keeping in step, and Gunning wanted to maintain the 'military' formation. Kickham was again taken to the hospital shortly thereafter, and that was the last I saw of him.

William Rountree, one of the men next to me in the quarry, at one point was in a very precarious state of health. He put his hand into his boot one day, and when he drew it out it was all bloody: not spotted with blood — as he slanted the palm of his hand, the blood dripped off. He was afflicted with haemorrhoids, and remained in that state for three months before he was admitted to the hospital for treatment. Declared unfit for duty then, he was removed to the invalid station at Woking.

Another day, Martin Carey was sledging; and as he swung the sledge the iron head flew off its handle. Carey knocked his hand against a rock and broke one of his fingers. He was taken to the hospital. The doctor wanted to amputate that finger, but Carey would not consent, in consequence of which the doctor would not allow him to remain in the hospital. Sent out to work the next day with his hand in a sling, Martin was seated on a heap of stones in a corner of our area, a hammer was given to him, and he was put to breaking stone there day after day for six weeks before he regained the use of his injured hand. When Carey wanted to get a load of large stone, I waited on him the first two or three days; but, the officers seeing that I took advantage of this to have a whisper with him, I was forbidden to approach him, and another prisoner was detailed to keep Carey supplied with work. Carey overheard the governor tell a warder to report some of us for 'idleness', and next day those of us reported were taken before this impartial judge to be sentenced to bread and water.

Visits from our friends and kin were occasions the authorities availed of in order to rile us. Every convict was allowed one every six months, but if the officers chose to have him on their books as 'ill-conducted', we might never see the face of a friend from the outside. My wife had written from Ireland to know if she would be permitted to see me, and the governor told me one day that — as a favour to her, not to me — he would grant her permission to come. I told this to my friends, and we thought it would be well if some others could avail of her coming, so we might glean as much news as we could. Martin Carey saw the governor on the subject, and told him the only friend he cared to see was his mother, but, as she was old and could not come to Portland without a lot of inconvenience and expense, he would be obliged if the visit the rules allowed him was granted by letting him see Mrs O'Donovan. She could convey to his mother, who lived in Eyrecourt, County Galway, anything he had to say. The governor said he would consult the directors, and in a few days Carey was sent for and was told that the authorities would not allow him to see my wife.

For weeks I was anticipating her visit and had nearly given up on it when one day at dinner-hour my door was opened and I was told, 'Come.'

'Where now?' I said.

'Ask no questions,' said the officer, 'just come.'

I was taken to the room where we had all been examined on our first day here, and on entering saw my wife, and in her arms the baby I'd never until that moment seen.

I hesitated before approaching her because I'd heard that in the visiting areas there were panels or partitions between the parties. Discipline was so much on my mind that I stood there until she and I were directed to go behind a separating barrier. Or possibly I was moved by pride to refrain from making an advance. The officer beside her said, 'You can come up here and speak to your wife for twenty minutes; but if you tell her anything relating to matters inside the prison, or if she tells you anything relating to outside matters, I must end the visit.'

I sat down and took the baby in my lap, but the little fellow didn't know me – he was then but three months old. Indeed, I think his mother hardly knew me. It was the first time she had seen me since I was shorn, shaved, and dressed in convict fashion. She felt my hands, which were rough as oyster-shells, and my face had been baked to the colour of an earthenware crock. For the first few minutes I kept talking to the wee one, wondering what I could say to the mother: I think we parted without saying much at all. The jailer was right beside us, and my tongue seemed to be paralyzed. At the end of twenty minutes, the deputy governor came by, and said that in view of my never having seen the child before he would extend the time ten minutes longer. I had messages from Roantree, O'Connor, Mulcahy and others, but when I attempted to mention any other prisoner, I was told I should confine myself to my own case. As we were parting I recollected that I had scratched a few notes on a bit of slate, but when I took it out of my pocket the officer seized it. My wife vanished; and I went back to work with a heart heavier than ever.

When my wife got home she sent me a photograph of herself and the baby; shortly after its arrival the governor sent for me and said it was his duty to return it. I observed that it was a very harmless thing to allow me to keep. But no, it would not be allowed, the prison rules did not permit it; discipline must be maintained, and my photograph be returned. 'However,' said he, 'as you seem to be improving your conduct lately I'll let you look at the picture before I return it.' I took it from him, and looked, and gave it back. I afterwards learned that the thieves were allowed photographs; but then, those were thieves of good character, and, unfortunately for me, I was in bad repute. Indeed, the governor told me that if he had been in the prison the day my wife had come he wouldn't have allowed her to see me in consequence of my bad conduct. Further, that the deputy governor had exceeded his discretionary power by allowing me to see her in the reception-room instead of in the usual place. I told him he need not be discomfited on account of any happiness or consolation my wife's visit had brought me, and I was very sorry that Captain Bulwer's kindness had subjected him to a reproof. The deputy was one of the most gentlemanly of the officers I met in prison. He always did his duty, but, in doing it, never gave that haughty, contemptuous look that others gave, and never wantonly wounded our feelings by arrogant remarks.

Time passed, and the day came when I was again allowed to write a letter. This was written to my wife. I had mother in America, and was anxious to send her a line, but the authorities would not, for any consideration at that time, extend to me the privilege of an extra letter. They would not even give me a scrap of paper on which I might write a few lines (to enclose in my wife's) to the old woman on the brink of the grave. I made especial application to the governor for it, and he refused me.

My letter was written and turned in. The governor then sent for me. When I was placed in 'attention' attitude before him, he said: 'What use your writing these letters? You know I cannot send them out.'

'Governor, have you read my letter?'

'I haven't read it – I couldn't, the writing is so small. Your letters take up more of my time than do those of all the other prisoners; and you've written between lines, a thing especially forbidden in the instructions.'

'Well, that's a thing you might excuse me for, seeing that I have but one leaf of paper, and, with such a large family, so much to say. I can read the letter in five minutes for you, and if you find anything objectionable in it, I'll scratch it out.'

I commenced, and ended without his objecting to anything. But still he said, 'No use. I can't allow that letter to be published.'

'Published!' I protested, 'Sure, the letter is for my wife.'

'But your wife publishes your letters.'

'And more than that. When those people come visiting here, they publish all they can learn about the prison, and bring a lot of trouble on me.'

'I'm very sure I wouldn't write letters like that to my wife if I thought she'd publish them; and I'm sure she wouldn't do that.'

'Well, if you write at the head of that letter that it is private and not to be published, I'll pass it.'

I took it, and wrote: 'Do not, love, make such letters as this public. I don't write for such a purpose. This one is confidential, as all my letters to you must needs be.' The letter itself follows:

23 August , 1866

My love,

I'm in doubt whether it is better to scold you or coax you into sending me what I desire from you at present, and have been disappointed at not getting. Scolding might be best if you were as much afraid of my voice now as before; but, as possibly you'd place scant value on my growling at you from my cage, I had better see what I can do some other way. I will not scold you, Mollie; I fear I'm not a good hand at coaxing, so I'll only ask you lovingly to send me a very, very long letter — six, ten, or twenty sheets of paper! You often gave me as much when I was not so much in want. What matter if they must be sorrow-laden? I've accompanied you in sunny hours; and cannot I have your company when the rain is pelting? No political news; all about yourself — how you've met the world since, and particularly when you went to Carbery. Who were kind and who cold to you, etc. Did the children realize their position? Did they say anything of me? And what happened you every day, hour and minute? For in so much of your life I am interested. If you have nothing to write a long letter about, write about nothing, and that will be something to me.

How many things I had to say which I forgot (in our visit); and that I would not be allowed to speak of, in that short space of half an hour! When you left, I felt I had relieved myself of very little of my burden; indeed it weighed heavier. A little punishment awaited me that day, and I thought I was being taken to receive it when you took me by surprise. I was fascinated by you, Mollie, exclusive of the baby. I did not ask about our fifth son, must needs speak of him in the fifth person, lest mention of his name might interfere with this transmission.

Regarding the four eldest — it is not pleasant that your father has the keeping of them when he has plenty of company of his own; but if my brothers or mother sent money for them I would rather they remained with him for a while than be separated. I have applied for leave to write to my mother. She might die any day, and then I'd feel so sorry that she had passed, thinking, perhaps, that she was forgotten by me. I shall go to the governor again tomorrow, and if successful will enclose a note for her; also, one for the children.

I am allowed to write now as a letter would be due me if I remained the same length of time in Pentonville. I might have had two visits there for my good conduct, which conduct I was not good enough to have had here. I had the misfortune to incur punishment discipline during the week of your visit. Such is tolerable, and preferable to punishment by harsh words.

The governor tells me he answers letters of inquiry from you as to my health. This he need not have done. Any kindness to you from anyone, I think more of than of anything regarding myself. You ought to keep a record of such things, that they may be available to me if I live again ever. You see that though my life is forfeit to the laws I'm unable to banish hope.

Write; and put one from each of the children with yours — their own handwriting and efforts, that I may be able to see these. If money be contributed by Irishmen for the maintenance of the children of the men imprisoned, I am not so

125

proud as to feel any qualm that mine are to be so cared for, though I would fling a contribution in the face of anyone who would tender it as charity. You are one of the trustees of money now; and I refer to this as I am anxious that when you withdraw from such responsibility you will be able to have your accounts in good order. Our enemies always make money a handle with which to hurl slander.

The governor says that you had a visiting ticket from the Home Secretary. You might try again. I would hope you'd get liberty to write more often. Do you write to Mrs Keane and to Mrs Duggan of Ballincollig? You ought. Have you anyone to rock the cradle when you write?

Love, ever fondly and faithfully.

After some weeks I got a reply. My wife asked me some questions about money matters, and wrote a special letter to the governor asking him to allow me to answer them. He sent for me, and said he could not allow me to do so, but if I wrote the answers to her questions on a slate and sent it to him, he would have them copied and sent off. I did so. On asking him a month later if they had been transmitted, he said, 'No. I could not be sending your love letters to your wife. It would be lessening your punishment.' I went back to my cell, and resolved that, fair play or foul, I would never stop until I had found some means of reaching the outside world and getting some account out of our treatment.

We fell in at chapel with a good fellow named Lynch. He was a Francis Street, Dublin man, but was sentenced in Bolton for seven years. He gave us writing materials; and I went to work to break the law by writing a 'surreptitious letter'. Lynch told us he could get this conveyed to the outer world for £3, and that out of that sum we could get ten-shillings-worth of tobacco. It was a novel thing to get tobacco here, and, as some of my friends craved a taste of it, I requested it with an order on my wife for that £3. But as I feared that letters to Mrs O'Donovan Rossa would be opened by the post office I directed this one to the mother of Michael Moore, and on the cover of the envelope wrote in tiny letters, 'For Mrs O'D.' Moore kept watch for me during the dinner hours while I

wrote. He lay down on the floor of his cell, and under his door
there was a space that would enable him to see through the hall.
Sometimes the slippered officer who kept watch outside would go
upstairs to have his peep at those in cells above ours. That was my
time for scribbling, but when Moore would see the jailer coming
down he'd signal to me, and I'd stop.

I kept watch for Moore many hours in similar position while he
was engaged in work far more dangerous than writing surreptitious
letters. He was trying to break a hole in the wall of his cell large
enough to admit him into the yard, through which hole he and I
meditated an escape. Hugh Brophy and Martin Carey were in the
next two cells, and if Mike found that he could do his work, the
three were to operate about the place where the iron partition
divided their cells, and the four of us would fight our way out. We
did not intend to harm anyone, but had agreed that, after we had
made our way into the yard, if any man came upon us before we
had scaled the wall (with the aid of sheets), there would be nothing
for it but to throttle him. Moore stole a small chisel out of our
tool-box on the works. I don't know where he hid the chisel in his
cell; but when he had it there, he would give me a signal to lie on
the flagstones and keep my eye on the hall. I would hear him
scraping away for an hour, at the end of which time he'd give
another signal that he was getting up. Through the slit in the partition he'd whisper that the work was going well. He had already
made a hole large enough to hide the chisel. He'd close it up then,
and plaster the surface with the whiting he used for brightening
his tins. The colour was very much like the wall whitewash, and
no distinction could be discerned when one stood at the door as
he had shaded the spot by an arrangement of certain of his cell furniture. Brophy, Carey, I and a few others supplied him with the
whiting. Day after day for a fortnight he worked at that hole in the
wall, and I kept my ear to the floor and my eyes on the stairs. At
the end of that fortnight Moore was half-way through the wall, and
we were half-way to freedom, for failure, of course, never entered
our heads. Once we got out, we would die game rather than return
to our cells. But as my ear was to the flagstones I heard Mike
groan, and he came to the slit in the partition. 'Rossa, 'tis all up

with us,' he said in an agonized whisper. 'The stones in the middle of the wall are fastened to one another by links of iron, and we can't remove them. We must give up. Lie down again till I shut the hole.'

Brophy and I had had another scheme of escape shortly before this. As we quarried a large rock one day we discovered a hole under it that appeared to be a cave. It had escaped the officers' scrutiny. When the stone had been removed we covered up the hole. We took five or six others into our confidence, who would keep the jailers engaged while we examined our discovery. We found it was a fissure between rocks that did not extend far, but ought to serve as a hiding-place. For three or four days thereafter, our friends were bringing their bread to the hole till we had sufficient to sustain me and Hugh for a few days. We would enter; the others would cover us up, leaving simply some airholes that couldn't be detected except by the closest search. We planned to emerge at night, make a raft, and paddle across the bay to the mainland about three miles distant. But when we actually tried to hide in the cave we found we could not get into it, and had to abandon the project as hopeless.

*   *   *   *   *

THE LETTER I had written to my wife was ready for delivery and I laid plans to pass it to Lynch at chapel one Sunday morning. But my first attempt to reach the world surreptitiously failed, and brought on me a long train of punishments.

When I took my position in the chapel, Lynch was two seats behind me, and not on my side of the aisle. But a principal who was on watch at the back of the congregation saw some movement on Lynch's part and, on leaving the chapel, he was detained and stripped. I was taken to the dark cells, and, looking behind me as I entered one, saw Lynch in the charge of another officer. I had to strip to the buff, my clothes were searched inch by inch and seam by seam. Nothing was found on me, and I remained in suspense until twelve the next day, when I was taken in *deshabillé* before the governor.

'You are charged,' said he, 'with attempting to get a letter out of prison surreptitiously to the wife of another prisoner. What have you to say?'

'The charge, as it is recorded, is a false one.'

He held up my letter. 'Do you deny the writing?'

'I deny or admit nothing; but I ask you to take down what I just said.'

The governor spoke to the officers: 'Take him away. His case is postponed till I hear from the directors.' And the Board being heard from, I was sentenced to three days on bread and water, and fined as many marks as would add a few months to my life sentence.

At work again in the quarries, I learned from Michael Moore that the governor had been serious when he charged me with writing to the wife of another prisoner; and whether or not the governor believed that I was intriguing with Moore's wife, he endeavoured to make others believe it. I first treated the matter as a joke, but when I came to have it corrected on the prison-books, found the matter to be no joke at all.

Moore had made application to the governor to be allowed to write to his wife, and the governor asked him if he knew that another man in the prison was in communication with her. 'What!' said Moore. 'Oh,' said the governor, 'I would not have mentioned the matter, but I thought you knew about it.' Moore insisted on his right to know all; and the governor told him I had been detected sending a surreptitious letter to his wife. Moore affected the greatest indignation, and kept it up when he came out to work, demanding an explanation from me. As at this time we were forbidden to speak, and as the necessity for explaining away the charge seemed superior to that of maintaining silence, I kept talking to Moore, and the more I talked, the more he remained dissatisfied. When the officers went in that evening, they reported that Moore and Rossa were on the verge of a fight on the works; and I demanded to see the governor next day, to learn why he had told falsehoods about me to my fellow prisoner. Next day, I was taken to the 'judgment chamber'. Luby, Keane, Duggan and three or four others were there also. I was called in first. I asked the governor on what basis he had told Moore that I was detected in correspondence with his wife; and he said it was by virtue of a letter he had in his possession.

'Cannot you look at that letter,' I asked, 'and see on the corner of the envelope the words, "For Mrs O'D."? Cannot you also see that it is addressed to Mrs Mary Moore? If you'll only look at your books, and find the record of the letters Mr Moore has received from his wife and his mother, you'll see that his wife's name is Kate, and that it is his mother who is named Mary. If you read the body of the letter you'll find allusions to "my children"; and Moore's wife has no children. I ask you to correct this charge on the books, and correct also any erroneous reports you have made regarding it.'

The governor would have none of it and ordered me to be taken to the cells. As the warders approached me, I looked directly at him, and said, 'You have shown nothing but meanness in your treatment of us ever since we came into your hands.' I was immediately seized, and with scant ceremony was shoved through the hall and tossed into a darkened cell.

Next day I was brought before the governor. What had I to say?

'Governor, you've been slandering me; and placing on record in government offices false charges that could be exhumed for the defamation of my character when I am dead. You can do what you please with me while I'm living, I suppose, but your torture should end there.'

The governor answered: 'I did not, until I got back your letter yesterday, see the words "For Mrs O'D" on the corner of that letter. They had been written so small that no one could see them unless his attention was particularly directed to them. If you had acted with respect before me and given your answers in a proper manner, you would have fared differently. I will not punish you now further than to fine you forty-two marks.' He ordered me to be removed.

'Governor,' I protested, 'Will you give me permission to write to the Home Secretary on this matter?'

'I cannot. You can see the director when he comes.'

I went back to work feeling that the director, upon being approached, would correct the reports made regarding that letter.

But there are many tricks in such affairs, and the governor of a convict prison is not without his quota. The day before the director came I was reported for talking while at work; and the day he was in prison I was on bread and water. It was one of his duties to visit every prisoner in the cells. My door was opened; I stood to attention; and, seeing Mr Fagan outside, proceeded to tell my story. I was told I was forbidden to make any complaint while under punishment, and that the next time the director came, he would, if I was in good standing, go into my case. But the next time he came, I was again under punishment, and the time thereafter, and every time up to my exit from Portland Prison.

Lynch, in whose possession the letter was found, got three days on bread and water, twenty- five days on 'penal class' diet, and lost three months of the remission he had previously earned. He was to have left the prison a few months after having encountered me; but I met him twelve months later in Millbank, and he told me they had continued to report him time after time until they had taken away every remission day he had earned, and he had to work out his full seven-year term. When he came to chapel after his twenty- eight punishment days, he passed me another lead-pencil, and told me, in a note that the package contained, that he'd have paper, envelopes, and a pen and bottle of ink for me the next Sunday.

The circumstances behind his promise were that someone on the works had heard of his being in communication with me, and of his suffering punishment without 'squealing', and had offered to procure the needed items for a consideration, which consideration I readily consented to. Sunday came; I was on the lookout; and the writing materials came into my possession. I had two sheets of paper, two envelopes, and a little bottle of ink.

8. A Petition to the Secretary of State

SO STRICT WAS the watch kept on me now that I had no chance of writing in my regular cell at any hour between rising and retiring. The 'eye' seemed to be ever at the spyhole. At night I racked my brains for some feasible way of writing, and thought of two. One was to talk on the works deliberately, thus being sent to the punishment cells. When you entered one of these there was a strict search, yet you were safe there, the 'eye' not so constantly on you as elsewhere. I could, I hoped, carry in bits of pencil with me; sit with my back to the door and, using the sole of my slipper for a table, write my story on closet paper. The other plan was to sit up in my hammock all night, and write there as well as I could. I had as much light from the gas jet in the hall as would enable me to see the paper; but I hadn't much paper, and, if I attempted to write small, might wind up writing one line over another.

Martin Carey told me that he had a book in his cell that was not registered to him. It was a religious treatise, not stamped with the prison brand – one of the officers had left it with him by mistake. It had large margins on every leaf, and Martin said I could write as much as I wished on it. I took it, and arranged with Jerry Donovan to be provided with tiny supplies of pen-and-ink. In my cell I would begin to write, and the officer on guard would commence his patrol of the hall. He wore slippers, but everything would be so still I could hear his footfall as he approached my cell. If necessary, I would suspend my labours; then, when he had passed on, would go on with my work, making up for my loss of sleep by sleeping during dinner-hours. When I began I could see little more than the piece of paper I was writing on, but with practice did tolerably well. I consulted with Jerry and others as to the best mode of packaging and directing the pieces I had prepared, and, of course, hiding them until a time came when we could get them out.

I already had two letters written and had copied from memory a petition I had previously written to the Secretary for Home Affairs. A convict, if he is 'well conducted', has the privilege of writing such a petition once a year; but after my year in Portland the authorities were not at all inclined to grant me any such privilege. My idea was that I would also write a copy of that petition in hopes of getting it out surreptitiously. In one way or another I would get that copy into the hands of one or other of our visitors who might in turn be able to pass it to some Irish member of the House of Commons. The member, in turn, might be able to present it, or use it, in an interpellation in parliament.. My petition did, in fact, reach the outside world. The authorities, for their part, held it for two months before they vouchsafed an answer. On Christmas Eve I was called out of my punishment cell and brought before the governor. Two English convicts were in position beside me, and, the three of us having been called according to our numbers, we were told that our petitions had been duly considered and no grounds were seen for granting what we desired.

Nevertheless, I did not relax my efforts; and lest the copy of the petition that I had written should be seized, I set to work to make another. But, on an evening I was due to shave, I commenced to pare my pencil with the razor and, glancing toward the cell door, saw 'the eye' at the spyhole. I kept looking at it, and it kept staring at me. The key turned in the lock, and Warder Russell stood before me. He took both pencil and razor, went out, locked the door; with other warders reopened it a moment later. They took me to an unoccupied cell on the other side of the hall and ordered me to strip. They searched my clothes inch by inch, but found nothing till they came to the pocket of the jacket, out of which they drew three or four sheets of the paper I had been writing on. 'What's this?' asked the discoverer.

'Don't you see,' I said, 'that that's my closet paper.'

'And what's written on it?'

I was marched to a punishment cell, and, taken before the governor next day, was charged with misusing the razor and paper given me, with having forbidden articles in my possession, and with many other things connected with these offenses, such as disobedience, insubordination, insolence and impudence. Asked what I had to say, I said I would give my reply in writing. But as I would not get writing materials I said no more. The governor told me that this was such a serious case he would not adjudicate it himself, but would refer it to the directors and send me to punishment on light diet until they were heard from. In due course I was sentenced to three days on bread and water, and an order was read to me (from the directors) to the effect that I was not to be supplied weekly with the regular supply of waste paper, but would receive some from my officer every time it became necessary 'for purposes of nature'. The reader need not consider my feelings in detailing matters of this kind, and may not entirely believe me when I say that I could never approach any of those officers for that paper without feeling the humiliation that such a transaction necessarily would bring to a fellow human.

I took the scraps of paper to my cell, and wrote on them as much as I could of my petition. I had no seat or table in punishment-cell. How to write without a book or a table to lay paper on was the problem. 'Necessity is the mother of invention'. My shoes had been taken from me, but in place of them I had a pair of old slippers. The sole of one of these, turned upward, answered me for a table, and thus I wrote what got out into the world and brought on the sham inquiry by commissioners Knox and Pollock.

I went to work again with my companions, but our masters determined that we should have no peace. The governor came to the quarry and, saying that he'd heard some talk among us as he approached, brought the officers to account for allowing us the privilege of speech. After we had returned to work from dinner, Jones, one of our officers, told us he would be reporting seven or eight of us next day. We asked him if he had received orders to do so, and he was honest enough to say he had.

Action on his report was delayed a few days. Then O'Leary,

Luby, Keneally, Keane, O'Connor, a few others and I were taken barefooted before the governor and charged with speaking while at work. Some got off with reprimands and the loss of some marks. O'Leary, Luby and Keneally each got twenty-four hours on bread and water, and O'Connor and I were sentenced to seventeen days on bread and water, with the additional penalty that when that time had expired we would no longer be allowed to rejoin our own working party, but must be assigned to another gang.

One man detailed to help me in that party had an ill-looking countenance and was blind in one eye. He wanted me to help him put a stone on the block, and when he addressed me with 'Mate, give us a hand with this,' I laid my hammer on the block, and, addressing the warder, said: 'I don't think I'll do any more work today.'

'What's that?' snapped he. 'Take that hammer in your hand.'

'No,' said I.

He sent for a superior officer. The supervisor came, and similar words passed between the two of us. He ordered me to a punishment cell. At dinner hour I was brought before Major Hickey, the deputy governor. He told me that the governor was absent, and asked me to return to work and behave quietly. I refused to go unless he sent me to work in my own party. He said he had no choice but to give me twenty-four hours on bread and water.

Next day I was sent out again. I learned that one of my companions was in communication with parties who would send out communications we wished to send. I had very little written, and set to work as soon as I could to write more. Put in possession of paper-and-pencil, I struck work again in order to get to punishment-cell where, alone, I would have opportunity to write. I wrote up a piece that I passed to James O'Connor when I came out. James passed it on; and I heard nothing more about it until Knox and Pollock, eight months later in Millbank, gave me to understand that the piece I had written had been published! It was printed in the *Dublin Irishman* under the heading, 'A Voice from the Dungeon'.

*   *   *   *   *

I WAS NOW very emaciated and reduced in strength. The weather was intensely cold, and I felt as if every blast of wind was cutting through me. I saw the doctor one morning, and, showing him the chilblains on my hands, asked him if he could not get me work indoors. Looking at them, he said, 'They are not bad enough yet. I will order you a pair of gloves.' And being taken to the officer in charge of such articles, I got a pair of mittens. They had thumb-fingers only, all the other fingers being exposed as they protruded from the large holes at the ends of my 'gloves'.

On making up my bed, I abstracted the single blanket and wrapped it around my body inside my shirt. I felt quite comfortable for a couple of days, but the third day it was discovered, and I got twenty-four hours on bread and water for 'converting prison property to an improper use'. Next morning, when I went out to work I thought it would be easier to stand anything than what I was suffering from the cold. I laid my hammer on the block, and made up my mind that this would be the last time I worked in that party. I don't know how many days of such abuse I had endured before something occurred that produced a change of tactics on the part of my masters. The papers that my companions had concealed in the shed in which they worked were by some mishap discovered. They found the wall torn down one day when they went out after dinner, and the next morning, O'Connor and I were marched out to work in company with them. All this time, the others were working inside a shed, but James and I would not be allowed in. We were ordered to blocks some twenty yards outside, and were kept there in the cold blasts, looking at the others under shelter. My first impulse was to kick against this, but the friends told me those papers had been discovered, and I worked on until dinner-time, knowing that something was bound to develop. O'Connor and I had been away from this area for about a month, and the object of bringing us back now was to legally connect us with the disappearance of those papers.

I was brought before the 'bar of justice' and charged with 'destroying prison property, converting such property to improper uses, having an ink-bottle and pen and pencil concealed in the prison', and with other offences. I was asked what I had to say;

and said, 'Nothing'. The governor said he would not set the punishment himself, would refer the case to the directors; meanwhile I would remain in punishment. Three days later, word came down – the heaviest dose applicable, three days on bread and water, and twenty-five additional days on punishment-diet. In addition, I was to be deprived of the use of all books (including the Bible) for six months. I had defaced prison property, had written on a *Think Well On It* and on a prayer book; but, had I had a fair hearing, would have beaten them on this head, for whereas all other books in the prison were branded with the prison mark, the ones I had used were not so branded; there was no evidence of them being prison property; and all the books supplied to me had been accounted for, as marked on my related record.

Twenty-eight consecutive punishment-days was the worst dose I yet had had, and time hung heavily, with nothing to read, and very little to eat. I managed to make a start on another 'surreptitious letter'. These people gave me work to do while on bread and water, put a pound of oakum in my cell each morning. I left it there all day without touching it; and in the evenings they took it out again. I refused to pick it unless they gave me a regular labour diet. Their reaction was to deprive me of the pint of stirabout and pound of potatoes a man gets while he is on punishment diet! This, I told the governor, was a flagrant breach of prison regulations. He should not bring in a second sentence to encroach on a first. His retort – he could do what he chose if I did not choose to work. One day he came to my cell with the doctor and the deputy governor. He posed the usual question – had I anything to say? 'Yes,' I said, 'I want you to place on your books a report against the governor for not allowing me to see the director the last time he was here, though I was not under punishment.'

'I'll do no such thing,' he said.

'Well,' said I, 'you're a contemptible creature; and I suppose I'll have to suffer being the sport of such a fool.'

He turned to the doctor. 'What's that he just said?'

'Sport of a fool,' mumbled the doctor, facing off, and away the three of them went. Next day I was charged with gross insubordination, and, again, received punishment.

Twenty-eight days in solitary is a long time. No book to read; nothing with your food but water; and very little food at that! No one to speak to, no face to look at but the face of a jailer; yet, to pass the time, I had to do the best I could. Memories of books I had read as a little boy helped me. I think it was in *Schinderhannes, Robber of the Rhine*, that I had read about Karl Benzel dancing with chains around his feet; and when I lay on the bare boards, pinched with hunger and shivering with cold, Benzel would come into my mind, and I'd jump up and go through the dance I had learned from 'Thady O', till I could barely shuffle from sheer exhaustion. Then I'd stretch again, and go to making verses. It was in this mood, and in such surroundings, that I began to string together rhymes about Jillen Andy. A verse a day, which I'd keep in my mind until the next, when I'd make another. I kept tacking on more verses, and sustained myself by reciting them aloud in my cell. The warder would cry out, 'Stop that noise!', but I'd keep at it. He'd put his eye to the spyhole, but I would continue. I argued that that cell was my house, that every man's house was his castle, and as long as I did not make such noise as would wake my neighbours, I had a reasonable right to solace myself as best I could.

But about Jillen Andy. I had often asked Charles Kickham, when we worked together on *The Irish People*, to poetise this story about Jillen. I knew there was no man who could clothe it in Irish feeling as he could, but he put the task on me. Jillen Andy had lived on the other side of the street in Roscarbery when I was a child. Her husband, Andy Hayes, was a linen weaver, and worked for my father ere I was born. He died before I came into the world, but when I did come I think I formed Jillen's acquaintance as soon as I did that of my mother. Jillen was left a widow with four helpless children, and the neighbours were kind to her. Her eldest son enlisted, and the first sight I got of a 'redcoat' was when he came home one time on furlough. The other sons were Charlie, Thade and Andy. Charlie was looking at Lord Carbery's hounds hunting one day. Going through a lonesome place he got a 'puck' from one of the fairy folk. He came home lame, his leg swollen 'as big as a pot'. It had to be amputated by Doctors Donovan and Fitzgibbon, and he went about on crutches till he died in '65.

Andy enlisted, and died in Bombay, and Thade and his mother fell victims to the famine legislation of '47. Thade met me one day, and spoke to me as I state in the verses that follow. I went to the graveyard with him. We dug and he shovelled out the earth till the grave was about two feet deep. He said then that it was deep enough; that there would otherwise be too great a load on her; and that he would stay and vigil with her a while. By and by, we saw men coming in the churchyard-gate with a door on their shoulders bearing the coffinless Jillen. She was laid in the grave. Her head didn't rest firmly on the stone on which it was pillowed; and one of the men asked me to hand him another. I did so; and, covering it with a red-spotted handkerchief, he gave it back to me, and I settled Jillen's head on it. Then I was told to loose the strings, to take out a pin that had shown, and to lay her apron over her face. To this day I can see how softly the man handled that shovel, how quietly he laid the earth on her feet, how the clay kept building up until it covered her head, and how the men pulled their hats over their eyes.

Jillen Andy

Come to the graveyard if you're not afraid,
  I'm going to dig my mother's grave.
And want someone to work the spade,
  For Andy's away, and Charlie's sick in bed.

Thade Andy was a simply spoken fool,
  With whom in early days I loved to stroll.
Often he'd take me on his back to school;
  And made the master laugh, he was so droll.

In songs and ballads he took great delight,
  And prophecies of Ireland yet being freed.
From singing them by our fire by night
  I learned songs from Thade before I learned to read.

And still have by heart his Cailin Fiune,

140

His 'Croppy Boy', his 'Phoenix of the Hall';
And could raise his 'Rising of the Moon',
  If I could sing in prison cell — or sing at all.

He'd walk the eeriest place a moonlit night;
  And whistle in the dark — even in bed.
In fairy fort or graveyard, Thade was quite
  As scornful of a ghost as any ghost of Thade.

Now in the churchyard gloom we work away,
  Shovel in his hand, in mine the spade,
And seeing Thady cry I cried myself that day,
  For Thade was fond of me, and I was fond of Thade.

But after twenty years why now will such
  A bubbling spring unto my eyelids start?
Ah! There be things that ask not leave to touch
  The fountain of the eyes, or feelings of the heart.

This load of clay will break her bones, I fear,
  For when alive she wasn't o'er-strong.
We'll dig no deeper; I can watch her here
  A month or so; sure, none will do me wrong.

Four men bear Jillen on a door — 'tis light.
  They have not much of Jillen but her frame.
No mourners came, for 'twas believed the sight
  Of any death or sickness then begot the same.

And those brave hearts that volunteer to touch
  Plague-stricken death are tender as they're brave.
They raise our Jillen from her humble couch,
  And shade their swimming eyes while setting her in grave.

I stand within that hole, nor wide nor deep,
  The slender, wasted body at my feet.
What wonder then if strong men fret and weep

O'er wraith-like Jillen in her winding-sheet?

Her head I try to pillow on a stone.
  It does but hang one side, as if the breath
Of Famine gaunt into the corpse had blown,
  And cast that frame in rigid lines of death.

'Hand me that stone, child.' In his hands 'twas placed.
  Down-channelling his cheeks are tears like rain.
The stone within his handkerchief is wrapped,
  And we pillow on it Jillen's head again.

'Untie the nightcap string; unloose that lace;
  Take out that pin. There, now, she's nicely. Rise,
But lay the apron first across her face,
  That earth won't touch her lips or blind her eyes.

'Don't grasp the shovel roughly — make a heap;
  Steal down each dribble softly; let it creep
O'er her thin body. Friend, do not weep,
  Tears would disturb old Jillen in her long, last sleep.'

And Thade was faithful to his watch-and-ward.
  Where'er he'd spend the day, at night he'd haste
With sods of turf to that churchyard lone
  Where he'd be laid himself before a month was chased.

And Andy died a soldier in Bombay;
  And Charlie died in Ross the other day.
Now, no one lives to blush because I say
  That Jillen Andy went uncoffined to the clay.

All, all are gone that buried Jillen, save
  One banished man who dead-alive remains,
The little lad who stood within that grave
  Stands for his country's cause in English prison-chains.

How oft in dreams that burial scene appears,
　Through deaths, evictions, prison, exile, home;
Through all the suns and moons of twenty years.
　And oh! how short those years, compared with ones to come.

Some things are fiercely on the mind impressed,
　And others faintly imaged there, it seems.
And this is why, when reason sinks to rest,
　Life's patterns show, and shadow forth in dreams.

This then is why in dreams I see the face
　Of Jillen Andy searching deep my own;
The poet-hearted man, the pillow-case,
　And spotted kerchief gentling rugged stone.

Welcome — these memories of my youth
　That nursed my hate of tyranny and wrong;
That helmed my manhood in the tide of truth;
　And help me now to suffer and be strong.

For all who ever won had to endure;
　And fortitude proveth good at last.
The painful operation works the cure;
　The health-restoring draught is bitter to the taste.

While I was composing the foregoing I made an attempt to steal
a Bible. I was moved from one punishment-cell to another, either
for 'a change of air' or as a precaution against conceivable escape.
The warder opened my door one morning; ordered me to strip;
searched me and searched my clothes. And when I put my shirt
back on, he said: 'Take the rest in your hands and go into No. 14'.
I went in; my eye fell on a Bible that lay on the window-shelf, and
quick as lightning I laid hold of it. By and by the officer came to
see if I was duly installed, and to lock the door more firmly than I
had shut it, by slamming it and allowing the spring to catch. He
left my cell without noticing anything amiss, and I cannot well give
an idea of the delight I felt in thinking I had something to help me

143

to kill the time. I sat with my back to the door and read for about an hour, when I was dismayed at hearing a key turn in the lock. The officer came in, looked around, and asked, 'Isn't there a Bible in this cell?'

'There ought to be if the rules were carried out.,' I replied.

'Have you a Bible on your person?'

'If you have, you'd better not put yourself to the trouble of stripping again.' And so saying, he drew his hands over my person, and was leaving the cell with a look of frustration, when my hidden treasure suddenly showed, and disappeared with him.

*   *   *   *   *

I WAS STILL under punishment; refused to work; and refusing, got bread and water every second day and penal-class diet alternate days. I refused to go before the governor to hear those sentences of 'bread and water' pronounced, since he refused to take down my words in reply to his questions of 'What have you to say?' I told him it was a mockery to be bringing me before him and asking me such questions; and added, 'This will be the last time I'll make my appearance in your presence. You can order your starvation process to continue; but leave me in peace in my cell.'

'You'll come before me any time it suits me,' he retorted.

Next day at the dinner hour my cell door opened, and I was brought before him to hear that I was to get no dinner. I refused to go. Two, three, four of the officers came and hauled me outside the door. I grabbed at the iron bars; they could not disengage me; the in-charge man called out for handcuffs; an officer went off for them; and there was a suspension of force till he returned. The handcuffs were put on me and hooked into a long chain; but, unless they pulled my arms out of their sockets they could not pull me away from those bars. In as imperious a tone as I could manage I cried out: 'Here — you with the key. Open these irons!' He did so when I showed him that I had one of the cell bars in my embrace. I was cuffed again; several of them laid hold of the long chain, and pulled. Further resistance was useless. I walked down the stairs with them, and they led me into the presence of 'His Highness'. He had heard the noise, it seems; and, with the dignity of ignorance, asked, 'Why is this man in chains?' New accusations of 'insubordination', 'insolence' and 'mockery of prison authority' were voiced. I was again asked what I had to say; and said, 'Nothing'. I was marched back to my cell, and that day got no dinner.

Two days after being led enchained before the governor, my door was opened, and I was commanded to 'come!' I refused; but, on being told that it was not to go before the governor, I consented. I was taken before the establishment's clerk. A list of the clothing I had been issued was read out to me; and on being asked if the list was correct I answered 'Yes'. I was told to sign the record; and did.

I was taken back to my cell and was ordered to strip. I obeyed, and was led naked to another cell where another kit of clothes was set out for me. They brought me a dishpan of water in which to wash my feet before I put on the shoes and stockings of my new outfit. I was told to hurry — 'your carriage is waiting at the gate,' they said.

'My carriage,' said I, 'will have to wait until I get breakfast.'

'Didn't you get your breakfast at half-five this morning?'

'Yes; but I take breakfast for dinner; and my loaf is still untouched in my cell.'

One of them went off for it, and brought back the nine-ounce roll. I was asked in a softer tone than usual to put it into my pocket, for they were in a hurry to catch the train. I obliged them in this, though they would not tell me where I was going. 'Let me get a drink of water,' I said, making a move toward my cell, for I had left a treasure there I wanted to retrieve. In a corner of my shirt was one of those surreptitious letters I had written. But I had to leave it in its hiding place, as an officer followed me into the cell. I've never since learned anything about the fate of that piece of 'contraband'.

As I was passing the punishment-ward, I came in sight of the area where the party of Irish prisoners was working. I halted, and very earnestly asked the officer who was conducting me if he would not let me bid goodbye to my friends. He put his hand on my shoulder, saying, 'Come on; I thought you had no friends anywhere.' And I turned my back on that group of twenty- four, who are scattered now to every part of the world, many of them in their graves.

9. Another Penitentiary; and an Impenitent

THE CARRIAGE WAS waiting outside the prison gate. I stepped into it without bidding goodbye to the governor and the deputy governor, who were there to see me depart. My keepers followed me in, we started off; and I pulled my nine-ounce loaf from my pocket and began to eat it. We were at the station some twenty minutes before our train arrived. My custodians marched me up and down the platform, but kept me at a distance from other travellers. A restaurant was nearby, and, hearing them talk of dinner, I asked for mine. Said White, the senior officer, 'Didn't you already have your dinner?'

'No.'

'Well, we have no orders to get you anything to eat.'

'Well, orders or no orders, if I have far to go, and am to get no food, I'm not going to accept it quietly now that I'm outside your prison walls.'

The train's whistle was heard. White went into the restaurant and returned with a package. He opened it, and its contents turned out to be soda-cakes. He spilled them onto the seat; and after eating one said, 'Rossa, you can have a few of those.' He handed me six of them. I could have made one bite of the six, so ravenously hungry was I. Two more remained on the seat, and White said, 'You'll manage those two as well.' And I did.

No question of mine could elicit where they were taking me. But after about four hours we stopped at a station where there was a delay for refreshments; I guessed from the bustling around us that London was our destination.

I persuaded them to let me go to the water-closet. When we

returned to the platform, our car had been switched in order to come back on another track. Passersby stared at me, some giving sympathetic looks. Thinking they might be Irish, I looked inquiringly at them; but when I did so was ordered by my keepers to face the other way.

White went into the refreshment room and came out again with a glass of water in his hand. Passing it to me, he said, 'You must be thirsty; I'm sorry I can't give you anything better.' I thanked him, and after drinking gave him back the glass, which he returned to its place. While I was alone with the other officer I had wondered what chance I might have of making a run for it, and whether I'd be able to get my hands out of those iron cuffs. Even with them bound I felt I would have an even chance, but second thoughts told me I would have a better opportunity when we reached the London terminus.

The train was re-readied, and I was ordered into it. 'What!' said I, 'you'll take me off without giving me dinner?'

One of them put his hand gently on my shoulder, saying, 'Now, then, now, then; no use giving us trouble. We'd give you dinner if we could.' We walked toward the carriage and I sat down inside. A crowd collected around the still-open window and, as I had an audience, among whom might be someone who might send the story to Ireland, I inveighed against the inhumanity of starving me in prison and taking me from Portland to London without properly feeding me. Finally White said, 'I think I might manage something'. But as he laid his hand on the door to go out, the train-guard's whistle sounded. Just then, a little girl with a basket on her arm cried out, 'Cakes!' 'Here, here!' yelled White. He put his hand into the basket and took out two; and put his other hand into his pocket and took out a penny. Giving the money to the little girl, he gave me the cakes. As I took them into my manacled hands, whatever blood was in my body seemed to rush to my face. I had an urge to throw them at him or out the window. But another impulse overrode that, for I sensed that the man was going against orders. There was kindness in his act, and the last thing I should do would be to hurt the feelings of a man who didn't mean to hurt mine. I ate the cakes, and, still pondering that escape idea of mine, said no more until we reached London.

Many possibilities of escape occurred to me. Assistance could be had somewhere, and I knew it would come if only I could manage to make myself known. There is no railway station in London that lacks Irishmen about it who would risk their own liberty in order to effect mine. As soon as I landed on that London platform, I told myself, I'd make the dash. The best way would be along the railway track itself, for there I'd encounter the most hardworking Irish, the poorest and truest, who would have least to lose. If I cried out, 'Ireland!' or 'Rossa!', someone might recognize me. But all those thoughts were driven out of my head by a new move on the part of my keepers. The train slowed down as we came into London. As we passed Millbank, White said, 'There it is; the prison.' He put his hand in his pocket, and pulled out another set of handcuffs. As they shone in the gaslight, I read in them my doom. And as he fastened one of the cuffs on my wrist and the other on Green's wrist, my spirits dropped to zero.

The train stopped; we emerged, entered a carriage, and when we came out again I was inside Millbank. It was after eight, and the prisoners were in bed. Most of the warders had gone to quarters, but a few remained. I was given over to the man in charge of reception, and, as White delivered me, he said to my new custodian, 'Rossa had no dinner. If you have any, give him some.' And White and Green bade us 'Goodnight,' and departed.

'Millbank' shut me into my cell, which contained a table, a stool, and six or seven tin-cans. By and by, the door was opened, and my new keeper appeared with a larger tin-can used for measuring out the prisoners' porridge. 'Put some of those tins on the table,' said he. I placed three. He filled out one pint, then, a second, and emptied his remainder into a third. 'Eat the lot,' said he. 'You'll be here a long time before you get that much again.' I ate the nine-ounce loaf, and drank up those tinfuls of gruel. I got my bed, and spread it out on the flagstones.

The morning after, I was put through the initiation process of Millbank Prison residence. My height, weight, and eye and hair colour were recorded. I was examined by the doctor; was registered on the books; and orders were given to put me to tailoring. The cell I was assigned was a particularly gloomy one, situated in an angle of the pentagon just behind the chapel. Upon occupying it I looked at its furniture. My tin plate and pint came up for inspection, as one occasionally used those articles, when burnished up, for a looking-glass. On the bottom of the pint I found scratched the words, 'The Artful Dodger', and my heart leaped as if I were shaking hands with Denis Dowling Mulcahy himself. This was the name we had called him in Portland, and this was his writing! This was the cell he must have occupied in Millbank, and this the pint he had used to take his porridge. Yes, whenever I used that pint, I would have memories of an old friend!

At a quarter-to-eight, the bell for the making of our beds sounded, and I made mine. At eight, a warder went around to turn off the gas jets and see that every prisoner was in his cell. He passed mine without putting out the light, and, thinking he had made a mistake, I halloed after him. He came back.

'Governor, you haven't put this light out.'

That gas is to be left on. Now, make no more noise.'

The jet was only about two feet from the head of my bed, and, with the light shining, I knew I wouldn't get to sleep. I had a water-bucket that served the triple purpose of scrubbing-tub, washbasin, and stool. I set it by the head of my bed, then took the large card on which the rules and regulations were printed, stood it on the bucket against the wall between the gas jet and the bed head; and it effectively screened off the light. Shortly, the night-watch looked in, and growled: 'What have you done?'

'Governor, I can't sleep with that light shining in my face.'

'Take that card down.'

'No!'

'Then you'll soon see that you will!'

I heard his slippered feet in the hallway as he moved off, and, in about five minutes, the tramp of several approaching warders. They halted opposite my cell and their supervisor, Power, speaking through the slit in the wall, ordered me to take down the card. 'Put out the light, and I will,' I said.

Said Power: 'Rossa, the prison keys have been given up for

the night. But if you don't take that card down, we'll have to. Which is it to be?'

'Well, anything to avoid trouble,' I told him, 'but can't you lower that gas a little, turn it down a bit? That's it...fine.' And away they went.

As I was doing my 'orderly' work next morning I noticed on a wall a card bearing my name. Opposite it was written: 'This prisoner to be closely watched, and the gas jet in his cell, left alight all night.' When I went back to my cell I began to think that I must really be a desperate character.

I was to be treated like any other prisoner — that was the stereotyped order set down for me on every occasion of an interview with the director, the governor, the deputy governor and every other official down to the lowliest. Yet by their petty acts they managed to deprive me of every puny privilege the convict system accords its children. My twice-a-week 'school hour' was voided before I was a month in Millbank. They screwed me down so tightly that I guessed that something had to be bothering them! You could see alarm in the countenance of every prison official. I write in the light of information I did not then have, and now know that on 7 March 1867 a rising took place in Ireland. The movement was a secret one, and England did not know whether it would be confined to Ireland, or would branch into England. But, with all her spies, she knew very little about it, or when, where or how she would be struck. Hence the alarm. A similar panic seized the government in December of that year when an attempt was made to blow up Clerkenwell Prison. Horse, foot and artillery were brought inside the prison walls and kept there day and night for months. Cannon were placed in the prison square, and every precaution was taken in the heart of London to meet an attack from those Irish revolutionists.

I did not escape scot-free for shading my face from the light. Next day, in the governor's presence, I was charged with an offense 'against rules and regulations'. My judge was Morish, a big, important-looking man with the air of a disciplinarian. He read me a lecture. But when he spoke of my coming to his prison with 'an exceedingly bad character', I couldn't forbear a smile. My sentence was forty-two marks. In Portland I had added a year-and-a-half to my life sentence by the forfeiture of marks, but here another week's worth was passed on me. If things went on this way, I concluded, I had scant chance of getting out of prison, either in this world or in the next!

Not long after this first encounter with the governor, two officers came to my cell and ordered me to strip. I had been stripped the day before as part of my initiation into the freemasonry of Millbank. But repeating the humiliation the next day, to me, was quite out of order, and I asked, 'What's up now?'

'Never mind what's up; just obey,' I was told.

I took off my jacket and trousers, shoes and stockings, shirt and wrapper, each of which they examined and felt inch by inch. I stood before them with the flannel drawers still on me. 'Strip off those drawers.' 'May I put my shirt on before I take them off?' 'No; take off the drawers; we have to see you naked.' I obeyed again; turned around; opened my mouth; and extended arms and legs. They discharged their duty to the law's letter; threw my clothes at me, and locked the door.

For three months, day after day, those officers put me through the same routine. I felt it more than anything connected with my prison life; and when the surveillance came so forcefully on me that, when taking a bath, I had to suffer a jailer standing over me, no words could describe the depth of my resentment. I am not overly sensitive or thin-skinned, but I own to strong feelings against my fellow man looking at me in a 'state of nature'. When I was at school, and heard the boys tell tales of how men were stripped naked when they enlisted, I imagined it to be the most arbitrary outrage they could suffer, and there was little fear of my ever becoming a soldier. I frequently reminded those in charge that this daily stripping violated prison rules that say: 'The governor and officers must at all times cultivate sentiments of morality and propriety of behaviour in the prisoners.' But the demands of 'discipline', and those regarding me, evidently had higher priority than the rules and regulations code.

Not long after my reception at Millbank the door of my cell was thrown open and an old man walked in, handed me a sheet of ruled paper and a pen, and walked out again. An orderly then came to the cell with about twenty little brownstone inkbottles on a board. 'What's this for?' I asked. 'School!' And he hurried off with his board to the scholars adjacent.

My next urge was to steal one of those brownstone bottles of ink, and a pen to boot. I had a foreboding that my guardians would not leave me long at 'school', and made up my mind not to let another opportunity pass without trying to avail of writing materials.

My first school-hour was spent writing my 'Jillen Andy' verses on the leaf of paper I got. The schoolmaster came a second time and told me I could write whatever I liked, but shouldn't write verses. I should write like the other prisoners, copying lines or passages from my books or the Bible.

Chance gave me a second hour at school, and also an opportunity to retain my bottle of ink when the school period ended. I also became possessed of a steel pen. When the schoolmaster came around to provide me with a pen he had a number of them in his hand, some of which were without nibs. When he left my cell I drew out the nib and put it on the floor, where the shadow from the leg of the table hid it. When he returned by and by, and saw me idle, he asked why I wasn't writing. I took the pen-handle that lay on the table, and, holding it toward him, remarked innocently that it wasn't easy to write with that. Had he made a fuss about having given me one with a nib in it, I could have made a fuss looking for it and finding it on the floor. But he merely said that he thought he had given me a good pen, and handed me another.

Being employed at tailoring, I had some black thread, which I tied to the neck of the ink-bottle, and the other end to one of the bars of my window. The roof of the chapel rose to within a foot of the window, and a gutter ran along it to carry off rain. In that gutter the ink-bottle lay hidden for three months before it was discovered. Whenever I wanted to use it, I hauled in my line, and, having used it, would put it back in its hiding place.

I applied for permission to write my 'reception letter', but the governor wouldn't grant it. I reminded him of the rule that said every inmate, on being received into the prison, could write a letter. But he told me that that applied only to prisoners of 'good character', not to men who had been sent there from works prison because of bad conduct. He said I could repeat my application to the director if I wished; and the latter said I could write the letter, but he hoped I would confine myself to 'legitimate' matter. Writing time was during the school hour, and I had not finished my letter the first day. I surmised it would never pass the censorship, as I had written about the treatment I was receiving; but I managed to write two copies on my waste paper before releasing it on the second schoolday. I intended sending out those copies surreptitiously if an opportunity should offer. The next time the director came, he sent for me and told me he could not let my letter pass, but would allow me to write another. I thanked him, and wrote as I had written previously. Again he sent for me; remonstrated with me for repeating the offence; ending, however, with an offer to let me try once more.

By this time I was alive to their strategy. If I refused to write they would put my refusal on record, and thus gain a strong point against me in the struggle for public opinion to which I was determined to bring them. If I wrote, stating nothing of my treatment, they could, in case I died and questions were raised about my ill-treatment, cry out, 'It is all false. Look at his last letter to his wife; not a word in it about ill-treatment!' In fact, every time I was allowed to write to my wife, I wrote of my prison life. Over three years they suppressed those letters, during which time she never heard from me.

Eventually I would lose my schooling: it happened in this manner: An English convict, born in Kilkenny, occupied a cell next to mine. He was there under the name of Scott; but he told me 'Scott' was not his true name. That he wished to keep secret, as he did not want Kilkenny folk to know anything of his whereabouts. He was only lately convicted, and as we stood inside our open doors mornings, waiting to have our numbers called to take our buckets of fresh water, he whispered to me many stories of the war in Ireland. Not being able to use his food at first, nearly every morning he'd throw a piece of bread into my cell as he passed by.

When I learned that he was able to tell me much about Ireland and 'the doings' there, I neglected my schooling to stand near my door and have words with him.

Officer Brown used to be in the centre of the ward, where he had a view of two corridors, but he put on slippers one day, and, creeping softly down, stole a march on Scott and me as we were talking to one another from inside our doors. We were startled from our *tete-a-tete* by his roaring out: 'Put out your brooms, and shut your doors!' And having taken away my writing material, he shut my door. He opened it again, and asked, 'Why haven't you put your broom out?' The putting out of your broom or brush was to signify to all persons passing that you were 'under report' and awaiting sentence: many a time my broom was out. The sentence passed on me was that I was to get no more schooling while in that prison. But Scott was not deprived of his schooling, though it was he who had done most of the talking. Didn't I feel lonesome every day afterwards when I heard that school-bell ring, and the doors opening, yet my door remained locked!

* * * * *

AT THIS TIME my fingers had been bandaged by the doctor. I had been so reduced from hunger and cold in Portland that I came to Millbank with the flesh literally rotting off my hands. I could use the needle pretty well, for it didn't require much bending of the fingers; but when I came to pick coir, I found it required the exercise of all my fingers, and, failing to do my task-work, got bread and water, and no bed at night.

If man ever felt cold, I felt it those nights. It was about the end of March, and I had no bed or bed-clothing but a light rug. I was not allowed to walk about the cell, had to remain prone with this rug around me. When I looked out through the hole in the wall next morning, the rooftops were covered with snow. During the winter season, a prisoner under punishment gets a rug and a blanket, but from 25 March to the end of September he gets a rug only. That cell had no window, but there was a hole about two feet long and three inches wide to admit a little light, and, as my bed-board was under the hole, the snow had drifted in on me all night.

I heard the prison-clock strike two. To sleep was impossible, so I got up to walk about the cell. I wore my punishment slippers, and shortly heard a voice outside: 'Stop that walking, and go to bed.'

'I have no bed.'

'Well, lie down, and don't be making noise.'

I sat on the board, and communed with myself how to kill time. I took off the slippers, and commenced walking as lightly as I could in my stocking vamps. The watch heard my footfalls, and tapped at the door again. 'Didn't I tell you to stop that walking? If you don't go to bed, I'll report you.' Rather than again be reported, I went 'to bed', and shivered the hours away until daybreak.

The rising in Ireland came; and immediately thereafter such a hubbub erupted that I guessed something had to be developing in the outer world. I had been in Millbank a month, and night and day, like any other prisoner, occupied one cell. But now things would be different. When my hour came for going to bed, I was taken from my cell and led through several corridors to another where I slept with the gas alight. In the mornings I was conducted back to my regular cell, and this continued for months until they had crushed the rebellion in Ireland. They didn't seem to know whether there might or might not be a rising in London, and took these precautions regarding me lest I be released from Millbank by force.

What I most regretted about this change was that I had lost the bed in which one of my outbound letters had been concealed. The mattress and bedclothes were taken out of my day-cell, and I saw them no more. I thought it might be better to try to send out the other than wait for a future opportunity that might never come. The next day, when I was scrubbing my cell, I broke my scrubbing-stone, and ground down a piece of it to about an inch square. I took out my letter, and enclosed the stone in it to make it heavy, so I could throw it over the prison wall from the exercise yard. I knew there was a road running outside the wall, but had scant hope of tossing it that far. There was a garden between the prison and the road, and I thought that if it fell there, some prison officer or prisoner might find it who, for the consideration I had stated on the letter, would send it to its destination. I had recourse to my ink-bottle, and penned a note to tell the finder to send the letter to a certain place and he would get a certain sum of money. I folded it tidily, hid it on my person, and went to exercise when the bell rang. This exercise consisted of walking around the yard for a half-hour and working at the pump another half-hour.

When I was walking around, a principal called me over. 'Open your jacket and waistcoat,' he ordered. I did so. 'What is this?'

'One of the six bags I have to make.'

'Take it off.'

I took it off; he took it away, and I was allowed to continue my exercise. I had that wrapped-up letter in my pocket, but, for a wonder, he didn't detect it. I knew there wasn't much time to spare if I was to throw it over the wall. When I came to the best place, and told myself no unfriendly eye was on me, I flung my treasure with all my might. High into the air it went, but my eye didn't follow it, for I espied an officer looking my way. A second later I heard something hit the roof. I looked up, and saw my letter fall back into the yard. The prisoner behind me gave a groan, and the one in front of me a curse. The wonder was that the officer didn't hear them or notice anything wrong. The letter had fallen into a corner where there were cinders. Snow covered the ground, and there was my missive on top of it. I would have had to get out of ranks to recover it, and this seemed impossible without an officer seeing me. Then, an order: 'Back to cells!' I had time for a last turn-around. Should I leave my letter? No; I would retrieve it. As I passed the spot I picked it up. Stepping into ranks again, I looked over to see whether Brown had seen me; but he hadn't, and I re-entered my cell and put my letter in its hiding-place. Minutes later, I was ordered to 'put out my broom'. When the judge sat, I was ordered twenty-four hours on bread and water for 'destroying prison property and converting it to improper use'. The destruction consisted in my having put stitches in the bag so I could keep it tight around my waist.

I asked the governor to put down my name to see the director on his next visit. He showed up the following Thursday. He was

Captain Gambier. I came before him often, and he would speak to me so sweetly that I began to think of him as a father. But all his attentions were bestowed on me in the form of reprimands. While pronouncing sentences on me that he knew were meant to bring me to my knees, he would say, 'God knows, I'm sorry for you.' Then the sentence: 'A month in solitary on punishment-diet; the first twelve days, bread and water. Take him away.' He had a glass eye, and this used to look at me as if it was shedding tears in sympathy with his pitying words; while the other seemed to gloat with satisfaction that he had me in his toils. I never could give this Captain Gambier an ill word, for he always spoke civilly. With his crocodile words he'd polish up the ugliest dose he could give, and I believe I vexed him as much as any prisoner he had ever met, for I never lost my temper with him, but would catch him up quietly whenever I caught him in error.

I came before him to ask for an increase in food ration. He refused it. I then asked that my friends on the outside be permitted to send me food; but this was entirely out of the question. 'Well, Governor,' I said, 'I am surprised. England would not see a sufficiency of food refused to the political prisoner of any other nation.' To which he replied: 'England has no political prisoners now-a-days. You are no more than any other prisoner here, and are treated like every other prisoner.'

'Ah, but Governor, I think you're mistaken. You don't keep the gas burning in the cell of every other prisoner all night; nor do you strip every other prisoner naked once a day. You don't take every other prisoner through wards and corridors from his day-cell to sleep in another at night; nor do you punish every other prisoner for not doing two work tasks at the same time.'

'Now, now — no use your going on with these frivolities. I just can't grant your application for more bread.' And out of his room I was marched.

10. The Struggle for Political Treatment

I TRIED TO disassociate myself from the English convicts, but to no avail. In time, however, the authorities had to change their tactics, and isolate me from them of their own accord. Later they kept me away from them altogether. I said to Captain Gambier one day, 'Governor, during my hour's exercise I'm put at the pump in company with your murderers and thieves, and I ask to be relieved of their companionship.'

'Certainly not,' said he, 'you are no more than any other prisoner here, and must exercise as do all the others.'

Working on the pump was not unpleasant: it developed the muscles; and while at it I got a lot of information. There were thirty of us in that gang, and fifteen stood to each side of the crank, facing those opposite. We laid hold of the iron bars, and the officer cried, 'On!' We pushed; our bodies bent; our heads came together at every revolution of the wheel; and remarks of some kind were passed. Those professionals could whisper without moving a lip or a facial muscle, and I took much interest in their flow of stories. They trusted me; knew I wouldn't 'stag'; and while I was with them I learned how several burglaries had been committed, who committed them, and what was done with 'the swag'. This was a reception prison, and new bodies coming in were a great source of news. I wanted news, and when I couldn't get near a newcomer, those who could would learn as much as possible from him about Ireland, and tell me next day how things were faring there. Yes, almost half of those men were of Irish parentage, and their crimes were substantially traceable to poverty or whisky. Some people today ask me how I was able to stand all the 'bread and water' treatment I got, but, in fact, I was sustained by those unfortunate criminal convicts.

We got a bath once a fortnight, and were taken to it during the exercise period. There were four troughs, with holes in the side-boards to let the water pass through. Four men would be called, and when they had bathed and dressed, four more, and so on till we were all done. Whether by accident or design, it scarcely ever happened that I was one of the first four called, and I seldom had water that was clean. The dirty suds would scum its surface. Some of the in-charge warders would make me strip and go in, but others would not insist, contenting themselves with having me wash my feet. This was the only matter remedied by Knox and Pollock. After their visit, and my representations to them on this head, I had clean water every time I bathed.

In May of '67 a change, but not a change for the better. I was at Sunday exercise, working the pump-crank in an isolated corner between two walls, for by this time that was where they had put me, surmising that otherwise I would be getting information or consolation from the whisperings of the other convicts as we pumped. As the crank was going around I heard an order, 'Halt!', and a call, 'Rossa!' I looked behind me, saw two officers beckoning. They conducted me to my cell and ordered me to strip. 'What's up now?' 'You know what's up,' said one. I stripped, but nothing was found on my person or in my clothes. 'Put out your broom,' they said. I did so and, when they'd locked the door, began to ask myself what was up. I made for the window and, woe of woes! there was no black thread tied to the bar outside; my ink-bottle was gone. I went to the slit under my bed-board, and my steel nibs were gone. I searched between the gas pipe and the wall, and my pen was gone. There had been a clean sweep of all my treasures! While I brooded over these misfortunes and the bread and water regime that clearly was in store for me, my cell was opened, and in marched 'Big Power' with several other jailers.

'Where did you get that inkbottle?'

The way he stood before me, and the domineering tone with which he put his question, stirred my bad blood, and, moving close to him and looking at him eye to eye, I said: 'I will not tell you.'

Summoned to answer to charges of having ink, pens and letters concealed, I was much amused to hear Power's complaint about the 'insolence' I had offered him. 'When I asked him, sir, where he had got the inkbottle, you should see the way he swelled up to me. If I was the commonest man in England he couldn't have spoken to me worse than he did. I am twenty-five years here, and never got such insult, never came across a more refractory character.' I was ordered seventy-two hours on bread and water, and it was further ordered that I not be allowed to approach any other prisoner; that I be exercised in a separate yard; and be taken to chapel separately. So that this was actually compelling them to do what I'd asked them to do in the first place — separate me from the other convicts. My whole fight had been to require them to recognize the difference between us 'politicals' and the ordinary convicts, and in the end they were obliged to do so.

After going to bed one night, I heard tapping on the wall at the foot of my bed. Hello, I thought, a signal from someone! And I set to thinking how to answer it. I turned my bed around, and signaled back in reply. I managed to convey a few remarks through the wall, and learned that the man in the cell next to mine was one of the Fenian soldiers. We exchanged signal codes in the chapel next morning and made arrangements to have a longer talk the following evening. Mind you, the conversation would have to be through the wall. But stone walls won't prevent comrades from communicating, and we managed to thwart our jailers. I became acquainted with Augustine Costello and Ricard O'Sullivan Burke before I ever saw their faces. I met John Devoy through those stone walls, when the authorities were resorting to all kinds of tricks to keep me from meeting anyone.

Next morning, at chapel, I recognized my acquaintance by means of the code given to me the night before. He and some ten or twelve companions were sitting behind me. That night I had a long talk with him; learned that his name was Keating and that he came from Clare; that he'd been in the Carbineers a long time; had escorted Clarke Luby to prison; and also had had the undesired honour of escorting John Mitchel on his way to banishment and penal servitude in '48. That Foley, who belonged to his party, used to make up my cell every morning after I had left it, and that any message I left there would be found by him and be attended to. I told him to tell Foley to look behind the card that was affixed to the wall and he'd find a letter from me which they were to get to the outside if they possibly could. It was one of those 'reserve missives' I'd prepared in case a chance offered of getting one out, and I placed it behind the rules and regulations card on the wall. That was to be the 'post office'. But the authorities seized those post offices of ours. I lost contact with the soldiers and did not see any of them after that. My cell was changed, my place in chapel was changed, and – most remarkable change of all! – my closet paper was changed to old rags.

My reputation followed me to my new quarters, and my new neighbours seemed to know all about me. They knew that paper and pencil, and pen and ink, were things I greatly desired; and as they swept and scrubbed the halls in the mornings they'd linger outside my door to whisper through the slit in the wall, 'Rossa – want a cedar?' I didn't know at the time what a 'cedar' was, but as I was in want of everything that creation contained, I whispered back 'Yes'. A lead-pencil three or four inches long was tossed in through the slit. But where was I to hide it? The stripping naked, and search of the cell, would come by and by.

I had to devise hiding-places, or be punished. There was a slit between my bed-board and the wall; when I probed it with my tin knife I could find no bottom; but, as I could think of no other place, I decided on this one. I would need thread. Well, there was my towel. I drew a couple of threads from it, and, twisting them into one, tied it to my pencil and let it down into the hole. I found bottom, and hitched the end of my line to a splinter I'd fashioned at the edge of the board. This was the first morning of my entry into the new cell. The report against me came the same day, and I got my three days of punishment-cell. When I came back, the first thing I did was try my hidingplace to see if my cedar' was safe; but it was gone. I couldn't find the end of the string, and the pencil lay in the hole below. How to recover it? There was but one way. Next morning I brought in a bucketful of water to scrub my cell and threw some of it into the hole to see if the cedar would float up. It did not show, but when the water had subsided I filled the hole a second time. No use. I kept working away till I had used up the entire bucketful, but no pencil made its appearance. I gave up the search and braced myself for consequences, for I knew that that water would show somewhere. I dried my cell, and went to work picking my coir. In an hour or so the water had begun to show, and oozed out from under my bedstead. My cell began to flood, and a warder came and asked me how come. 'Governor,' I told him, 'I spilled my pail today.' That was true – I had spilt the water; and had made sure that some of it would go down that slit. I never told these gentlemen lies, but never told them the whole truth either. I was told to dry out my cell and, as the water kept seeping in, I had to keep drying it out. Next morning I was temporarily ordered into another cell and, when I got back to my own, found that the slit had been plastered up with cement, no hole being left that a pin's point could enter.

I related my misfortune to my neighbours, and wasn't long without another pencil. The greatest difficulty I had was to make them understand that I needed paper, too. At last they threw in some, and by next morning I had written a note telling them just what else I needed. Soon we established another post office (in the water-closet), and every morning I would find messages there. It was here that I got something like an account of what had happened in the world outside since I had left it; that I first learned how everything had failed and how our initial hopes had been disappointed. Johnny O'Brien was in another part of that ward; he had called at my 'post office' and gave me a detailed account of how things were faring in Ireland. He had been a druggists's clerk in London, but left his situation and gone to Ireland to enlist in a regiment there so he could teach love of country to the Irish who also were in it. When 'the troubles' came he was seized, got a military trial, and was sentenced to servitude for life. His sentence was read to him in the presence of his entire regiment, and when all the 'degradation' ceremonies had been accomplished he gave an hurrah for 'the Irish Republic'.

When my neighbours were taken out for their hour's exercise I was marched a distance behind them, but for no consideration might I approach close enough to the most rearward man to be able to whisper to him. I cheated the warder sometimes as we'd descend a winding stair into the lower yard. The last man would tarry behind the others and I'd step up quickly to catch what he had to whisper or give to me, while the warder unlocked the lower gate.

We had to go through a small yard where I was left in an officer's charge while the others were taken to the exercise ground. When the hour was up, my party passed through again, and I would have to go in after them. But lest any signal should pass between us, I had to turn my face to the wall while they were entering, the officer standing between us so I would not be able even to squint at them.

When I was shaving one day I cut my neck, and the blood flowed freely. There was a wee pool of it, and the sight brought to my mind the story of the duke of Burgundy, wounded on a battlefield, exclaiming in French: 'See how flows the red blood of Burgundy!' I got my slate-pencil, and, dipping it in the blood, wrote on the door of my cell, *Le sang rouge d'Irlande coule en Angleterre*. After I had shaved, the officer came to take me to exercise, and while I was out the writing was discovered. Ordered from exercise before the hour was up, I was told to 'put out my broom'.

Next day, taken before the governor, while the officers all around looked daggers at me, I was charged with writing on my door: The red blood of Ireland will rise in England.

'What have you to say to the charge?'

'It is false.'

'You say those words were not written on your door?'

'I do.'

The 'evidence' was taken: one officer had gone to search my cell and had seen the writing; he sent for another officer and then head-warder Power, who decided that, as the writing was in Latin, it was better to send for a 'schoolmaster'. The schoolmaster came, and then sent for another schoolmaster. In the end, three or four of those 'masters' translated the 'Latin' and the translation was entered in the report book. I told them that someone had given the words a most malicious turn and asked that the sentence be taken down as it was written on the door, but the governor would make no change. He said I had violated rules by writing anything, and gave me forty- eight hours on bread and water.

Coming from chapel one morning, a man passed me whom I was sure I knew. I kept wondering who he might be. It continued to be a puzzle for some days; then, espying him again, I recognized him as Edmond Power. I arranged to communicate with him, and having succeeded, learned that several other movement men, recently convicted, were now fellow boarders of mine – John Devoy, St Clair, John Warren, John McCafferty, Tom Bourke, Augustine Costello, Edward Duffy, Stephen Meany, Patrick Walsh and Denis Cashman. By and by I got into communication with Costello, who told me the story of how he and others had come in a small craft from America to Ireland. She made Sligo Bay, and, not being met there to satisfaction, came around to Dungarvan, landed her men, and made her way back to America. It was all new to me, and I got as much out of Costello as I could, until the fates intervened and put us beyond each other's reach.

Edmond Power prayed at chapel three or four benches from me, but soon we managed to communicate, and bulletins passed regularly. I was given a package one morning. When prayers had ended, and I was leaving my seat, Power's eyes and mine met and I saw him put his finger to his mouth. This I took to mean that I was to keep the message contained in the package in my mouth,so that, if I were suddenly seized, I could swallow it. I had a sense of danger, and when I got to the exercise yard made a signal to go to the water-closet. There I opened the package, which contained a bit of lead-pencil, and a note informing that, a very strict search was under way: Power had been stripped three times the preceding day, and I was to keep the bit of pencil safe for him. I destroyed the note after reading it, and secured the pencil in my shirt-collar near to where it buttoned, so that I could, if taken by surprise, have the best chance of passing the item into my mouth.

I was not allowed much time for reflection, for two officers approached. 'Rossa — this way!' They led me into the tower, and there they ordered me to strip. I began stripping with zest, so as to keep them engaged and make them less watchful. I had given the jacket, trousers and waistcoat to them in less than a minute, and as I was unbuttoning my shirt-collar the bit of pencil passed from its hiding-place into my mouth. It would not do to keep it there, for the mouth would be examined next. I had to swallow it. The first effort failed, and I had to let it moisten before I could get it down. The searchers found nothing, and for once I evaded my accustomed bread and water.

The establishment's chief medical officer was a Dr Gover, and I thought I would test him on the question of the starvation of the Irish political prisoners. When he came by on his rounds one day, I represented to him that I was not provided with a sufficiency of food — something, I declared, that no civilized nation refused its 'politicals'. After some conversation on my punishments, and on the weight I had lost because of them, he decided he would have me weighed, and, if I had lost weight, would consider my application. You must know, however, that it was next to impossible that I could have lost weight, for I was so light upon arrival in Millbank from the cold and hunger I had experienced in Portland that I couldn't have lost much more.

Indeed, I was down to skin and bone. Dr Gover said he'd be very happy to give me more food, but, as I had not lost weight under his charge, and as there was so much particularity about my treatment, he had to let normal discipline take its course. But some months afterwards he put a veto on my getting further punishment-diets; which decision was shortly thereafter re-vetoed by my genial director, Captain Gambier.

11. A Second Visit from My Wife: The Confrontation Sharpens

TAKEN FROM MY cell one day, I was led through corridors I had never travelled before, and was ushered into a place that somehow resembled a menagerie. A door opened, and my wife stood some feet away. Two wire screens separated us. She was in one compartment with Warder Power beside her; I was in the other with my guardian; and we had twenty minutes to talk across the intervening space, with those two listening and the head-warder interrupting our conversation whenever I touched on the treatment I was receiving.

She was going to America to earn a living. She had written to the governor, asking him to tell me that she was coming to see me before she sailed; but he had never told me that. Her visit took me completely by surprise, and this undoubtedly was what the authorities desired, so that I could have no story prepared for her. She told me she had written a letter to Portland six months earlier, informing me of her intention to emigrate. I had never seen or heard of that letter, and Power said it had never come to the prison, but subsequently I learned that they had told me lies about it.

She also told me there was to be a 'commission of inquiry' concerning our treatment, but was at once commanded to give me no information on the point. The public might want a little light thrown on the matter, but it was absolutely necessary to keep me in the dark, so I wouldn't be prepared for what was coming. Everything was to take me by surprise; to disconcert me; and render me unable to defeat 'the ends of justice'.

The bare twenty minutes was allowed for my wife's visit. No

chance of a handshake at parting. Her last words — to have hope, and not let my spirits sink. It puzzled me why she would speak this way, particularly since she spoke with a firmness that indicated there were reasons to have hope. Now, however, she tells me that at the time she was fully confident of being able to have me spirited from prison. She had borrowed £100 to effect my release, had the money with her, and had had wax impressions made of the keys that opened doors that stood between me and the outer world. But, in consequence of my many removals from one cell to another, the men who were assisting couldn't get access to all that would have been necessary. She had to give up the endeavour; paid back the money; and went herself to America.

*   *   *   *   *

ONE MORNING AT chapel, while the priest was repeating the litany and the prisoners were responding aloud, I heard a voice to my rear addressing me at each response. 'Have mercy on us,' cried the congregation.

'I'll get you paper...' intoned the voice.'

'Have mercy on us.'

'...and pen and ink.'

'Have mercy.'

'Our baker will send the letter...'

And so on, the prisoners in my immediate vicinity responding all the louder when they noticed we were communicating. On leaving the chapel I glanced at the man who had spoken to me, and the next morning sighted him some seats behind me. By and by, word was passed to me to get ready, and in the process of our rising and moving out, something was passed to me which I covered up with my kerchief. After getting back to my cell I opened the package. It consisted of a letter, a pen, a sheet of paper and an envelope, and a piece of flannel saturated with ink. My first move was to put out the red end of my signal-board through the wall slit, to signify that I wanted to go to the water-closet; and in my hiding place there I secured all that I had received except the letter, which I brought back to my cell. The writer was a Castlebar Irishman. He had heard of the straits I was in for writing materials; and had made arrangements with a fellow prisoner who worked in the bakehouse to get a letter out for me. He would keep me supplied with ink, because he got 'schooling', and when the ink-bottle was left with him would spill some ink onto the flannel.

By now, I had in my hiding place a supply of fine white paper – five or six sheets – but this I had stolen. Before chapel one morning I was taken out of my cell and made to stand in a corner till the other prisoners had passed. The warder was in my view, and when he looked away I made my own observations. I noticed on his shelf a large book in which he kept an account of his work. I opened it when the chance offered, saw that the book wasn't paged, and that I could take sheets out of it without the loss necessarily being noticed. I was the last to go into chapel from my ward, but the first to come back. My cell was near the corner where the book rested and as I passed that corner I went to the account-book and hastily tore out several sheets.

A week after my wife's visit I was writing in my cell about ten in the morning, which was the hour when I attracted the least observation. I was scratching away when, tramp-tramp, I heard officers approach. I stuck paper and pen inside the waist of my britches; the keys turned in the locks; the door was thrown open and Big Power snapped, 'Come.'

'Wait, Governor,' I said, ''till I go to the water-closet.'

They did let me, but stood at the door of it, and I had no further chance of concealing the pen and paper I had on me. I was led into the governor's office; the warders withdrew, and I stood at attention before two gentlemen who sat inside. They introduced themselves as Messrs. Knox and Pollock, and informed me that they had been commissioned to ask me some questions regarding my prison-life.

I questioned them as to how they had been appointed, and what the circumstances were that called for their inquiry. They wouldn't tell me, but I wasn't long under examination before I surmised that something I had written had gotten into the world and had caused a little stir. They queried me principally on Governor Clifton of Portland, and my 'letter to another prisoner's wife'; and I learned that Mr Clifton had told them lies. I suggested that, if this was to be an honest search for truth, I be brought face to face with him; that the Portland Prison books be produced, together with the relevant correspondence, and that I could then convince them that my words had been true, and his false. They had examined Mr Clifton, they said, but he was not now available; they would, however, be seeing him again, and might call back to see me in a week's time. However, I never saw them again. I was under their examination for about four hours, and, as the proceedings came to a close, I made motions to adjust the pen and paper that were still inside my trouser-waist. When I made these motions, however, they showed signs of alarm.

I really believed from their looks that they thought I had some concealed weapon with which I might assault them; and, to allay their fears, told them the truth — that I had been writing, and had had no time to adequately conceal my pen, which had been bothering me all the time I had been talking to them. They assured me I might regard anything that passed between them and me as if it had passed between a priest and myself at confession. They were extremely polite. We parted, seemingly, on the best of terms; yet, in their report, they cut my throat. Here are extracts from it:

> We now come to the main grievance — namely, that the governor had charged convict Rossa with writing a love letter to the wife of another convict, Michael Moore. As a fact quite unconnected with this occurrence, Moore had asked for permission to write a letter to his wife. The governor, wishing to know whether Moore had had any participation in Rossa's letter, observed, 'This is very strange; only a day or two ago, Rossa tried to pass out a letter to your wife.' He said nothing to him about 'love letters'. Moore flew into a passion, and Mr Clifton was convinced from his manner that he had had nothing to do with Rossa's letter. A few days afterwards, when the governor saw Rossa in his office, Rossa charged him in the most insolent terms with having accused him of writing a love letter to Mrs Moore. Mr Clifton replied he had told Moore that Rossa had written a letter to Mrs Moore, but he'd said nothing about a 'love letter', adding words to the

effect that he didn't mind telling him (Rossa) his own opinion, that when a man writes a letter to another man's wife, begins it with the words 'My love', fills it with expressions of strong devotion, signs his name to it, and forwards it in a surreptitious way, the facts have a questionable look. Mr Clifton expressly added, 'A reason that makes me think all the more that this letter was never intended for your wife is that I have too high an opinion of Mrs O'Donovan Rossa to think for a moment she would help you to infringe the prison rules'.

Said Knox and Pollock's report: "'Mrs O'D.' will scarcely stand for Mrs O'Donovan Rossa; and the further explanation that Mrs Moore was Moore's mother, not his wife, sounds unsatisfactory.' Yet they had the record before them showing that Moore's wife's name was Kate, and his mother's, Mary. Again:

On June 3 we visited Millbank, and, as our sole purpose there was to converse with Rossa, we need not dwell on arrangements at that prison.

Rossa admitted he had nothing in particular to complain of, except that on various occasions he had been unjustly reported for punishment. He complained that everyone was unjust to him. It is but fair to add that everyone complained of him. He had the most ingenious contrivances for concealing fragments of paper, for hanging inkbottles out of his cell window by wires, and obviously managed to maintain contacts with the external world. He has driven matters finally to a point where he has been committed from Portland to Millbank as a thoroughly unmanageable subject; and at Millbank the authorities are obliged to keep him apart from his fellows. He recently concocted a letter stuffed with the most absurd accusations; and contrived (no one knows how!) to convey it to another convict who was about to be removed. The letter, dropped on the railway, was addressed to the editor of any one of several papers. It contained the story of his wrongs, and was meant to set the country ablaze.

We could not but regret, as we saw this active young man before us in the prime of manhood, and in strong, vigorous health, that such energies of mind and body had been misapplied, and that the end of all was a convict-cell and a duel between him and the authorities as to whether they could keep him in prison or he could set them at defiance and effect an escape. His letter contained the usual farrago of falsehood and exaggeration. For example, that he had been denied the privilege of writing to his mother in America. It turned out he had never asked permission to do so at all. He complained to us that he had been reported for abstracting at his tailoring work a portion of cloth, and for concealing it inside his jacket. It turned out that he had done so, but he said he had not intended to hide it, had just put it out of the way for 'temporary purposes'. Convict Rossa is a dangerous man, and must remain the object of increasing anxiety to the authorities. The senior warder at Millbank, a man of no mean experience with convicts, said that over his whole career he had never met Rossa's equal. Rossa has no ill-usage to complain of. He must mend his ways, or abide his fate.

*   *   *   *   *

AFTER THIS INQUIRY the authorities put the screws on me in earnest. The cell in which they now lodged me at night was full of fleas, though it is but just to say that my prison life in England was otherwise pretty free from this condition. In this cell, I got out of bed one June morning at about three AM. I couldn't sleep, and, having my writing materials with me, planted myself with my back to the door, in a position where the watch couldn't see me. Shortly he appeared, and hollered through the slit: 'Where are you?'

'Here,' said I, standing up and holding a prayer book in my hand.

'You must go to bed, or be reported.'

And to bed I went, taking my materials with me, and making every effort I could to finish my letter. I wrote under the blanket, and had the clothing so arranged that if he looked in again, I could tell him I was merely hunting the fleas.

But now came the winter of my discontent — one more injustice that made my whole soul rise in rebellion. They gave me forty-eight hours on bread and water, and I got twenty ounces of coir to pick each day. The officer gave it to me at four in the evening, and took it from me at the same hour next day. On giving it to me, a cord was tied about it, and on giving it back I bound it with the same cord, so he could place it tidily on the scales to be weighed. I had made up my bundle, and, feeling at ease, stretched out on my bed-board with a book in my hand, but was immediately startled by the voice of Big Power roaring out, 'What are you doing there?'

'Reading.'

'Reading! Why aren't you at work?'

'Governor,' I said, 'I've done my work.'

He opened the door, called Percival the ward officer, and scolded him for allowing me to be idle. No man was to be idle in that prison. I should keep at my work till the end of the work period; or, if I had done it before then, should ask for more. And he wound up by ordering me to put out my broom. Next day, taken before the governor, I was charged with idleness. Power told his story, and I told mine. The governor said it was a serious breach of discipline, and sentenced me to a 'dark cell' for two days. I asked leave to appeal that decision to the director, but he would not accede. 'Then,' said I, 'I'll not go to the dark cell; nor will I do anything else while you treat me so outrageously.'

Off I was taken. As I was passing the tower that led to the punishment ward, the officer commanded me to turn left. 'No,' I said forcefully, 'I'm going to my own cell.'

They let me get there, shut the door, and came back by and by with Big Power and four or five others. I would not obey a single order. They came into the cell, and ordered me out. I said, 'No,' and on the instant Cooper and Brown sprang at me and seized me by the throat. I couldn't even relieve myself by a screech. I was thrown down and dragged out. The hands were released from my throat, and Beresford raised his club, but Power caught him by the arm, saying, 'Don't strike him.' They turned me face to the ground, caught me by the hands and legs and dragged me off. My arm joints felt as if they were being twisted out of me. When I was laid opposite the door of the dark cell I was ordered to strip, but I refused. They went at me again, and when I resisted, they had a little trouble. A civilian who was working as a plumber in the ward came to their assistance.

At last my clothes were torn off, and I lay on the flagstones naked. I crawled into my cell, they throwing my tattered garments in after me. The forty-eight hours passed, and when I returned to my regular cell I was again ordered to put out my broom. 'Put it out yourselves if you want to,' I told them. Next day, ordered before the governor, I refused to go. Power came, but could not get into my cell, for I had placed my bucket between the cell-door and the wall. 'You'll come,' said he, walking away, and in a minute I heard a tramping as of an entire squad. I had an earthenware chamber-vessel, and when I heard them coming I smashed it on the flagstones and put my towel around large pieces of it. The bucket would allow the door to open just wide enough to admit a man's head, and, as sure as I write, if I had had a chance at the heads of Brown or Cooper, who had lacerated my throat days before, I would have given them the benefit of my loaded towel. But neither had come this time, and I would not strike at anyone else. Chief Warder Handy parleyed with me but to no purpose. I wouldn't take the bucket away. He put his head in, but I warned him not to venture further. Enraged, he yelled: 'Knock him down if he moves to strike anyone!' Said I: 'You keep away, too; and if you want to see me knocked down, bring Cooper or Brown up here.'

Some warders who had been brought from other wards took a peep at 'the wild animal' through the spyhole; and, catching hold of my waterpint, I shouted: 'If anyone else stares at me through that, I'll fling this water in his face.' Deputy Governor Wallack came, but, again, to no effect. Ultimately they sent for the priest, and since I wouldn't let him in without getting a promise from all the others that none of them would enter until he had gone out again and I had perfected my barricade, he went away, and they sent for the establishment's blacksmith, who came by with a sledge and a crowbar. He battered at the door, and smashed it; but as he was about to tear it off its hinges I yelled, 'Enough. I surrender.'

And taking the bucket away, I let them in.

In minutes I again stood before my judge, charged with resisting and assaulting, three days before, six officers discharging their duties. The governor said he would refer the charge to the director. I was brought back and lodged in the cell next to the broken one; but they took away the bucket that was there lest I should raise another barricade. My 'broom' was out for four days until the director showed up; and as I was led into the place where we waited until we were called to go before him, I saw one man with his face turned to the wall. I had to pass him and stand three yards away, but, passing by, I grasped him by the hand and exclaimed, 'Devoy! How are you?'

'Well enough. How are you?'

The officer intervened; even so, as I took my position, I said to Devoy, 'Here is where we get civilized, right?'

'Never mind,' said Devoy, 'we'll have a day for that ourselves.'

'I don't think you knew me at first,' said I.

'Know you,' said he, 'I don't know who you are yet!' He looked again. 'Great God, it's Rossa!'

I was before the director again, the indictment this time: 'resisting officers, assaulting them, refusing to be stripped, refusing to do anything'. What had I to say? 'Governor,' I said, 'will you please ask those officers if they can show you proofs of my assaults?' Neither of them could, but all said that I was extremely violent, and would have continued to assault unless I was restrained. I pointed to my neck, which had scabs on it, for they had torn it in the choking they had given me days before. 'Look at this. You can see the marks of their assaults!'

I was conducted to a punishment-cell, and the deputy governor, following, informed me of my punishments. Four months in solitary in dark cell on penal diet, with the first twelve days on bread and water; in addition to this I was to pick oakum, though for those four months I never picked a thread of it. The bundle was put into my cell every morning, and remained untouched until evening, when it was put outside, where it remained until the next day. No milk, meat, tea or coffee; indeed, I was fortunate if I got enough salt to make 'dip' for potatoes or porridge.

The twelve bread and water days brought me severe attacks of something like cholera. The first attack seized me in the middle of the night. The watch, hearing me groan and vomit, asked if he should call the doctor. 'You needn't,' I said, 'your doctors know that this treatment is meant to break down my health. I'm not going to give them more trouble.' He reported the case, however, for, by and by, Dr Pocklington came, clad only in his pants and shirt. He said he'd send me something to stop the retching and would change my diet for a few days. I got hot milk for breakfast and supper, and rice pudding for dinner, or rather as dinner, for the pudding was the only dinner I got. It was flavourful and sweet, and great was my regret that I couldn't keep it on my stomach.

My changed diet continued for three days. I recovered somewhat; the bread and water began again; and, again, a relapse of my illness, which affected me for several days. Dr Pocklington was as kind as man could be. I don't know what his feelings toward me were, but I felt warmly toward him for the promptness with which he came to see me those nights, and for the fact that I never heard from him an unpleasant word, or saw an unpleasant look, during those twelve Millbank months.

After the bread and water days the months of punishment-diet commenced. Toward the end of it, my body broke out in pustules. Not an inch of me was free from them, and they looked very ugly with their white heads. I showed them to the doctor, and he said it was a natural result of the food I was getting, of confinement in a dark cell, and want of exercise. A fortnight thereafter, as the officers were stripping me, one, Cooper, expressed shock at the appearance of my skin. I told him I had shown them to the doctor, but, as the doctor had said it was 'the natural result' of my punishment, I thought I ought to let nature take its course. Said he, 'When he comes by, show them to him again.' I said I would not. 'Then,' said he, 'I'll report the case.'

He did report it, and I was taken to Dr Gover's office. After he had examined me, he ordered me to dress, and to be taken back to my cell. I afterwards learned that the medical department had had a fight with 'administration' about my treatment. Gambier wanted to continue my punishment to the ultimates of discipline, no matter what ensued as to my health; and, after the four months had ended, I believe I would have gotten more bread and water for not working during that time, except that now the doctors intervened. Dr Gover told me he was trying to keep me off such punishment, and hoped I would assist him by my good behaviour. To which I replied, 'I need only be treated like any other prisoner, to act like any other.' I have nothing harsh to say about the Millbank doctors. They gave me milk of magnesia three times a day to help me digest my punishment-diet; they acted like gentlemen; but I have other things to say of their doctors elsewhere.

For my first days of that four-month stretch I had company, for John Devoy and St Clair were undergoing sentences of four months in penal also. The charges against them — attempting to break out of their cells. They had made such attempts but, as in unsuccessful revolutions, got punished because they didn't succeed. When the director asked Devoy if he was sorry for his offense, John told him he was sorry he had failed. He seemed to be dissatisfied with his escape attempts, for one day he attacked two warders who were overseeing him while he was sweeping out his cell. He knocked one down with a blow of his brush-handle; his second blow was warded off by the other's club. The handle broke; the officer ran to give the alarm; and John, seeing that the cause was lost again, commenced to dress the wound of the officer he had knocked down, and allowed the wounded man to have the credit for locking him up before the others came. It was when he had been brought before the director for that offense that I had met him in the passageway and had shaken hands with him.

We had daring spirits in Millbank in those days and, with our ways of communicating, were developing a plan to seize on the officers' armoury and make a fight. It was a desperate idea; but, with all that has ever been said about the Irish never making an effective fight, we had pledged each other that in this affair we would fight to the death.

*   *   *   *   *

AT ABOUT THIS time the Devil became aware I was in prison, and decided to pay me a visit. He did it with images of womankind. Do not conclude that he came into my cell, or that I saw him and hurled my inkbottle at him as Martin Luther is said to have done when he was in prison. But if what the theologians say about the old gentleman is true, he was with me to a certainty.

Yes, he appeared in woman guise, and did not cease to disturb and preoccupy me for a long, long time. Why he hadn't laid siege to me in my first prison-years I don't know. Possibly my mind was then filled with the hopes and concerns attendant on our fight in Ireland; and when that was seen to be a failure, the ground lay fallow, and the weeds of temptation sprung up. But certain it is that the Old Boy did attack, and never more persistently than when I was in most miserable condition. On starvation diet, and in a black-hole cell where not a ray of light could enter, the devil would remind me of how pleasant it could be, even there, to have female company. My defence for a time was an algebraic problem, or a proposition of Euclid that I took to bed and worked on until I fell asleep. But, as if my jailers knew that I resisted in this manner, they took my Euclid and my algebra book, on the pretext that I could have no books for refusing to work while under punishment. The Devil, seeing how I was fighting him, must have gone to Gambier and encouraged him to deprive me of those books. But I didn't give up easily. I told the jailers that if they didn't return my books I'd give them no peace, would break everything I could; in short, I'd keep the Devil away by playing the devil! Father Zanetti told me that Gambier had seen him about the schoolbooks, asking whether I would be more incorrigible with them than without them. To which the priest had replied that he supposed it would not make me worse to get them. In the event, they were returned to me.

*　　*　　*　　*　　*

IT WAS WHILE I was undergoing that four-month ordeal that the door of my cell was thrown open one morning, and Governor Morish stood outside with paper and pencil in his hand. 'I've come to learn if you'll volunteer to go to the penal settlements of Western Australia,' he said.

'Volunteer, Governor, did you say? To go there as a prisoner, and be a prisoner when I arrive?'

'Yes.'

'I'll do no such thing. I suppose you can send me; indeed, do anything you please with me. But I'll do no volunteering.'

'The government won't send you otherwise.'

'Then I'll remain. I prefer to receive their tortures and starvation here than in the wilds of Western Australia. If you're taking down names, you can put me down as not volunteering. I'm a prisoner; they can do what they please with me; but whatever they do must be their responsibility.'

'Then I'm to put you down as not desiring to go?'

'It is not a question of my desiring to go or not go. The authorities care very little about my desires. I don't know what their motives may be in sending me to Australia. But when you tell me I am to be a prisoner there, I prefer to be near you here, where I can make my needs known, than thousands of miles away where there may be orders to "civilize" me in the fashion you're following in London. No, Governor, I'll give the authorities no such opportunity.'

He pencilled something on his paper and went away. Any change of life at that time would have been a godsend, and I was hoping I would be sent to Australia; but I was determined not to give them the satisfaction of volunteering. If anything happened to us they would say we had volunteered, and I didn't want them to be able to say this. But, as one might guess, my desires in the matter were nothing. In a few days a government doctor came by, examined me, and days later I was officially told I was to be sent to Australia. I got a sheet of paper to write a farewell letter to my wife. I wrote; but it was pronounced 'non-transmittable'. I wrote a second, against which the same sentence was pronounced; and then I learned somehow that 'the Australians' had been sent off and I was to be left behind.

The secret of all this was that between the time the governor first spoke to me about going and the time of the ship's sailing, Colonel Kelly and Captain Deasy of our organization had been rescued from the police in Manchester. This changed the government's decisions, and it was evidently considered safer to keep some of us in England than to send us overseas.

I can never forget the vexation that seized me when Fr Zanetti met me one day and I asked him whether John O'Leary and Thomas Clarke Luby had been sent. They had been in Portland with me, and unsurpassable barriers of locks, keys and stone walls had since separated us. I had a fierce urge to know, one way or the other, however unhappy the truth might make me. And I asked him. He stamped his foot in a rage. 'Don't ask such questions,' he stormed. 'Don't you know that my honour is pledged and that I can't answer you?' That was the last question I ever did ask of that scrupulously honourable man, who was a perfect example of the union of Church and State!

My four months of penal served, I was taken back to my regular cell. They brought in skeins or coir cord, and directed me to pick them and wind them into balls. But I refused to pick or wind. There was no further talk of task-work, and for a while I was left alone. I went to chapel every morning, and there became acquainted with James O'Brien. No formal introduction: the prisoners who sat between us told me who he was, and told him who I was. In course of time we passed letters to each other, and he briefed me on many things about the movement in Ireland.

Once, when his cell was searched, a letter of mine was found, and it again brought me misfortune. My name wasn't signed to it, but it contained evidence that no one but I could have been the writer. I had stated that I had applied for a visit from Richard Pigott and a lady friend and got permission; had informed them that the permission had been granted; and that the director had been as 'hypocritically civil as possible' in granting it. I was brought before Gambier: the letter lay before him. 'So,' said he, 'I was hypocritically civil?'

'Governor,' said I, 'you want me to admit that I wrote that letter. I will admit or deny nothing. Prove your case; but this you may be sure of – that if what you hold in your hand was written by me, it contains nothing but the truth.'

'Then I shall stop your visit, the ticket for which has been sent to Mr Pigott.' And orders were immediately given to write to Pigott that I had forfeited my visit privilege.

The day my letter to O'Brien was found, I was stripped three times. I went through the procedure without resistance because I knew I had nothing contraband about me, and was anxious to learn what was up. Nothing was found in my cell to warrant a report. I was charged with my writings having been found in the cell of another prisoner. Being asked what I had to say, I said, 'Nothing.' I was put into a darkened cell to await the director's decision, and after three days was taken out and told that he'd directed that I be kept from Mass and morning prayer for the remainder of my time.

I was told that my punishment for writing to O'Brien would be six days on bread and water and twenty-one on penal diet. The black-hole cell was truly black, one where no ray of sunlight ever entered; and the punishment-cell, a darkened one where a perforated metal sheet kept out the full light. I made a solemn address to the officers one day: 'Officers, I am here a political prisoner. By all the laws of civilization, and the rights of man, I'm entitled to food and to God's daylight. I cannot command food, but can do something to get myself light; so I ask you to take away that metal blind before I do it myself.' They smiled at each other.

'Well, if you won't, it's my duty to go to work on it.' Laying hold of my wooden spoon, I proceeded to scratch out little bits of cement until the spoon broke. It had been left with me to eat a pint of stirabout that is given to a prisoner every fourth day he is on bread and water. The stirabout arriving, I asked for a spoon, but was told that the governor had ordered that I was to get no more spoons while I was in prison, as I had broken the one I had. The doors were locked and I was left in darkness with my pint of stirabout. With my hands in cuffs, I put the dish to my mouth, but it was thick, not running, stirabout, and it wouldn't come near my hungry lips. I was determined it should find its way to its destination. No way, evidently, to get it down but to lay the dish on the floor and support myself on knees and elbows. You may call this eating on all fours if you like, but it was the way I had to take my dinner that day; and when I had it taken, I turned the bowl upside down, leaped on it, and broke it into pieces.

I thought it would be a good thing if, when the officers came by,

I could make them stay with me until my time in that cell was up. So, taking a piece of the broken dish, I broke it into smaller pieces with my teeth, and commenced stuffing the keyhole of the inner gate. It was duly packed when my nocturnal visitors showed up. 'What now?' queried Beresford. 'Show that lantern here.' And when he looked, he nodded and said, 'Well, well...to be sure.'

Awls, wires, corkscrews and gimlets were put to use before they could get out all those wooden splinters. They spent much time at the task, while I kept begging them to go away and let me live in peace. When the keyhole eventually had been cleared my time was up, and I was taken back to my 'blind cell'.

When the twenty-seven days had passed, I got twenty-eight more for breaking my dish and spoon and writing on my wall. From 20 December till the 24th day of February (the latter the day I was taken from Millbank to Chatham) I was on bread and water.

12. Christmas Day on Bread and Water

THE PUNISHMENTS REFERRED to in the last chapter commenced Christmas Week, and on Christmas Day I was on bread and water. The bell rang for dinner. I heard doors opening, and began to ask myself was it possible that these Christians, so strong on the Bible, would leave me on Christmas Day without dinner: precisely that was possible. My door was passed. I set to work to find something to do, wanted to banish my dinnerless reflections. I had an iron screw in my pocket I had picked up when I kicked the trapdoor open days before, and with this I set to work to take down my metal blind; but though I sweated with my effort I didn't make much progress. Exhausted, I lay down on my bed-board, and rapped on the wall to learn if there was any prisoner within hearing. I got a response from a cell below me, and asked 'Who are you?' The answer tapped out: JOHN DEVOY. I signalled back 'Rossa'; and we both rapped a Te Deum on the wall and commenced our conversation. Hungry as I then was, I was happier to have made this acquaintance than over the best Christmas dinner I had ever eaten.

We talked until John had to go to evening prayers, but there would be no prayers for me. When he returned we talked again till bedtime, when he was changed to another cell. Next morning he was brought back, and we renewed our contact. Our conversation was about Ireland and the movement. He was one of the men who had sprung James Stephens from Richmond Prison. It was into his arms Stephens fell when he slipped off the prison wall, and I got the full story of the affair from him. It was strange to find it industriously circulated in America that Stephens was spirited out of prison with the connivance of the English government. Stephens was taken out of prison by men who were true to Ireland; and whatever may be said of him in other respects, this at least could be said with assurance: he was as free from the taint of English gold, and as unlikely to be corrupted by it, as any man of his name.

For three or four weeks I was in this cell over Devoy's. I had covered the walls of it with writing; and as my jailers appeared to believe that I would disfigure in a similar manner every cell I went into, they may have thought it better to allow me to remain where I was. It was amusing to see those inspectors come in and take note of that writing. 'This land of Bible hypocrites, where they worry men to death under medical superintendence, so none may call it murder.' 'We won't kill these Irish rebels publicly; will starve them privately.' In another corner they could read: 'With one hand they pass me a Bible; with the other, the bit of bread that slowly starves me.' All this was literally true. When a prisoner was put on bread and water, the Bible followed him to his punishment-cell; and if he was changed from one cell to another, that Bible followed him. Once when I was taken to the black hole, Cooper brought my Bible along; and as he was about to lock me in, I asked: 'Aren't you going to give me my Bible?'

'Why? You have no light to read it by.'

'But can't you leave me one of those lanterns?'

'I wish I could,' he said. 'Your Bible will be left outside your door until your time is up, and then will be taken to your other cell.'

'Stop that knocking! What are you doing?' they'd cry out when they'd catch me telegraphing to John Devoy. And I'd tell them I was trying to strike up 'Garryowen' on the wall, as I had no other way of killing time.

*   *   *   *   *

AT THIS POINT, another change. I was moved from one side of the pentagon to another. My new cell was an improvement on those I had had previously. It had a small window containing two panes of glass. The warder opened it each morning to give me fresh air,

184

and many an urge I had to reach it and get a look at the world outside, but the window was beyond my reach. I'd leap for the sill and try to hold on; but, light as my body was, the effort was too much for my strength, and I'd drop after a few seconds. I piled one on another all the things I could lay hold of. My gutta-percha pot was the foundation stone, my mealtime stirabout dish would be next, then my pint, and my jacket and vest on top of these, each folded up to afford me as much height as possible; and on top of all I positioned a wooden plate that belonged to the cell and had not been removed. It was as neat a feat as you could imagine, to plant my toes on the rim of this plate and keep hanging on to that sill while I held a conversation with a prisoner in another cell. My hands would tire, I'd lean on the structure underneath more heavily than I should, and the pile would totter. My first attempt to open up communication thus was a success, but a melancholy one. When I had raised myself to a position where I could see the windows of the other cells, I whispered urgently, 'Any one there?' After several such attempts, a whisper came back, 'Who are you?' 'Rossa. But who are you?' 'Murphy, from Manchester.' 'Murphy...Manchester?' 'Yes; I met you there in '64. Remember?'

We had words as to how and just where we had met. And I did remember, and asked him what had brought him here.

'Didn't you hear of the three who were hung?'

'No. Who were they, and what was it about?'

'You didn't hear of Colonel Tom Kelly and Captain Tim Deasy being rescued? Kelly and Deasy were arrested; and we rescued them. One of the police was shot; and three men were hanged for it, and seven transported. You must have known one of the hanged – Mike O'Brien of Cork.'

These last words unsteadied me, and the pile that was under my feet fell. I clung to the window sill, and asked, 'Not Mike!'

'Yes; he went to America; and came back to fight.'

I dropped to the ground, and heard no more. Mike O'Brien! One of my best friends in the organization. As artless as a child, devoted as a lover, courageous as a lion. Hanged! I'd made his acquaintance in Cork in '59; introduced to him by a relative of mine, Denis Downing, both of them then working in Sir John

Arnott's establishment. Denis was arrested in Skibbereen in '58 on a charge of being connected with the Phoenix Society. The movement was then in its infancy, and Denis sixteen years of age. After his release he left for America, went into the service there, and raised himself to the rank of captain. He lost a leg at Gettysburg, was marshaled into the regular army after that war, and was stationed in Washington. He fell into ill health, got a leave of absence to go to Ireland, and died there. Mike O'Brien went to America, too, and, learning that Denis was in the Army, made to join him. Denis's brother Patrick, now a colonel in Washington, also imprisoned in '58, was commanding in the 42nd Tammany Regiment. Mike met the brother. They were going to fight: he should go with them. And providing himself with a weapon, he went in as a volunteer, and came out of the conflict without a wound.

I had met him in New York in '63. One day he said to me: 'Rossa, I must get more knowledge of the use of arms; so, I have made up my mind to join the 13th New Jersey. Will you come to see me off?'

I went, and saw him take the oath, the recruiting sergeant tempting me by saying I'd make a splendid soldier. I saw him on the train that took those recruits to regimental headquarters, and that was the last I saw of Mike O'Brien. God — that man to be hanged as a criminal! Well, if he was one, then Tone, Emmet, Fitzgerald, or any who had died in our country's cause were criminals, too.

Murphy told me that Captain McCafferty, St Clair and others I knew were in the pentagon and within communication range. I felt timid about calling their names out, for they might be acting the roles of 'good characters' and be averse to doing anything against regulations. I whispered them a few times, and, getting no response, didn't trouble them further. I had met St Clair in London in '64. He then had the reputation of being imprudent, used to march his men in military style through the streets. He had been in penal with Devoy and me on charges of attempting to break prison, and when Murphy told me he was in the vicinity, I called his name. At the other side of the pentagon he heard me, and, instead of whispering across when he recognized my voice, bawled out a hearty congratulation on our encounter. It drew the attention of the officers, and our cells were changed.

O'Brien's fate preyed on me for days. Then, as I lay on my bed-board one morning when the prisoners were coming from chapel, one of them put his lips to the ventilator, and whispered, 'Duffy. Dead! Ned Duffy.' Duffy — another 'confessor of the faith'! The man who gave me the word was Lynch, who was detected in Portland Prison trying to pass out the letter to my wife that I had directed to the care of Mrs Moore. He was then within months of being released, but, in consequence of his having been detected trying to assist me, the authorities laid it on him. The warders kept reporting him for imaginary offenses; he lost all the remission he had earned; and had to serve his full sentence. In Millbank now, and learning that I was in the same ward, he had communicated with me.

I had travelled Ireland's West with Ned Duffy, and we had had many an adventure. We found ourselves one night struggling through bogs and brakes in the triangle of Ballaghadereen, Boyle, and Ballymote. The meeting place was on a hill within view of rocky eminences that were full of caves. I think they are called the Keish Mountains.

We were to meet a large body of men, but a mistake was made in the designation of the rendezvous, for we only encountered half of them, the other half having assembled on a hill some three miles distant. This we discovered after we had ended our business about midnight. Our men knew that the boys from the other district were to assemble also; and a few of them shouted calls in code. There was dead silence; then, in the stillness of the night a reply came. Our men gave a general shout of 'All finished.' This was immediately returned; and we broke up, scattering in various directions.

A serious question had come up for resolution that night. Another society was active in the district, and its members were averse to our United Irishmen being introduced. Our men were beaten at fairs, markets and on the highway whenever they were met by the others. This had been going on for quite a while; but now that the United had become strong enough to command respect and power, some of them wanted to force the other party to merge with them — to actually beat them into the revolution's armed ranks. Duffy and I would not approve. We told them that forbearance was our strategy, that it was better to use persuasion than force. There were many good men in the other camp who had been bitterly opposed to joining at first, but now were ardent workers in the good cause. There was nothing to prevent any of them from being a member of both societies. There was, however, one difference — the other organization had been started to defend people from aggression, while ours had the object of making war on the aggressors and destroying their rule in our country. We admitted to our brotherhood Irishmen of every class and creed who would swear to fight for Irish independence. They admitted adherents to their particular creed only. They were sectarian, and defensive against the enemy; we were national and aggressive, organizing ourselves to fight.

All seemed pleased with our intervention, and it was gratifying to learn shortly afterwards that the two groups were working harmoniously together.

Ned Duffy at that time (March 1865) was in delicate health; yet he travelled for us night and day, was up late and early. One night we passed by his mother's house. 'Hold,' said he to our driver, 'a light in the window; they are still up; we'll go in.' His mother kissed him, saying, 'Eddie, won't you stay over? You'll kill yourself.' 'Not yet, mother,' he answered. They kissed again; and we mounted our jaunting-car and went to meet the friends.

I had had a sight of Ed once in Millbank. It was when I was allowed to go to chapel, and I saw him one Sunday morning receiving Communion. I would have given much to have had his eye catch mine, but he never raised his head going to or coming from the altar. He had a sort of stoop to his carriage, and it looked as if his treatment was bending him to the ground. When his last days were approaching, an officer in the prison told me that Duffy would very much like to have a talk with me. There was no way of having it by code, he being in the hospital, and I, in punishment. But I resolved I would do anything I could to gratify his wish, and had my name taken down by the officer to see the director on his next visit. When he showed up I was brought before him, but he told me that visiting Duffy was out of the question.

Duffy's death, following so closely on Mike O'Brien's, threw me into a sombre mood. When I went to bed, and couldn't sleep, I fell to rhyming, rhyming verses to keep the memory of my comrades alive.

The world is growing dark to me, and darker day by day.
  The stars that shone upon life's path are dimming fast away.
The tyrants setting and some shifting, but there's one that changes
      never,
  The guiding star of Freedom blazing bright and clear as ever.

'Liberty' sits mountain-high, and slavery has birth
  In hovels and in marshes, in the lowest dens of earth;
The tyrants of the world o'erpave the path between;
  And palisade with scaffold, prison, block and guillotine.

The gloomy way is brightened when we walk with those we
    love.
  The heavy load is lightened when we bear, and they approve.
But the path of life grows darker as I journey ever on,
  For the truest hearts who've travelled it are falling one by one.

*   *   *   *   *

MY FOURTEEN DAYS punishment was up, and I was expecting the light and diet of an ordinary cell. But no, that wasn't for me yet. Hauled before the director, I got fourteen more for not doing any work the preceding fourteen. Seven of the second fourteen had passed when I found myself taken to a first-class punishment cell, and got four ounces of meat for dinner. I got porridge for supper with my bread, and, in the morning, three-quarters of a pint of cocoa. I asked the officer what the change meant, but he couldn't tell me. I was getting the regular working-diet, yet they would not put me in a regular working cell, or let me go to chapel. In fact, I was about to be transferred.

My last week in Millbank was a pleasant one, for I could look out my window and watch the prisoners exercising. Devoy was now in a cell two floors below me, and we were able to speak to each other without raising our voices. During breakfast hour one morning we noticed an unusual stir. We saw some prisoners taken from one yard, others from another, and concluded that a transfer of a number of the prisoners to a works prison was imminent. Amid speculations as to how we might be involved, my door was opened. I was ordered out, and irons were readied for me. In moments I was bound, and on my way to a waiting coach. 'Big Power' and two other warders entered the carriage with me, each of them wearing a belt in which were stuck a short sword and a revolver. The prison gates opened; we drove through London for a half-hour before being transferred to a railway carriage. The four of us had a compartment to ourselves. Power, feeling he had me well secured, began to get jolly, and talked of my skill in providing myself with writing materials.

'Rossa, we're going to a place where they make the closest searches possible; so, if you have anything on you, just fling it out the window, and don't give it to them to say that we didn't do our duty.'

'There's no doubt but that you did your duty. But if you did it with an easy conscience, I don't envy you. Anyway, I have nothing about me that will get you into trouble. But where are we going?'

'You'll know soon,' said he; and as he spoke, the train slackened speed. I heard 'Chatham!' We all stood up. I was conducted to the platform, where other armed men shook hands with my guards. Coaches were obtained. And in another half-hour I was in Chatham Prison, and didn't see its outside until three years later.

13. A Military Prison

MY NEW GUARDIANS conducted me to my wing, and one of them ordered: 'Turn your face to the wall.' My blood leaped, but I mastered myself. I was measured, weighed, stripped, searched, bathed, re-dressed, shaven, shorn, and entered on the books. Principal Warder Alison read me a lecture. He told me I came here with a pretty bad character, but hoped I'd become an altered man. And I told him I felt pretty well altered already. 'You should have seen,' said I, 'what a handsome man I was when I was in the world.' And you, reader, should have seen the confused look he gave me.

The cell was ten feet by seven. My bedstead was nailed to the ground, and its pillow portion was raised four inches. The bedclothes were folded, and lay on a mattress that was also folded. My table was a board embedded in an angle in the wall, and my stool was two feet high, part of the trunk of a tree, and fastened to the floor alongside the table. Again that detestable metal screen with holes in it to admit as much light as would enable me to see my misery.

On my second day I got a sheet of paper to write the 'reception letter'. I wrote it to my wife, and next day was told it wouldn't be allowed to pass, for I had written about my treatment. On my third day I was sent to work with a group of nine thieves. The youngest of them was twenty-six, and the eldest, seventy. They had worked previously with the other convicts in a place called Mary's Island, outside the prison. We wheeled rubbish from one yard to another. Each man had his barrow, and if I didn't fill mine as full as the others, Supervisor Thompson would make me take the shovel to lay more on. We were allowed to talk moderately.

191

After dinner, the ten of us were sent to break stone. I wasn't long at it before I noticed the officer's special attention being directed toward me. I am left-handed, and when I began working my hammer in that hand, the officer ordered me to use the other. I told him I couldn't; and he told me I must work in the same mode as the other prisoners. I hoped that this wouldn't be an indication that the screws were to be put on me here, too. But it was an ill-founded hope. Two left-handed men came into our party subsequently, and that warder never interfered with their using hammers with their left hands.

I tried awkwardly to use my right. Sometimes I'd strike the block instead of the stone; or at other times, the round hoop of iron with which I held the stone in a fixed position. Jobler, who worked next to me, told me to strike more lightly until I became dexterous. But, objected Thompson, 'Your stroke is too light.' I said nothing; kept hammering away. 'Your stroke is too light,' came again. I raised my eyes, but said nothing. Whispered Jobler: 'Just work away.' And away I worked, sensing that my companion was giving me sound advice.

'Stroke's too light,' sounded again; and Jobler muttered, 'God help you, Rossa.' 'Too light, too light, too light,' was repeated several times. At last, in as mild a tone as I could manage, I replied, 'Officer, the wages are light, too.'

The principal officer coming around soon after, Thompson made for him, and I heard, 'Rossa!' The supervisor motioned to me with his sword to approach. I did so, and received a lecture. In explaining myself, I raised my hand to illustrate the action of the hammer. The principal immediately raised his sword as if to strike, and ordered me to keep my hands by my side. This again set off my ire, and when he went on about my 'insolence' and 'impertinence', I said: 'The prison rules don't permit me to be insolent to an officer; nor do they permit any officer to be impertinent to me.' He turned on his heel, telling Thompson to report me when we went into supper; and I returned to my 'too light' stroke.

That evening, upon entering my cell, the first thing I did was unbosom some old news-scrap items that Pratt had passed to me earlier in the day. I read about two brothers named Desmond who were on trial in connection with the gunpowder plot at Clerkenwell. The key turned in my door. I stuck the scraps inside the waist of my trousers. Alison and another officer entered, and ordered me to strip. I was caught in a 'violation' the first week of my Chatham novitiate, and there was little doubt but that preparations had been made to catch me. Pratt was afterwards hunted out of our working party because he was believed to be an informer. When I went out to work again after getting ten days on bread and water in dark cell, on my telling the others what had occurred, Cosgrove, who had been orderly on the evening of the stripping, remembered that Alison had gone to Pratt's cell before he came to mine.

I was told I had forfeited my right to write another letter in place of the one that had been suppressed. Taken back to my cell, I looked around, and, seeing my gutta-percha pint, laid hold of it and dashed it against the gaslight fixture, smashing the fixture and the pint to smithereens. The noise of the breaking glass brought the warders around, and in minutes I had been lodged in one of their black holes. Here I passed another forty-eight hours with scant food by day and scanty covers by night. In addition, seventy-two hours on bread and water. Satisfied that I deserved this punishment, I went through it quietly, save that I refused to salute the governor and other officers when they came to visit.

The Protestant chaplain visited me daily and endeavoured to reason with me. He spoke very kindly, and asked me if I wouldn't grant him a favour. I said I would if I could; and he asked me to conform to the custom of the prison in the matter of standing 'to attention' when the governor called. I told him I would; and I stood in the middle of the cell, with my hands by my side, the next time Captain Powell appeared. I thought that this would settle matters, and that I would be sent out to work when my three days were up; but no, authority had to be upheld, and I would get three days more for 'insolence' and 'insubordination'. Then I was sorry I had made that promise to the chaplain; but, since I had made it, I kept it, and at the end of ten days found myself breaking stone again at Jobler's side.

Jobler's real name was William Crane, and he came from

Hampstead. He entertained me with stories about the Derby and other great races, where thieves would attend in organized gangs. He told me how watches were 'prigged', and how other robberies had been committed, but hoped I would never divulge these 'secrets of the profession' if I chanced to get back into the world. He and the others often used 'professional' slang, and the secrets of that he wouldn't tell me; but, from my constant listening in on their conversations, I developed familiarity with their codes, and he was quite surprised one day when I told him something in code.

Cosgrove, the head of our working party, was as well built and handsome a man as one would wish to see. He had served in the English army, and was now serving time for a burglary in Nottingham. He was the only one of the party I made free with. I used to call him 'Cos', but used to 'Mr' the others when I had to speak to them. Our work inside the walls was varied. We piled brick and timber, emptied lime-carts, and stacked material that was brought into the yard.

If Cos caught me behind a pile, out of the officer's view, he'd go on with tricks of jugglery, often setting me to laughing. One day he made me accessory to an attempted theft. We were tearing down an old shed in which one of the officers had his office. Cos and I were on top of the shed, tearing out the boards, and Jobler and another man were taking them away. Cos saw a coat (belonging to one of the warders) hanging in the office below. 'By golly,' said he, 'there may be a pencil or a plug of tobacco in that.' He signaled to Jobler, and, telling him to be on watch, told me to keep an eye out also and to cough if Thompson was sighted. He jumped down, but was back up in a minute, cursing the old coat because its pockets held nothing.

These months were not without interest, and I had variety, for hardly a week passed that I didn't have a day or two on bread and water. Besides the punishments that came to me from the urge of the authorities to keep me in hot water, I gave myself three days in the cells every month. This was a sort of protest against having to work with thieves. As I had no political companions, I did not fear to be showing a bad example; but if any of my treason-felony friends came in there afterwards, it would be cited to them that I had associated with criminal prisoners, had never refused to work with them.

While the convicts were never allowed outside the prison walls when I worked with them, every day I was held in punishment they were taken out. They were thus given to understand that their rigorous treatment was due to my presence, and, if relieved of me, would be relieved of the extra punishments that made their durance time more than usually miserable. Several asked to be sent back to the ordinary prison area, but only one succeeded. This one was Scotty. He suddenly discovered he was a Presbyterian, and by rights should be attending those religious services rather than the Episcopalian. He asked for the chaplain, and told him he wished, in future, to attend his own services. But to take Scotty by himself to another congregation would have required another guard; accordingly, it would be easier to remove him from his party. In the event, he was transferred.

'Irreverence at chapel' was one of the heinous crimes recorded against me in those prison-books. Two strangers preceded me to chapel on Sunday. They came from my ward, and turned out to be Harry Mulleda and Ricard O'Sullivan Burke, who had been convicted on charges of purchasing arms in England. Burke attempted to have a look at me some rows behind him, but was immediately ordered to look to his front.

Our chapel on this occasion was a hall of the prison, with cells to each side. Each prisoner brought his stool with him, but we had no stools, and had to take some from adjacent cells. When placed in position I found myself in a row of one. Behind me were two strangers. How to get a look at them was the problem, and getting it was the 'irreverence'. I was seated on my stool as the preacher preached. When I came to kneel down, I turned around so my eyes would sweep the faces of the men behind me. Albeit, I didn't recognize them. But when I went back to my cell I was ordered to put out my broom, and next day was ordered two days punishment for the offence of looking around.

Captain Du Cane, chairman of the board of prison directors, ordered that the prisoners be seated four yards apart when they were breaking stone, and that they shouldn't speak to each other; also, when it was necessary to draw stone, that I be kept to my work, the others being sent to draw the cart. The prisoners were angry at being kept so far apart and prevented from conversing; and some of them began to look darkly at me as being the cause of their discomfiture. One fellow said that if he were in my place he'd fling himself down the stairs or commit suicide rather than be keeping a party of 'innocent men' in 'torment'.

On the morning of 1 June we were sent to work on a large heap of small stones. We were not allowed to sit down, but were permitted to place one knee on a stone and strike at the smaller stones with our hammers. It was not an agreeable working position, and I had previously made up my mind to 'go on strike'. Thompson and a principal officer were standing on a pile of wood that overlooked the stones. I stood up and asked Jobler if he thought I could throw my hammer over the prison wall from where I stood. While he looked at me in amazement, I flung the hammer with all my might. The warders approached, and asked why I had done that. I told them I'd need the hammer no more, as I had finished my work in that place.

I got three bread-and-water days for that. I told the governor I would work no more in that party, and he said I'd have to. I told him I'd salute him no more; and he told me I should. I told it was not to him I meant disrespect, but to the government that was sending him orders to treat me as I was being treated. The three days passed; and I got three more for not saluting the governor and not having my tinware bright enough. When these days ended, I got a repetition of the dose; and they kept repeating it until 17 June

On 15 June I told him I wouldn't come into his presence any more. Next day I refused to go, and several warders came to my cell and dragged me to his office. When I entered, they let go their hold of me, and I leaned against the wall with my arms folded and one leg across the other. I was ordered to stand to attention, but kept leaning against the wall. I was laid hold of and brought to the rail. One officer caught my left hand and held it by my side; another caught my right; another came behind, settled my heels

and toes in position, and straightened me up. I told the governor
it would be a good idea to have a picture of this taken for the edifi-
cation of those English people who were so fond of passing
judgments on foreign customs.

I went back to my cell raging at the thought of these people
laying hands on me, and having no way to be avenged of them.
Father O'Sullivan the chaplain came in, and the tears rolled down
his cheeks as he counselled me to bear patiently and offer my sufferings to God as 'satisfaction for my sins'. 'Father,' said I, 'don't
talk to me that way.' The priest left my cell, and as he did, that
thought of an offering recurred to me, and with it, the possibility
of making a 'real' offering and paying the governor a compliment
that would afford me some satisfaction. I fell on my knees, and
prayed, 'Almighty God, I offer Thee, in atonement for my sins, the
punishment and suffering that will come on account of an act I
contemplate committing tomorrow.' I rose from my knees, and
instantly felt relief.

Next morning, when I took my pail to the water tank, I brought
it back to my cell half-full. Twelve o'clock came. The governor was
making his rounds, and, hearing him approach, I braced myself.
The inside door was unlocked and thrown inward. The officer
outside cried: 'Salute the governor!' The governor looked through
the bars to see where I was, and as he did, got my salute full in his
face. It was the fairest shot I'd ever made; and as the water
streamed down his clothes, 'That,' I said, 'is the salute I owe you.'
And slammed the cell door with a force that shook the building.

The day of the assault I was allowed to rest quietly in my cell.
But next morning, about ten, Principal Alison and two other
warders came by to tell me they had orders to put me in handcuffs.
'Here,' said I to Alison, who had the irons; and held out my
hands. He took hold of one; another took the other; and they
brought them behind my back and bound them. I neither said nor
did anything on that occasion to provoke further violence, yet they
were ready to act very harshly if they got an excuse.

At twelve, Brown and Douglas brought me my dinner. They
took off the irons; and I thought they were going to leave them off
until I had eaten; but that would have been far too generous. They

cuffed my hands in front, and left me to eat as best I could. When I had eaten they came back and unbound me, but only in order to put the manacles on behind again. At two, I was taken out of my cell, and my irons were taken off. My shoes, cap, stockings, handkerchief and braces were laid before me, and I was ordered to dress myself. My hands were again tied behind my back and I was led to the exercise yard, a special officer having charge of me. The hour being up, my hands were untied, and, giving up my shoes, stockings, braces and cap, I gave my hands to the warders to have them again fastened behind my back. At a quarter to eight the cuffs were taken away altogether, and I was left in peace until morning. At a quarter after five next morning my hands were again tied behind my back; half an hour afterwards they were untied, and tied in front to enable me to take my breakfast; then, with it taken, they were again bound behind till dinnertime or the exercise hour, whichever came first.

This was the history of one day's cuffing and uncuffing. It continued day after day for thirty-five days, and before a week of that time had passed I could count eight bloody marks on my wrists. I got those from the spite of two of the warders, Brown and Thompson. Whenever the two came to change the irons they always made 'the dogs' bite by allowing the spring part of them to rest on my hands while they cuffed me. I showed the wound marks to Dr Burns who asked Alison how it had happened. 'Oh, sir,' said Alison, 'that might happen with the most careful officer. I've often nipped a man; couldn't help it.' 'I see,' said the doctor, and no more was done about it, other than that Thompson and Brown 'nipped' whenever they did their jobs.

Now, I had no braces; and no way of keeping up my trousers from slipping down as I walked my cell. I gnawed two holes in the front of my vest; and, using these, managed to button my trousers. Brown reported me for 'tearing my clothes'. The vest was taken away, and I got it back again; two patches sewed in where I had made the holes. I gnawed at it again; made two more; and the next time my hands were changed to the front, rebuttoned myself. Thompson came to change the irons, and, noticing that my trousers were 'hitched', went to the trouble of unhitching them. I was afraid that, to torment me, they would resort to cutting the buttons out altogether. My body-clothes were taken from me every night and placed outside my cell door; and every morning, I took them in. Thompson opened the door one morning, and, as I was stooping to pick them up, kicked them into my face. No use my friends or my enemies saying I hadn't patience: I had. Thompson had his club, but I cared little for that. I could have throttled him before he could use it; but it could never have been proved that I didn't make an unprovoked assault on him; and the other warders would have been up immediately to finish me, for in consequence of the assault I had committed on the governor all were eager at this time for any excuse to have at me.

When once after dinner they were putting the irons on, they gave me a very wicked 'bite', and the blood flowed so freely it dripped onto the floor. Laying the forefinger of one hand on the wound that had been made on the wrist of the other, I wrote on my door: 'Blood for blood!' Fr O'Sullivan came by, and, seeing the writing exclaimed: 'Terrible! You'll only make matters worse for yourself. Wipe it out, I implore you,' and he drew from his pocket a white handkerchief. I thought it would be wrong to allow him to soil it, and promised to wipe the stains off when he had left.

The summer was hot, and it was hard to pass a day without a stretch. I would rest on one of my hands whenever I lay down, and my arms were pretty unmanageable at first, but by and by they got used to the pressure of the metal cuffs. From time to time I'd fall asleep; then wake with the arm that was under me entirely numbed. But by rubbing it against the wall or against my body, sensation and motion would be restored. The heat became so oppressive in my cell that I thought it would be a relief to have my jacket off and be handcuffed in my shirtsleeves; and I decided to arrange for this when Brown came in with the irons. 'Where's your jacket?' queried he.

'My hands would be freer without it, and the weather is so warm I think I can leave it off.'

'Put on your jacket.' He put the irons on and at dinner-time, when the deputy governor came around, reported me to him for the offence and for the 'insolence' I had given him.

A week after the 'wet salute', Jobler, in the cell next to mine, knocked on the wall. I knocked in return, and listened. 'Goodbye, Rossa; remember me and Cos.' I rapped back; but then the doors were unlocked and a whole party marching out with bag and baggage. 'Goodbye, Rossa; remember us!' they called. The tears started to my eyes, and I let them flow. These men had treated me with kindness. When I had met them, after days on bread and water, Cos and Jobler made arrangements, with others of our party whom they trusted, to give me their dinner bread as we were going up the stairs. Cos, being an orderly, would slip his meat out of his tin and pass it through the bars of my door, and fill water into my can; and this would be done at the risk of the officer seeing him, for, if seen, he could have lost months of remission.

Fourteen days of the thirty-five had passed; and, my dinner eaten, the irons were not put on as usual. I wondered if the torture might not be at an end. My door was opened and I was conducted to the adjudication room where sat Captain Du Cane. He read a statement of charges to me, and asked what I had to say. I said that when I was brought before Captain Harvey the day after I committed the offence, he had told me I would get a sheet of paper to make out a defence for the director. I had gotten no paper. 'You can't have it,' said Du Cane. 'Have you any reply to make?'

'I'll make no reply except in writing.'

'Do you admit the offence?'

'Oh yes.'

'I'm sorry to see that, instead of improving, you're getting worse.'

'And worse I'll be getting as long as you get worse.'

I was left for an hour with my hands free, and began to think that a new sentence had been passed and that the irons were being laid away. Not so: they were put on again. Next morning I heard the triangle being placed outside my cell window where the prisoners came to be flogged; and as I heard the whistle of the lashes in the air, and the victim's cries as his back was cut, I nerved myself to go through the same operation. I was prepared for anything, and felt a grim satisfaction at thinking that these people would flog me. I knew that that act, degrading them, would stimulate us Irish to ever greater exertions to be avenged.

Du Cane reported:

> Ordinarily he would have been punished by flogging; but it was thought this punishment should not be inflicted without special authority. If it should be deemed not advisable to inflict it, I can only suggest that he be sentenced to twenty-eight days close confinement on punishment-diet, and be placed in penal class for six months; also, to prevent his repeating outrages of this description on officers obliged to visit him, that all moveable articles and utensils be removed from his cell, whatever is necessary be made a fixture, and that in the daytime he be kept in handcuffs. It is for consideration whether the prisoner should be allowed to remain in this prison after having committed such an outrage on the governor, especially if it is decided that the severe punishment for such an offence is not to be inflicted.

And Henderson, chairman of the prison directors, taking a week to consider and to consult the Ministry as to whether or not the prisoner should be flogged, wrote:

> I am unwilling, except as a last resort, to employ corporal punishment in the case of this man, whose conduct savours of imbecility. Carry out the director's recommendation — twenty-eight days on punishment-diet in close confinement; six months in penal class; and remove all moveable articles from his cell.

These people would have not hesitated to flog me if they had been able to do it unknown to the world; but they knew the story would get out, and do them more mischief than they could do to me.

Not a fortnight passed in this prison that the shrieks of flogged unfortunates didn't make my flesh creep. The first strokes generally brought piercing wails, but after that, till the two or three dozen were given, I would hear no more, though I'd hear the whips cutting into the naked back. An odd case occurred where a prisoner would utter no cry; and that person, in the estimation of his jailers, would be a 'hardened wretch', while his fellow prisoners would consider him a hero.

From time to time, by putting my fingers in the holes of my metal blind and drawing myself up, I managed to view a flogging. There was the triangle — three bars of iron coming together at the top, and extended and stuck in the ground at the bottom. The prisoner's hands were lashed above; and his feet, which I couldn't see, I suppose were tied below. Two doctors, the governor, the chaplain, and several warders, stood around. The prisoner, naked to the waist. A jailer swung the cat-o'-nine tails — pieces of hard cord tied to a stick about a foot-and-a-half long. Every stroke he gave, he drew the cords through his hand to clean away the flesh or blood that might have been on them, and to make them even for the next stroke. A principal warder cried out, 'One – two – three...' and so on till a dozen had been counted. Then, to relieve the first man, an assistant flogger took the lash, and began at thirteen, continuing till he came to twenty-four, when the other flogged again, and was again relieved at thirty-six if the victim was to get more than three dozen. My whole being revolted when one day I saw an unfortunate tied up, with his head hanging on his shoulder as they slashed at him while the high officials (with umbrellas over their heads and mats under their feet to protect them from catching cold from the drizzling rain) looked on!

Du Cane had told Henderson that the governor of my prison was 'as temperate and judicious a person as it was possible to find.' Of course he was! Where could you find a governor of an English prison who was not so? And the officers in charge of me 'selected for their judgment and fidelity.' Undoubtedly. What did that mean? Simply that they were officers who would be faithful to their masters' behests and would give a prisoner no quarter.

About a week after Du Cane's visit I was changed from cell 6 to cell 13; and next day, when I got my exercise hour, I saw that two large holes were being broken into the wall of number 6. I surmised that they were preparing for my permanent placement there,

and I was right. As I passed by, my guard officer was talking to
Alison. Both were examining the holes, and Alison, loud enough
for me to hear, said, 'I think he'll be brought to his senses now.'
They were installing an iron closet in the cell, and otherwise
making it damage-proof. While the changes were being made I was
lodged in 13. The two cells above me were occupied by Rick Burke
and Harry Mulleda, and I soon managed to contact them. We con-
versed by knocking on the walls. I kept myself occupied all day
sitting on my gutta-percha pot and telegraphing on the wall with
my knuckles, and, when they got sore, with the knobs of my handcuffs. The two above me had to work for their daily bread; and I
had to contact each of them in turn, so as to give one time to pick
his oakum while the other was giving me news.

I had had about a fortnight of this life when number 6 became
finished and my Lenten season commenced. Deputy Governor
Alison and two other officers entered 13 one evening, the deputy
holding in his hand a foolscap document. I can't remember the
exact words, but its substance was this: I was to be kept in 6, and
never be let out of it, for twenty-eight days. I was to have no book
except the Bible, and my clothes were to be taken from me every
night, and be given back to me every morning. And now my handcuffs were removed.

14. A Fortress Constructed, and Breached

A THICK PANE of glass inserted in the wall of my new cell was protected on the inside by a plate of perforated iron also worked into the wall, and another such plate protected the spyhole. The position of my bed had been changed in order to allow room for the installation of a water-closet. The closet had no cover, and its seat was a slab of formed flagstone. The whole cell had been so fashioned as to frustrate any attempt I might make to damage or destroy it. After a few weeks, however, I had breached that fortress.

New pipes had been laid and a water-tap had been installed in my cell. This tap was one device that I had control of. Turning it on, I stretched out, and the water merrily spouted away. Before long the warders surmised that something was wrong. Alison came in, and, making for the tap, asked why I was letting the water run. I told him – to keep the water-closet fresh. He twisted and turned, but couldn't turn it off; and sent for the engineer. This man came, and decided that the device was in working order. Alison threatened all kinds of punishment, but I told him they were doing their worst with me already. He went out; came back with a pair of handcuffs. 'Now we'll quieten you,' he said, and, manacling my hands behind my back, led me into a black-hole cell. I was kept there for two days and two nights, and when brought back to cell 6 found that the tap had been changed from the inside to the outside. In consequence, when I wanted water I had to ring a bell for a warder.

English prison law declares that a prisoner is not to be put 'in irons' unless he is violent. There was not much violence in turning on a water tap, but Lord Devon's commission would not have it so. Here is what they had to say: 'The statement was that he was manacled for thirty-five days. It is to be observed that, having been released from handcuffs at 2 PM on July 20, he was, for a further offence of grave character committed in that interval, replaced in manacles on the same day at 4:15 PM, and they were not finally removed until noon on the 22nd.'

When the handcuffs were removed this time, I told Alison I'd break the water-closet if he didn't put a cover on it; and he challenged me to do so. After he had gone I espied the bell-handle, and made an effort to break it. I couldn't manage it with my naked hands, but thought I'd do better by taking off my jacket and twisting it about the knob. I gave a long, strong pull, and the bell-handle and I sprawled on the floor. I knew that the jailers would be in on me, and, hearing the doors open, hurled the bell iron against the closet basin, and broke off a piece of it.

Thus, one breach had been made in the fortification. I got the-black hole again for a few days; and when I came back had a bell-handle that couldn't be broken. But I resolved anew to work on the closet. I found a piece of the smashed crockery, and with this scraped away some of the cement and pulled out a piece of brick, with which in turn I made another assault on the citadel. My next effort was to pull my table out of the wall. Indeed, I showed them pretty clearly that I could knock their impregnable cell into a cocked hat.

After a fortnight's series of blows and counter-blows, Director Gambier visited the prison. In his silveriest tones he said he was glad to have good news for me — my wife was doing well in America; he had seen newspaper accounts of her 'readings', and had met my attorney, Mr Lawless, who had told him to tell me that my children were well also. As he talked in this strain he laid hold of my arm, and my whole frame trembled at feeling his touch on me. His fingers couldn't find much between them but skin and bone, and, for all his kind words, he left the prison that day with orders that I was to get no bed that night.

Up to this time I had got my bed at half-seven each evening; but, as I was in 'general insurrection', I refused to take it to the bathroom each morning, on the ground that it was being taken out of my cell during the day in order to punish me, and I shouldn't have to be the agent of my own punishment. Sometimes I'd remain lying down until the warders would come and pull the bed from under me. The deputy governor continually threatened that unless I removed my bed I wouldn't get it at night; but the threat wasn't carried out until Gambier came; and that night and the night after, I lay in the 'black hole' without anything to cover me. I was deprived of body-clothing also. With two nights experience of these deprivations, I accepted the bed on the third night when Alison offered it to me if I would agree to carry it out in the morning.

When my twenty-eight days on bread and water had expired, the six months penal diet commenced, and they gave me oakum to pick in my cell, and an hour in the open each day. I took the hour, but didn't pick the oakum. So, for not working, they took my exercise hour from me, and put me back alternate days (sometimes two at a time) on bread and water.

On one occasion when, deprived of my bed, I refused to put my clothes out, Alison came by with warders Hibbert and Giddings. He repeated the demand that I put them out, and when again I refused, the three of them rushed at me. I tried to keep them off by holding them at arms length; made no attempt to strike them; but they struck at my hands with their clubs to make me let go my hold whenever I caught at one of them. I was overpowered and flung on the ground, with Hibbert's knee on my neck. Alison pulled the breeches off me. It was necessary to turn my neck while this was being done. In fact, as I was on my back, he gave a leap, and with his knee foremost, came down on my torso. The air shot up my throat as it would through the neck of a full-blown bladder if you leaped on it. The blade bones must have been very strong to bear such a strain. When the warders had stripped me, they moved to leave; and I attempted to raise myself from the floor, but Hibbert, who was the last to go out, turned, and gave me a kick that threw me against the wall. My door was locked, but in a minute or two they came by and opened the trap to see how I fared. 'Assassin dogs!' I yelled, laying hold of my gutta-percha pot and flinging it at the trap. The opening, however, was too small to allow it to go out, so I seized the three little loaves of bread I had as a reserve against hunger, and hurled them one by one at my enemies.

The night of the assault I felt pain in my chest; was sore in many parts of my body; and heartsore also. Burke and Mulleda were in cells above me. They'd heard the noise; kept rapping to learn what the matter was; and when I was composed enough I answered them. We kept up our knocking for half the night, and their sympathy was balm for the wounds of my flesh as well as for those of my spirit. In the morning I asked for the doctor, and when he brought me from the black hole into the light of the hallway, we both saw that my chest was swollen and black-and-blue. I received some liniment to rub on it, and by degrees the soreness and swelling went away.

Captain Du Cane visited. 'Can you not get on in prison like your fellow prisoners?' he asked me. 'They are all doing well; and when I was telling some of them in Portland the other day how foolish you were for yourself, they were sorry for you.'

'When have I been treated like my fellow prisoners?' I replied. 'Was I not separated from them in Portland and sent to work among thieves? Have I not been separated from them in Millbank and sent to work among thieves?'

Said he, 'If I give you a chance now, will you promise to do better?'

'I cannot promise anything. But if I'm treated like a human, I have no desire to give trouble.'

'All right — let's forget the past. I'll remit the rest of your punishment, and send you to work tomorrow with Halpin, Warren and Costello.'

I knew that the three he'd mentioned were in the prison for I'd seen them through holes in my blinds the first Sunday they had exercised in the yard outside my window. And I had been annoyed, for they were walking around, one after another, some four yards apart, instead of being exercised in twos and allowed to talk as the other prisoners were. I thought they should have had pluck enough to kick against such treatment, and was vexed at seeing them, with all their Yankee bravado, submitting so tamely.

But they did resist afterwards, and Warren and Halpin often made me laugh at the way they kicked against discipline. Indeed, at the very time Du Cane was speaking to me they were on strike, having refused to work because of the provocations of the warders.

I had been in communication with Costello. He had become laid up with a sore leg, and the doctor, instead of sending him to hospital, ordered him into the cell next to mine, so I had opportunities to learn through the wall much that was going on. Costello had a lot of news about my wife giving readings in America, and, as she and I had had no communication for years, I made the black hole my frequent abode. I managed to do this by giving 'readings' myself. As soon as my first forty-eight hours in 'the underground' were over, I was taken back to cell 6, and, as soon as I was locked in, commenced a recitation from Thomas Davis (the poet), but was immediately pounced on for making noise, and was taken down again. This was what I wanted, but before I got tired of 'talking' with Costello, they got tired (or ashamed) of keeping me so long in the black hole. It began to look as if they'd given me up as a bad job, for ultimately I couldn't get myself sent to the dungeon! I'd dance, sing, recite and they wouldn't notice me; I would tire of declaiming and singing. Even so, I felt I had won a victory over their discipline and was magnanimous enough to ask for oakum to pick. When I commenced to pick it, they gave me a library book.

The morning after Du Cane spoke to me, I was sent out with Costello, and we were put in Warder Pepper's charge. He took us to the tool-box, gave us shovels, pickaxes and wheelbarrows, and sent us to wheel a heap of broken stone along deal boards to the top of another heap. I worked so hard the first day that Costello asked me if I was going to be a 'driver' on him. I was pale as a ghost and reduced to a skeleton, and no wonder, for I had been in dark and close confinement since the 1st of June. To counter the effects of the cold I ran the wheelbarrow up the hill as fast as I could, but soon exhausted my little strength, and after an hour or so Costello's reproofs were not needed to persuade me to take it easy.

Warren and Costello were among the volunteers who had come

to Ireland in the *Erin's Hope*. They landed in Waterford, and were arrested on the first day they set foot on Irish soil. The fact that this small ship was three or four weeks off the Irish coast fully demonstrated that men and arms could be landed in that country in spite of naval vigilance. Her commander, John Kavanagh, on making his official report when he took her back to America, said: 'During eighteen of the twenty-four days I was in British waters, I was sought by the English fleet deployed there; and, in proof of their vigilance and efforts, I record the loss – lost in hunting for us – of these vessels: the *Lapwing*, first-class gunboat, lost in Killala Bay; the *Revenge*, also a first-class gunboat, lost on Daunt's Rock; and the third, a second-class gunboat, foundered in a gale off Cape Clear. Yet there was no point of the coast where I could not have landed any amount of men and arms, had preparations been made to take them from me; and the military officers who were with me will confirm this statement.'

*   *   *   *   *

THE FACT THAT we were getting, and using, writing materials had alarmed the authorities, and they set to work to counter our efforts to get our cases before the public. They kept us from religious services nine or ten days, during which they were making a doorway in the gable end of the chapel. When it was finished we were admitted and placed in a separate corner. While the services proceeded, our keepers sat on benches in front of us, their backs against the altar and their faces toward us. A very religious person might pray under such circumstances, but I candidly confess I couldn't show much devotion with those gentlemen looking straight at me!

When our party went to Communion there was such a parade as turned the eyes of the whole chapel toward it. Other communicants, up half the length of the chapel from us, were allowed to approach the altar without the warders stirring from their seats. But when one of our party went up, a warder followed him through the chapel and stood over him with club or sword drawn while he was receiving the sacrament; then, gave him a 'right about face' and followed him down again in the same manner.

When the door was being broken in at the chapel's gable end, we continued to frustrate the discipline. The priest would visit us each morning after the regular service. Our doors were opened, and we would be ordered to come into the hallway to pray. But Burke, Halpin, Warren and Costello refused to leave their cells. They said it was a mockery of religion to pray where open water-closets were in view, while the chapel facility was there for the other prisoners. I came out and knelt down, and Mulleda came out. Costello and Rick Burke left their doors open, and knelt in their cells while the priest prayed outside. But Warren and Halpin wouldn't countenance this exceptional treatment and slammed their doors as soon as the warders opened them. This situation continued for ten or eleven days until the chapel had been readied to receive us.

In January 1869 Costello was taken from us, and on 4 March Warren got his marching orders. We hadn't as much as a goodbye with them. Six of us went to dinner one day, and came out without Costello. During the dinner-hour he was removed from his cell to one under mine. I heard the clank of chains, and later, by knocking on the wall, learned that he was in irons and was to be taken elsewhere. At brick-cleaning one morning a warder called out, 'Warren! This way!' And that was the last we saw of him. A writ of error had been filed in his case. He was taken to Dublin, and two months thereafter was released.

Cleaning bricks was a most unpleasant task, for we had to handle them in frost and snow. Often we worked in a corrugated iron shed so constructed that we couldn't get a sight of anyone passing through the yard. It faced the prison's high wall, so not a ray of sunshine could enter to lessen the cold's rigor, and here we worked at clipping old mortar off the bricks from daydawn until nightfall. Halpin called it 'the refrigerator'; and if you were stony-hearted enough to laugh at a 'free American' doing time in an English prison because of his conduct in America, you could laugh at Halpin hopping from one foot to another to warm his toes while his hands beat time with his brick-chopper. But he didn't stand it very long. Laying down the chopper one morning, he turned to the warder, and said: 'Mr Mabbot, the cup of my affliction has overflowed.'

'What do you mean, Halpin?' 'I mean to do no more work. This refrigerator is enough to kill a saint. You can send me to the cells. Please to send me in.'

'I don't like to be reporting you,' Mabbot told him. 'If you feel the cold, take a run up and down, and that'll warm you. But don't be going into cell.'

This was a great concession. Earlier, Halpin's words would have been a gross breach of discipline, severely punishable; but as Mabbot afterwards said, Halpin had 'joined the service in a good time'; and on this occasion his 'bad conduct' was winked at. We prevailed on him to take that run up and down; then, each of us took similar exercise, and Halpin was able to stay with us.

He had caught a severe cold, and currently was suffering from a very bad cough. All through the night we'd hear it echoing through the wards. The doctor sent him to hospital, but his doing this seemed to interfere with existing orders to keep us at all times to ourselves and not let us be seen by other prisoners. An iron screen was put outside his hospital-cell window. But this didn't seem to meet the authorities' requirements, and Halpin was sent back to us after a few days. During the three winters he was in Chatham this cough afflicted him, and Dr Burns would not give him any hospital treatment other than to allow him a spittoon in his cell, in order to enable the doctor to judge how the cough had progressed, from the increase or decrease of the quantity of blood he had thrown up.

15. New Arrivals, and
A Handshake with John Devoy

COMING IN FROM 'the refrigerator' one evening, we found that three additional cells of our ward had been occupied. By knocking on the walls, we learned of new arrivals from Millbank. Next morning I was orderly, and on my rounds had a handshake with John Devoy and Charles O'Connell. I didn't know the third newcomer, but he turned out to be John McClure, who had been arrested after fighting with O'Neil Crowley at Kilclooney Wood, and had been sentenced to be hanged.

McClure, Halpin, Devoy, Burke, O'Connell, Mulleda and I had worked for several days in the 'refrigerator'. Then, one of the directors visited, and arrangements were made that we be kept at work inside our own ward. The governor had his adjudication room there, and over his courthouse was a small room about twelve by eight, into which we seven were put, with two warders in charge of us. Our occupation — mending the prisoners' stockings. These were given to us after being washed; but after we turned them inside out, such a quantity of sand and dust issued from them that it almost suffocated us. Nine of us worked in this small space. Summer days came on, and after repeated protests to the doctor and the governor, we got them to take down a partition that divided us from another small room, the change making the work space more airy and less disagreeable.

But Halpin 'struck' work, refusing to darn in consequence of being refused letter and visit privileges that the rules accorded to ordinary prisoners. He got three bread and water days for the first refusal, but that didn't prevent him from laying his needle down again when the warder handed it to him on the fourth morning.

We thought his punishment would continue, but it didn't. The authorities by this time were tiring of their attempts to civilize us by ill-treatment; and they left Halpin alone. Every morning, his needle and yarn were handed to him; he graciously received them from the warder; and as graciously laid them down on his stool. He then amused us by telling stories all day long. His example had an evil influence on me, and I suggested that we should invent a game to kill time. It would have helped if we had had a draughts-board, but as we hadn't, we fashioned one by making a 'fox and geese' on the bench, and made 'men' out of bits of coal and scraps of paper.

The checkers game was fine recreation. The back pain that had been troubling me became very intense at times, but worse whenever I allowed my mind to dwell on the matters that affected me and mine; and I had no surcease from pain then but to let my thoughts fly to some game, however trifling. Either that, or to some scheme inimical to the powers who governed us. But as long as they left us alone, I was content to let them alone, and live in peace.

Home Secretary Bruce, when questioned in parliament at this time as to my ill-treatment, said I was now 'the quietest man in the prison'. Here is his comment as it was reported in *The Irishman* of 12 June, 1869:

> Another statement is that his appearance has quite changed, and that he has suffered sorely from confinement. Since he became an inmate of Chatham his weight has increased from 163 to 171 lbs. (Laughter in the Chamber). His general health is stated to be good. After what I have given you of this unfortunate man's career (here, the Secretary referred to his papers), I find that he had told twenty-four lies about me. It is a real pleasure to say that since September, '68, the date of his last offence, his conduct has greatly improved and he has not incurred further punishment. Captain Du Cane, on visiting the prison, told Rossa that his conduct had been outrageous, and he was astonished that 'a man of his position' should have been guilty of it. Since then, not only has O'Donovan behaved well and received no pun-

ishment, but Captain Powell had said that 'Of all the Fenians now under confinement, he is the best behaved'.

We well understood that any warder placed in charge of us was due for promotion if he performed to the satisfaction of his masters. Since my arrival in Chatham, the fellow who had drawn the blood from my hands, and one who had torn the clothes off my limbs and kicked and trampled me in the black hole, had received rewards for 'faithful service'. Pepper and Mabbott now sported yellow bands on their caps, indicating their promotion to the rank of 'principal'. But currently the test of faithful service was not so much to worry us about work as it was to isolate us and render it impossible for anyone outside the prison to know anything about us. These were the times when government were lying about us in parliament and sending commissioners to the prison to manufacture reports to be read in parliament about us.

On Sundays, before we went to chapel, we were paraded for inspection by the doctor, and some of our company were already getting so rebellious as to refuse to take off their caps when this gentleman appeared. Halpin and O'Connell began the fun, and kept it up for some Sundays. A few others joined in, but I obeyed the hats off! order till we all agreed that it shouldn't be obeyed, and that if they began giving us bread and water for our disobedience we should stand it to the point of starvation rather than uncover. Next Sunday, when the doctor appeared, Alison cried, 'Hats off!', but the hats remained on. 'Hats off!' he roared again in a voice that startled me, but no hat stirred. I was most happy at this spirited stand. The doctor and his aides wheeled off; we were marched into chapel; and I had much difficulty, during prayers, muffling my laughter when I thought of the ridiculous figure the officials cut in the presence of our rebellious bonnets.

O'Connell elicited from the doctor the strangest admission I'd ever heard a medical man make. Lamed from the heavy boots he was wearing, he asked Dr Burns if he could wear his Sunday shoes instead of the workday boots. 'No,' said the doctor, 'unless your leg is sore.'

'My leg is so sore I can't walk with these boots.'

'Can you show me a sore?'

'No; but I'm sure it'll get sore if I have to wear them.'

'Well, when you can show me a sore, I'll try to cure it.'

'Isn't prevention better than cure, doctor?'

'Yes; but in some cases we're not allowed to prevent.'

* * * * *

IN NOVEMBER, '69 it was manifest that something extraordinary had occurred 'out in the world' that called for the most extreme vigilance regarding us. The exercise we got in the open air wasn't given to us in the usual place, nor given in the same place on any two consecutive days. The secret of our being so handled was that the Tipperary election had taken place. The rebel spirits there had chosen me as their representative, and a rumour had gone out that I and my companions were to be rescued. In consequence, the authorities were in great alarm. They couldn't bring themselves to trust their own employees; and, lest a warder should be able to tell an attacking party where the prisoners would be exercising on a particular day, our venue was changed each day. Every precaution was taken to secure us — extra locks on our doors at night, additional guards on our cells. If the citadel had been besieged we couldn't have been more vigilantly guarded. This was ridiculous; but those who mean to fight England may take lessons from it — first, as to acting on her fears, and the measures that may be necessary to strike terror into her; and secondly, as to provisions and precautions that may be needed to protect us against surprise and defeat.

In spite of the arts resorted to to keep us in the dark, we had 'wires' laid down that kept us well acquainted with what was going on and learned of the Tipperary election before its results were officially made known to us. The governor sent for me, and, reading from a paper, said: 'I am instructed by the Home Secretary to inform you that the county of Tipperary has elected you a member of parliament; but I'm also requested by him to tell you that that in no way is to change your prison treatment.'

I affected surprise; and told him to take my name down to see the director to ask to be transferred to Millbank so that I could be convenient to the House of Commons and be able to attend to my parliamentary duties there at night after picking my oakum during the day. The director came, and I joked with him on the matter. Said he, 'Take my advice, and don't have anything to say to the authorities. You're getting along well lately, and should do nothing to injure yourself if they are disposed to favourably consider your case.' As he had spoken reasonably, I thanked him, and said I would take the new situation quietly. The government were embarrassed enough without my trying to discomfit them further. Thenceforth, with the officers, I assumed the personality of a live member of parliament. I would work to have good people promoted and the bad ones given indefinite terms of prison life.

Some of my companions took the new development seriously, and believed I might actually be taken before the House. They discussed what I ought to do — take the oaths, or refuse to take them; act like a member, or continue to rebel. Further, that if I were taken before the House, I should talk Irish to the others; and, if they couldn't understand me, insist on an interpreter. After all, I was an Irishman representing an Irish county, and I had a right to be heard in the language of my country. This may be a new idea for members who are presently discussing tactics in the House — whether to vote, or not vote; to go there, or remain away. Let them speak Irish in the House, and insist on speaking it. That may be considered ridiculous, but is no more ridiculous than to think that the votes of a hundred Irish members can get a really independent Irish administration against the votes, prejudices and interests of five or six hundred English and Scottish members. If a London parliament ever grants Home Rule to Irishmen, it will be another sham like the Tenant Right she grants to Irish tenants.

The Tipperary election, to my mind, was the grandest thing that had ever occurred in Ireland. As a protest against foreign rule the Clare election was nothing to it. There the popular 'freeman', O'Connell, had been chosen by the people. But Tipperary had chosen a man who had been condemned to imprisonment for life, was dead in law, and subject to every indignity England could heap on him. No compliment was intended to me in this matter. I felt no better, nor did the people consider me better, than anyone else.

The upsurge had been a protest, and a defiance of English administration. Said John Mitchel: 'A great event has befallen. Tipperary
has been wiser and bolder than her sister county of Clare. That
election, to be sure, won what was called Catholic Emancipation,
for the Claremen elected the disqualified Catholic to represent
them in parliament. Now, Tipperary men have elected from all
those imprisoned the very one England most especially abhors –
because he most loudly defied and denounced her government,
her traitor judges and packed juries.'

In December, '69 our company was reduced by the removal
from among us of Rick Burke. He had been taking medicine the
week before, and was visibly falling away. In the end he seemed to
imagine that poison was being administered to him, and he was
spirited away from us one morning without anyone knowing
where he had gone. A few days before his removal, Dr Burns, in
my presence, told him that possibly his problem was that he was
mentally troubled on account of his crime. Rick told him he
wasn't; and the doctor told him he should be.

Having learned that McCarthy Downing of Skibbereen had
been returned from Cork to the English parliament, I thought it
would be well to have a visit from him, and applied to the director
for a ticket, which I sent to Downing. My idea was to get him to
speak in parliament about those 'suppressed' letters to my wife.
The government would aver that they were suppressed because I
had told falsehoods in them; and if I could have the letters in
point produced and read, I would have attained my objective of
having the interceptions exposed. Mr Downing visited me toward
the end of March. He seemed to be very intent on getting us
amnestied, and greatly displeased at a speech that Colonel Warren
(after his release) had made at a banquet in Cork on St Patrick's
Day, as it could interfere with our releases. He wanted me to
express my disapproval of Warren's action, but this I would not
do. I said Warren was accountable for his own acts, and if he had
said or done anything wrong, the law would have its remedies. We
had had an idea before Warren left us that this would happen if
he was released. Certain people would want to fetter him outside
because we were fettered inside; and we distinctly told him in 'the

refrigerator' one day to tell our friends not to be deterred from any work they were minded to do in the cause by any fear that it might lengthen our stay here.

When McCarthy Downing visited, he asked me if I would promise to leave the country if I were released. I told him I was sensitive to anything being said about my seeking release on conditions, or about his seeking such terms for me. I told him that if I had a chance to go to Siberia and be my own master, I would prefer to go there to remaining where I was, but that I would promise nothing. After a lengthy discussion, I said that if he got me a leaf of paper I would reply to his question in writing; and, the deputy governor consenting to give me some, I wrote as follows: 'Responding, Mr Downing, to your question as to whether or not I would leave the country if released, I reply that I would, with the understanding that if found in Ireland or England again without the permission of the British government, I would render myself liable to be recommitted.' I would not promise not to return, having in mind that if I did return, it could not then be said I had broken my word.

Mr Downing said I might as well make up my mind that whoever would be released unconditionally, I would not. He put the statement in his pocket, promising to make no dishonourable use of it; and I believe he never did. But when I learned a year afterwards that he had shown it to my father-in-law, I was afraid it might bear the construction that I had sent for Downing in order to get him to intercede for my release; and I wrote to him to return me the paper. He did so, and I kept it in my cell. When the government officials subsequently asked me if I would leave the country if pardoned, the reply I gave was to send them this same statement.

Downing paid me a second visit a few months later, and brought with him another member of parliament (Mr Blake of Waterford). This interview was solicited by them, as questions had been raised in the House of Commons about my hands being tied behind my back for thirty-five days. Downing said that I had never told him this, which was true; but that was not why I had initially sent for him.1 The question again came up of my leaving the country. Mr Blake talked of my possibly going to Australia. He said he had some very influential friends there and would give me letters of introduction to them. I thanked him; but was so suspicious at the time as to think that he might be speaking with knowledge of where the government wished me to go; and that the friends to whom he would give me letters would be government friends.

Blake and Downing questioned me as to my having had my hands tied for thirty-five days, and I told them it was true. The deputy governor was present, and didn't deny it. Mr Bruce, the Home Secretary, had said I was tied 'for only part of a day'. Downing asked the deputy governor if he could see the record books. At first the deputy agreed but, on reflection, he thought he would be acting improperly by showing them in the governor's absence, and he begged off.

I had a visit from Richard Pigott and John O'Donnell, and managed, despite many interruptions by the deputy governor, who presided at our get-together, to tell them much that would enable them to make a noise when they got home. Pigott's object in visiting was to ascertain if I would be willing to give evidence in a libel case that had been brought against him by A. M. Sullivan, the editor of *The Nation*. This was the second time *The Irishman* had been prosecuted because of its publication of a letter of mine concerning Mr Sullivan. I agreed to give whatever evidence I could in the case, and a few months thereafter, a commissioner, accompanied by Sullivan and by counsel from both sides, came to the prison to examine and cross-examine me.

16. Revelatory Letters, Personal and Official

THE CHAPTER OF letters now before me reveals a troubled existence and intense suffering. It was a question with us in Ireland whether men who had committed themselves to the revolution should marry at all. I know many who had put off the 'happy day' until the war would be over, but I wasn't one of them. I married when the work was hottest; and the day after, started for England and Scotland to meet men who would be calling for someone from headquarters to visit them. Months after returning, I was sent to Connacht with Edward Duffy, and spent time there. After Connacht I was sent to America, and when I came back, my wife, who had left her father's house to go to Dublin, must have had serious doubts as to whether I intended a honeymoon at all. She had very little of my company during the months preceding my arrest. I was out of the house all day; and, in the excitement of the times, more often out at night than I had need to be. So that, looking back at our married life, it is not to be wondered at that a wife, now alone, and troubled and friendless, should write bitterly to me.

I, in prison, should have been spared the pain of thinking that my wife and children were neglected; and the men still in prison should be spared such pain. And if Irishmen here were what they ought to be — if their professions of love for the old land were to have corresponding action — they would have some society to provide for the dependents of those fighting for it. Irish-American patriots cannot fight for Irish independence in America; and if they don't assist and encourage those who mean to in Ireland and England, they do nothing.

Here is my wife's first letter from America. Let the men of the Irish societies read it (the Fenians and the *Clan na nGael* included), and ask themselves are they doing anything even yet but repeating the humbuggery that has operated all too often in the past.

6 Dominick Street, New York City,
19 July, 1867

My dear husband,

I write in a graver mood than usual. Only today I read the report of the commissioners who investigated the prisoners' treatment, and must confess to feelings of annoyance that you should make yourself so conspicuous among men who are as sensitive of their condition as you are, by the number of complaints you make and the number made against you. What is the use of bringing so many successive punishments on yourself, by defiance of a rule that holds you in its grasp? Who can assist you, or what end is to be gained? It seems so boyish a temper you have become possessed of that I should fail to recognize it in the report, if I didn't mark your irritations during my visit to Millbank, and the manner in which you seized on every word uttered by the warders.

I will write as I have never before written to you. It is necessary, perhaps, that you should have some incentive to act in a more rational manner. O'Leary is a sensitive, high-spirited man; so is Luby. Yet with admirable dignity they hold up their heads and take no insult from creatures who are beneath their contempt. They have less reason to be farseeing and politic than you; for think, what reasons have you? Need I set before you the fact that you have six sons – four of them in my father's house and likely to remain there if the poor man can keep a house over them, for I have failed in getting them any shelter here? Need I remind you that you have a wife whom you took in her ignorance and inexperience, whom you afterwards left unprovided for, and who at present is drudging for a pittance and wearing her heart away yearning for the infant who must find a mother on the other side of the ocean? Ah, Rossa, Rossa — think of these things, think which has most trouble: you who took it on yourself and drew it on me, or I, who, depending on your love to do that which was just to me, find myself a married woman without a husband, a child without a parent, and a mother without a child? In poverty, misery, and labour of heart and hand; far from home and in the midst of friends and strangers who are suspicious and critical of my youth. Who suffers most? Who has most reason for complaint? I against you; or you against the authorities?

Is there any hope for me? I see none except what may ensue from a writ of error or clemency of the Crown. Toward the expense of such a writ, let me tell you, the American people, after four weeks from the publication of Miss Mulcahy's petition, have not given a single cent. That speaks volumes. The families have joined in an appeal, and nothing goes home in answer to it, and the west of Ireland is famine-stricken again, and America sends no relief there.

I solemnly tell you that if you escaped tomorrow, I would not live with you unless you atoned to me for the past by minding your family and your own affairs in the future. You told me before our marriage that I could 'simulate and dissimulate'. You were right. Every day after that 25th of October opened my eyes wider to the madness of our union, but I loved you and would not pain you by showing my unhappiness. I looked to the future, disbelieving your talk of prisons and battlefields, and hoped for the life I had coveted after your Fenian business would be over. Philosophy came to my aid; and I bore what few wives would unreproachfully bear; and simulated happiness while my heart was sore, to make you happy. After this, continue to act against your own interest, if you love it and me so little as to feel so inclined. You would never know this much if I did not think it necessary to tell you, lest, mistaking my mind still, you plunge yourself and me into yet more misery. What use is my life if it is to be no more than a distant accompaniment to your protracted sufferings; and where do you think the strength can come from that is to help me to bear it?

Up to this time, in public, I have taken firm hold of the chalice of bitterness you have filled for me, and have drunk it down with brave eyes and unrejecting breath. But if the draught be deeper still, my breath may fail, my courage strangle me, or my strength desert me. Save me if you can. I have one good angel far across the water that looks through the eyes of my child, my bright little boy. This angel smiles on me through my sleep; stretches tiny hands across the sea, lisping my name; and with tiny feet tries to tread the waves that divide me from him and the sunlight. The spray gleams on his child hair and over the ruddy little face. While this angel appears, a firm anchor holds me to life; but if he goes, my heart will sicken; and I pray God to spare me so deep a grief and leave me my one object to live for. So far, my letter can be of little comfort to you, but I cannot in honesty make it more pleasant. You will be angry, wounded, but I must be satisfied with that, too. If you understand me, you will believe that the one pain I give is at the cost of ten or twenty to myself, for I find it easier to take than to give pain or trouble.

I must break off. But by and by shall recommence and tell you of my voyage out, my reception here, and what I have done since.

Ever affectionately,
Mollis

Friday evening
Some day I may be sorry for having written this letter. I'm sorry for writing it now, but don't see how it could have been avoided. When you write, do not reproach me for my words. I do not deserve reproach, and feel so wronged that anything harsh you would say would have an effect contrary to what you would intend.

When I left you, after that interview at Millbank, I went to Dublin, and from there to Clonakilty. Mr Pigott offered me money for my passage to America; and I took it, trusting to be able to pay it back as soon as I should arrive here. I have not been able to do so; but as that incapacity relates to the details of my efforts here, I shall let it pass till you know of the journey that preceded it.

I reached Clonakilty unanticipated by Papa; was received with open arms by the family; and was expected to remain some time. I had my passage engaged, but only two days at my disposal. That dear child of mine clung to my neck the whole time, and would not take his little arms away. He waked me mornings, kissing and patting my cheeks with his rosy fists. Oh, the pain of parting with him! I had been away a month, and had only those two days to be with him before leaving him perhaps for years or for ever. Mama was distracted at my going to a country where there was neither kith nor kin of mine. My father came with me to Queenstown. The morning I left, your letter to him came. I can't say that either he or I appreciated the arguments you drew to satisfy him that what is is best where I am concerned. On 30th of May I went on board the *City of Paris*, and the last sight of my father is stamped on my memory, a care-worn look over his grey face, a wan shadow on his lips, and lights of suppressed anguish in his eyes. I know as well as if I had followed him that he went back to that boarding-house on the beach, locked the door of the sitting-room we had left, and sat at the table with his head between his arms to cry out the agony of a father's heart. It chokes me, that memory. My poor, poor father.

I was known on board and very kindly treated. There were American families returning from a tour, and they made the voyage pleasant for me. A Frenchman was my good angel. The first day of the voyage I was so seasick that after crawling up on deck I had to lay down. He brought me lemons and ice-water, and folded all the spare rugs about me he could find; and so I spent the first day after the evening we embarked.

The next day, I was able to sit up, and the day after was looking about for something to employ my mind on. The Frenchman gave me pencil and paper, and I sketched a few of the passengers. There was a good library on the ship — a small one, but good books — and I read at intervals *Hard Times* and other stories. The Frenchman translated German legends from a beautiful little book he had. Evenings, after supper, we all gathered aft, and watched the phosphoric fire that rolled from our foamy wake. Then, nearing land, there were promenades up and down the deck in the starry nights. I shall long remember the kind words and advice a fine old gentleman from Louisville gave me. I say 'old', but he wasn't old, he was as light-hearted as a boy. His sister and his niece were with him, and the interest they all took in me stemmed from the coincidence of my being at Roscrea School with a cousin of theirs. They left me invitations and addresses to their places, whenever, if ever, I should be in their vicinity. I could have gone with that family as a governess, but I won't go to any family till I know a little more of America. The last day of our voyage was a stormy one; we were in sight of land, but had to put to sea again from the heavy swell. In the evening, we reached Sandy Hook. 'Twas Sunday, and we all had to stay on board till next day. I felt very lonely as the tender reached the Custom House. At sea I had been free from trouble, but with the first step on dry land my cares and perplexities returned. I had been given many affectionate adieus by the friends of my voyage; and looked sadly after them as, group by group, they disappeared, and I was left alone. The Frenchman saw my luggage safe, and ordered me a carriage; then, said goodbye, and went with his charges in another direction. I was seeing my things into the carriage when Tim Donovan came up. He joined me in the carriage, and we drove to Mrs Healy's where I remained one week and was kindly treated. I did not feel it pleasant to live in any house on sufferance, not even in my father's; and, sensing that I was putting the family to inconvenience, I left Brooklyn and went to board with an American family at 13th Street and Second Avenue. To do this I should have to have money, so I engaged myself to the *Irish People* to supply them weekly with poems or stories, under my name (yours), at a salary of

$10 a week, equal to £1/10 of our money at present. This is very inadequate to live on here.

I couldn't put by money to reimburse Mr Pigott; and that frets me. I would mention to you the names of many men who called on me — none with material aid — but 'twould make a long list, and the authorities might view it with objection. I told them the reasons for my journey, about the children, etc; but civility and a welcome to their houses was all I could get from the warmest of your friends here.

'Very hard the children to be in such a bad way.' 'Strange they weren't seen to.' 'Awful responsibility for a young woman,' etc., etc. I got lots of advice and sympathy, but no assistance. The 13th Street boarding-house proved too expensive for my purse, so I moved here (to Dominick Street), an humble neighbourhood, and a house more like home to me, as they are Clonakilty people who knew my father before I was born.

I was at Patrick Downing's in Newark, and, if his circumstances would admit, I believe I might expect that he would help your children. He is a spirited, generous fellow, but his family is increasing, and he has not yet established himself. I like him well. Denis Sullivan of the *Irish People* treated me kindly. He, too, I believe to be sincere, but his situation is not the best. Colonel Denis Burke and his family have shown me much friendship, but are only beginning to recover from the reverses they suffered through their connections with Fenianism.

I write as much as I can, and shall see if I can get into papers or periodicals besides the *Irish People*. Mr Meehan promised to get me into a fancy store as a saleswoman, if I choose to go into business. I will look around for a while. I may soon be able to send for your children, and they would be taken to trades or business here without fee.

I don't think that I have more to say now, except that I got a letter from my father and one from Tim since I came; and I wrote home once. I expect that you will write me, when you do write, in a cold strain, to punish me for having opinions

different from yours on several points in this letter. I'd say 'forgive', but don't feel I have done anything that needs to be forgiven. I haven't space to argue — as you see — and must simply sign myself, fondly and truly, your wife.
M.J.

This letter vexed me. I didn't relish my wife thinking of me in such a manner as would suit the English government to represent me to the world. Knox and Pollock would not bring me face to face with my accusers; would do nothing to afford me justice. Their duty was to whitewash the government and blackwash me. And to be asked if I couldn't act 'in a more rational manner' or like Mr Luby or Mr O'Leary annoyed me, when I had no chance of explaining or even replying.

I was allowed pen and paper to write to my wife; but when I had written the letter it would not be sent out because it contained the explanations I thought it proper to give. A year-and-a-half elapsed before I heard from her again. During that time, I wrote letters to her; but, as I harped on the same strings, the letters were again suppressed. Her prospects, during this time, appeared to grow brighter, and the next letter I got from her was not as gloomy as the one before. She had been turning her talents to earning a livelihood, and was beginning to entertain the notion of getting me out of prison when she would have earned a sufficient amount of money to employ counsel.

At the time I received this letter, my jailers were hitting me pretty hard. It was just after they had been trampling me under foot and chaining me, and I wasn't in a humour to write very kindly of them, or forgetfully of their treatment. Nevertheless, I wrote; but my letter shared the fate of the others. When I tried again, six months later, the same result. But the next half-yearly letter was allowed to pass. Mary's second letter came:

Utica, N.Y.
13 December, 1868

My dear Love,
    I don't know why I write tonight unless it is that I feel

more than usually lonely. I haven't been fit to write to you for a long time. My heart is a dormant volcano — by avoiding thoughts of you or my child, I avoid brooding on my more than three years widowhood and my far away baby, though my soul is shaken to its depth, my heart, convulsing with discontent.

I'm impatient to have a line from you. How do I know but that you have mentally buried me and caused a resurrection of your dead loves? If what the governor said was true about your breaking the rules so often, you certainly did not, or do not, care to write to me. I don't mean to write a long letter until I know. Let me know any ideas you may have as to how I could serve you; and tell me — have you really grown so indifferent to what I may think or feel at your silence that you make no effort to win the goodwill of your jailers, or share in the favours extended to your companions in misery?

I enclose my likeness, taken a month ago. I wonder, if you were out and free now, would you love me as well as you did four years ago. I am changed, Cariss — harder, imperious, self-willed, and irritable at times. I should love you better now if you had not been spoiled from prison. There is no man living, if I were free to choose, I could love better. Comparison with the best men in Ireland or America would not injure you; on the contrary, you appear brighter in the scale. But there were some points in your character the little woman of '65 bore most patiently. I would not promise the same forbearance from the exigent one of '68. But I suppose there will be time enough to resolve all that when you are released.

Faithfully and affectionately,
M.J.

The next letter (in significant order) is one from my lawyer friend, Timothy F. Donovan.

> 202 Broadway, New York,
> 3 September, 1869

My dear Cousin,

By my suggestion your wife recently commenced legal proceedings to obtain (out of a fund now in the custody of our courts) the amount due you for your outlay and services expended on the *Irish People*. The proceeds of the suit are to be applied to the education of your children, under the direction of a guardian to be appointed by the court. I may here state that her best friends in this city have warmly advised this proceeding, and, under their direction, the matter is being pushed. The suit would never have been brought were it not that its successful outcome is assured. But a clique headed by O'Mahony are striving to secure the award for division among themselves. He has made his newspaper here the vehicle for a most villainous attack on your wife, with intent to break her down in her readings before the public – in fact, to steal her bread, because she has foiled him and stopped the money from going into his pocket. It is the fixed determination to apportion this fund to the children of the prisoners for their education and nourishment; and your friends have put in a claim for your children. It is necessary, therefore, that you keep aloof in this matter. Do not give an expression either way relative to the case — and this becomes the more important as your wife's success in her readings may in great measure depend on her success therein.

Therefore, keep a steady silence about it; and please to send me authority to commence in your name all suits I may deem necessary to pursue for your children their rightful claims. An expression to that effect will suffice.

All the folks, deploring your fate, and hoping to see you free once more, send their love

My response to Mary Jane's, sent from Chatham on 2 November, 1869, follows:

Mollis, what's the matter? It looks as if 'absence makes the heart grow fonder' is to be knocked into smithereens by us; that is, if we are to judge by our correspondence, or rather, by the absence of yours, for I, at least, have made efforts to convey to you assurance of your engaging a fair share of 'my thoughts by day and my dreams by night'. But those efforts have failed, my letters have not reached you; you begin to think I have forgotten you; and cease to write. Your father tells me that these are your fears.

Your memory can not be so bad as not to recollect that I told you in that Millbank visit to write me every two months whether you heard from me or not, and you have written once in two years. Our short life together did not, perhaps, afford you time to know me thoroughly; and you may incline to think that my true character is that given by my enemies. Yet I do not believe that this is so. Should fate place us together again, I should like my happiness to be such as it has been, but you would have to do some penance to atone for your distrust of my affection.

'How do I know but that you have mentally buried me, and caused a resurrection of your dead loves?' I recollect your giving me a touch of this once before 'in the world'. I suppose the thought disturbs all men and women who marry relicts. I have been thinking how to meet this poser of yours, and could not find a better way than to ask you: would your affection for your first-born be divided if he had a little brother?

If you come to Ireland about Christmas (as your father expects), you may wish to see me. I have spoken to the director about the matter; he says no difficulty would be placed in your way. I would ask to have a ticket sent to you, but really do not wish that you should incur expense in so doing. A look at me for twenty minutes would do you little good.

Feeling the dreariness of solitary confinement, I have often reflected on how often I left you alone in Dublin, and how uncomplainingly you endured it. I remember you were sick one Sunday; I got some medicine for you; then, went out and left you alone till dinner hour. This was almost cruel, yet you took it as a matter of course that I had to be out, and never grumbled. At the time, I was thoughtlessly violating a wife's privileges. Your 'feigning' to be happy, 'to make me so' had the desired effect, and made me fonder of you, too. Whether

231

I am ever to return the compliment, God alone knows. I got the letter you wrote to me after your arrival in America, and the photograph that accompanied your last letter. I have it fixed at the back of my door — a queer place, you will say! — but my door is ever shut when I'm at home; and then, you are looking over the whole house and its sole occupant.

The four boys sent me a photograph of themselves. I do not have it in my cell, but, upon application, can occasionally get a look at it. Mr Lawless asked me if I would signify to him my approval of your sending those boys to school in Belgium, and I told him I had repeatedly signified to you that they were at your disposal if you could do anything for them. But there is something here to be explained. You cannot have as much money as would insure the continuance of such a programme. Public funds cannot be so plentiful as to obtain such attention for all the children of my fellow sufferers; and I do not like for mine more than others can have. Of course, I would like them to have a good education, but, with the loss of my ability to do a father's part, I yield the right to speak in affairs that depend on finances.

From your father I learn that the squabbles of party have brought you into a circle of contention, too. This I regret. I should wish you had kept aloof from those disputes. Perhaps you deemed it necessary to adopt a party in order to secure audiences; if so, it is deplorable. But when you are on your own, I must give you liberty of opinion, and cannot be thin-skinned on the subject of my wife becoming a manly character.

As to disputes regarding your father's treatment of the children, I suppose those were what you alluded to in your letter of last December. When you become a public speaker or 'reader' you invite criticism, and must make up your mind to endure the vexations of the position. Keep me informed. Send me a copy of the worst things that have been said of you. I have no objection that you should open the sorrows of your heart to me; and if you wish to reproach me with neglect of the welfare of my family, that is fair enough, but have nothing to say about my prison conduct – you can have only one side of that story.

From your father's letters to Halpin and Warren I learned much about you, when directly I could learn nothing. I suppose you have met Warren since his release. I believe that the last words I said to another companion (Costello) were to write my remembrances to you if he himself became released. Do not waste money attempting to get me out of prison by an appeal to the House of Lords. You might as well (as I said to your father) throw your purse into the deep.

I suppose you know that I'm now located with strangers; that is, have none of the old companions of '65. Now that we're allowed to talk somewhat, I wish we had Luby and O'Leary with us. I cannot write here without feeling sick. The restraint, the effort to avoid some things, and to seek others, agrees not with my present frame of mind. People like to be quoted; and, as want of space obliges me to conclude, I will do so with one of your expressions, and say, 'I will not write you a long letter until I know.' You will have seen my letter to your father ere you receive this, and I have said in that things for you which need not have repetition here.

Remembrances to all my friends. Goodbye, Mollis. God bless you. Be strong. Affectionately as ever,

Rossa

In February 1870, a few months after writing this, I had a visit from my wife. There was much talk in the newspapers about an amnesty, and friends had been telling her that we were very stubborn in prison and would listen to no terms of release; that the Ministry could not be the first to knuckle under; and that it only needed an approach from the prisoners' friends, with a request for releases, to get a favourable answer from Mr Gladstone. When I heard that my wife was coming on some such mission as this, I felt troubled. The authorities had been trying for years to reduce me to the level of a thief or pickpocket, and I had been trying to show them they could never succeed. I could write a petition myself, and did write some, but to have anyone else act for me is what I wouldn't allow. When one so near to me as my wife was to write or speak in the matter, it would, of course, be taken for granted that she spoke with authority; and though I did not doubt her ability to state her case honourably, I had a very uncomfortable anxiety lest things be said that would give my enemies satisfaction.

When we met in Chatham, I expressed some misgivings as to the propriety of her interfering with 'the cause of justice', and she gave me every assurance that she would do or say nothing that wasn't Irish and principled. How far she kept that promise may be judged by the following, which I copy from her scrapbook:

My Proposal to the Premier Regarding the Release of my Husband (There is no reason why I shouldn't set out the terms I was prepared to make for my husband's release. They were honourable enough to meet the approval of the most unbending patriot, and I supposed them complaisant enough to meet the views of the reputedly merciful Premier. They are contained in the letter copied here which, when Mr Gladstone refused to see me, I laid in Mr Motley's hands to be by his kindness delivered to the Prime Minister.)

To the Rt. Hon. W.E. Gladstone
Sir,
　　You have denied me the favour of a personal interview; and I am deeply disappointed. I have travelled more than 3,000 miles in midwinter for the sole purpose of pleading a cause that you will not hear — the cause of a husband, to whom, were he a sinner against any other government than that of England, or a native of any other soil than that of Ireland, I have no doubt that your ready sympathy would flow, in recognition of his sacrifices and sufferings for principle and liberty.

I have no wish to write a single word in vindication of my husband's conduct in anything that the law under which he suffers has condemned. It would be unbecoming in me to advance anything in my husband's favour which it would be contrary to your duty to entertain. But, as far as I can gather from the expressions of your government on various occasions, your resolution in the matter is founded, not on the necessity of inflicting further punishment on the political prisoners, but on the danger that would result to the public peace by setting them at large. I cannot deny that there may be reason for that view of the case, but anxiously hope that I have found a solution to the difficulty.

In my recent visit to my husband at Chatham I obtained from him assurance that, to regain his personal liberty, he would be willing to submit to any terms not inconsistent with his personal honour and character that the government might propose. He would consent to leave these islands forever, under penalty of arrest, and forfeiture of his pardon, in case of his return without permission. He would prefer to go to America because I have made that country my home; but if the Crown should insist that exile to any other part of the globe should be the price of his freedom, he is willing to accept the condition, and I am willing to accept it also.

These terms were extended to Mr Hamilton Rowan and others implicated in the insurrection of 1798 by the government of that day, and they were not found to have endangered the peace. It is to be hoped that justice has not grown more unrelenting, or the quality of England's mercy more strained, since that period.

In submitting this proposal I entreat you to bear in mind that I anxiously, though patiently, await the result; and while feeling miserably unequal to the task of influencing your judgment on such a subject, humbly address my prayers to God that He may show you some way by which you can reconcile your desire to be merciful with your sterner sense of State policy and State justice.

I have the honour, sir, to be your most obedient servant.
Mary O'Donovan Rossa

Mr Gladstone replied:

11 Carlton House Terrace, S.W.,
18 March, 1870

Madam,

Circumstances not under my control compelled me to announce in the House of Commons last night at very short notice what I should have preferred to communicate to you in the first instance individually and privately — namely, that we are forbidden by considerations of public duty to allow any further release of political prisoners until we can procure such a change in the condition of Ireland as shall afford a greater degree of peace and security to the people of that country, now in several parts of it exposed to violence, distracted by alarm, and apprehensive of a dissolution of many of the ties by which society is bound together.

During the interval since I wrote to you I have made inquiry to learn whether there were any particulars that would enable the government to draw a line in favour of your husband without injustice to others, but I grieve to say I have been unable to discover any such.

You will be well able to appreciate the gravity of the considerations that have weighed on my mind and on the minds of my colleagues, and I hope you may at least join with us in earnestly desiring the arrival of better days.

I remain, Madam, your very faithful servant.

W.E. Gladstone

I had nothing to say to this reply; but was so uneasy at my wife having anything to say that I wrote her the following a few days after she had visited me (and before she received his reply):

My dear Wife,

Now that you are gone, afterthoughts come to remind me of how often I interrupted you, and how a few times I made remarks which you didn't appear to take as I meant.

When you told me at our encounter that Mr Motley promised you an interview with Mr Gladstone, and when I said that I did not see how you could honourably intervene, I fancied your brow darkened a little; and I thought I might as well let you have your experience, as you were confining yourself to what I stated in my letter to your father regarding what passed between me and McCarthy Downing. When I questioned the propriety of your intervention, it occurred to me that Mr Gladstone was not disposed to countenance my release; and I have a serious objection to seeing you in the position of offering what there was no intention of accepting.

I felt I was in a false position, for unwittingly I had laid myself open to it being said that I had given Mr Downing authorization to intercede for my release, and I wrote to your father directing him to withdraw that paper from Mr Downing. You have that letter of mine to your father; and as you tell me that your letter to Mr Gladstone contains nothing more than what I have stated to Mr Downing, I have no fear that the honour of old Ireland is compromised by what you have done.

Now that my friends would compliment me with parliamentary honours, the most polite way for me to put it is that I do not wish you to seek any influence to embarrass the minister by pressing him to do what he does not intend doing. When you told me my election was annulled by parliament, but that some of the Irish members believed that that proceeding was illegal and they were to have lawyers' advice on the matter, you seemed not to catch the spirit in which I said that the issue was of little concern to me. I meant that any honour conferred on me was that conferred by the people of Tipperary; and any compliment or meaning their vote conveyed was not, for me, changed by a vote of the House of Commons. You let me know once that you had your share of what you called 'wife pride'. Is it strong still — strong enough to aid you in your hard struggle? Summon it to your assistance in this emergency. I have a firm trust that you will 'suffer calmly and be strong'.

Our countrymen seem not to be uninterested in our fate. I recommend your not spending any time at home beyond what you intended. I do this, apprehensive of that sickness of heart which is caused by your deferred hope. The minister may not answer you decisively, and some of his admirers may suggest to you an unendurable waiting. The wisdom of a Solon advised governors to keep the people always expecting something; and the people, afraid of losing that something, would be sure to do nothing. Do not, Mollis, waste your energies in this manner. Do not, on the other hand, imagine that I hurry you to America.

Write, and tell me what you intend doing, etc. Of course, remember me to all my friends. Donchadh has not answered my letter to him. Tim grew wonderfully big, entirely out of proportion, with that moustache of his. I suppose all your brothers and sisters have moved forward also. If you would not be jealous, I would particularly desire remembrance to Isabella. I suppose your little son has grown big, too. May God bless and strengthen you.

Rossa

At about this time, I took the first and only action I was to take on Timothy Donovan's letter to me from New York of 3 September, 1869. My response went, not to Mr Donovan, but to my wife. It follows:

My Love,

I send you this ugly letter of my cousin's. How you engaged in this Belmont-O'Mahony lawsuit, influenced by anyone who could use such contemptible reasons to influence me, is what I cannot understand. If this is the only thing you regret since we parted, I suppose I may pass it over. But though it may tend to make you self-opinionated, let it be a caution to you to beware of acting on the advice of others against your inclination. If you are much led by others, it is ten to one you will be led astray.

You say that in America, the party that befriended you most, of all the groups, was the Roberts group. I must tell you that Mr Roberts did not make the most favourable impression on me. I heard him say he would have nothing to do with Fenianism if he knew there were so many difficulties to overcome. He tendered his resignation there and then. The

Council pressed him, begged him to hold on, and it has often surprised me since to hear with what tenacity he has held on through such a sea of difficulties.

It is not often that tears start to my eyes, but I felt the woman in me at witnessing that scene. I said to myself, 'This man will never do.' He aroused a prejudice in my mind, and if I had heard any time since that he had withdrawn from Irish politics, I would have more confidence in him.

You said you spent an evening at Mr George Moore's, in London. I don't know did he remember that it was your husband he met at Moore Hall on one occasion. I liked him immensely and very much regret his death.

This spinal affliction is troubling me. If I leave you entirely, 'A place in your memory, dearest'.

Rossa

I publish Mr Donovan's letter under protest from my wife. She says there is no man in America who acted more friendly or more honourably toward her than William Roberts, and she grumbles at my expressing a thought about him at any time. But I am writing of my prison life, and her critical impressions should not alter the record of anything I wrote or did.

Anxiety of mind and depression of spirit brought on an illness that rendered her unable to write, and her medical adviser said she should have rest and country air to save her life. Mrs Spillane was making preparations to afford her these when Mr Roberts, having learned the circumstances, sent his wife and his carriage for her and took her to his house on the Bloomingdale Road, where she was treated for a few months with the greatest attention and kindness. This is a debt I have no way of requiting, and for which I must forever feel obliged. But as most of my indebtedness comes from trying to serve Ireland, I cannot allow any of it to suppress matter that was written when I was preoccupied with Ireland's interests. It is in the dark days of a nation's distress that the truest of her sons cling closest to her; and those who are ashamed to associate their names with her fallen fortunes, or who, by dangers or difficulties, are scared away from giving their assistance, are not the men fitted to raise her to a position of national independence.

Strand House, Clonakilty,
27 April, 1870

My dear Rossa,

I have been cleaning an old picture of yours — 'twas broken in Cork the day you last sailed for America — and dispatching it with voluminous directions, and an exact description of the colours of your eyes, hair, beard and complexion, to an eminent artist, that he may get me a decent oil painting from it to console me, now that Mr Gladstone refuses me the original! And if you only knew where that little picture has been in the meantime! Do you remember any young lady who would feel so deep an interest in you that she wouldn't scruple to bribe a servant to steal it for her from my unoccupied room at home; and, after possession of it for a couple of years, would find her conscience urging her to disgorge her unlawfully obtained property? Do you know where you might look for such a person? I won't tell you her name; but it is a fact that the picture, after a disappearance of seven years, has turned up much the worse for wear.

I happened to be a fellow traveller of Mr McCarthy Downing on Saturday evening from Limerick Junction to Cork. 'Twas so late on reaching the city that I went to Victoria Hotel for the night, and had only just finished supper when he sent up to know if I would see him. I went downstairs and met him; found, that like myself, he had to break his journey home to Cork, and that we would be together on Sunday morning as far as Bandon. He showed me that document you gave him some months ago, but did not offer to give it to me; and I didn't like to ask for it, though I told him you regretted having written it. At first I was not agreeably impressed by Mr Downing. I thought he looked and spoke like a man who had a big opinion of himself and a little one of everybody else; who would be prone to look at people and things through rather dark and narrow glasses; but my opinion improved on Sunday morning when I heard him bring forth the most convincing arguments, and over-whelmingly pour them on a 'loyal' Bandon physician who 'couldn't see what in the world the people were continually complaining about'. From that moment, when his grey eye dilated and lighted to his subject — while he mourned the exodus caused by the Coercion Bill and inveighed against the shortsighted policy that had led to it — I began to admire and like him, and was really sorry when Bandon was reached and our roads had to separate.

I was at Mullinahone the week before last, and learned the dumb alphabet in order to talk to poor Charles Kickham. He is apparently enjoying good health, though he complains of weakness and inability to pursue as arduously as he would wish his literary occupations. He is presently engaged on a serial story entitled *Knocknagow; or The Homes of Tipperary*, for the *New York Emerald*. I stayed at his place. Some of the Rossa and Kickham election committee were also present with ladies of their families; and we sat up all night and went to bed at sunrise. Mr Kickham monopolized me from the time I came until I went to the Lecture Hall. You would have been awfully jealous if you could have but seen the amount of attention he lavished on me, and how complaisantly I received and returned it. He came as far as Carrick with me when I started for Waterford; and, on parting, kissed me before all the people at the station! Now, don't you feel aggrieved? You needn't, my dove — a million kisses from any other wouldn't be as sweet as one from you.

It is close to 1AM. There was a fire in the grate, but 'tis dead out. The room consequently is chilly, and I shall have to bid you goodnight — or goodmorning — lest I retard, by acquiring a fresh cold, the recovery of my sore throat. Must tear myself away, but hope to go to sleep without thinking of you. Says the old song:

If only land or sea had parted him and me,
I would not now in tears be wailing.

Land and sea, and prison walls, part us. It must seem exas-perating to you, who always managed to have your way in everything, that the force of your will and all its concentration are powerless to level the walls of Chatham, or bring you one step closer to the object you desire. And it's no less disheartening that the object for which I strained all my powers is at such an aggravating distance from me. I can't grow contented.

Goodbye; and a hundred kisses from your affectionate wife, M.J.

This letter was soon followed by another:

Thursday,

This morning, the papers bring intelligence of the sudden death of George Henry Moore. Great public regret is felt. And I am much saddened to think that Ireland and the prisoners have lost so faithful a friend and good an advocate in the British parliament. Of the few who are generous enough to see the interests of the country before their own, or too independent to sell their sense of right, Mr Moore was the most generous and fearless.

I may be infringing on my privilege by writing anything that could be regarded as political news. However, as you were allowed to hear of your election for Tipperary, you may now be allowed to hear the reason you were not renominated. It was credibly stated that the Sheriff would not accept your name again, taking his cue, it was supposed, from the action of parliament. Kickham was nominated, and his name couldn't be refused. Unfortunately, Tipperary was so sanguine of success that it did not put out its full force in the second election, and Mr Heron, it is said, has fraudulently secured a seat in the House.

I have written at length; really seem to have told you nothing; and to be only now in a condition to begin. I hope with all my heart they won't detain it from you, and that you will forgive my delay in dispatching it. The whole family send love; and, with wishes for your health and resignation, I remain, dear Rossa, your affectionate wife,

Mollis

*   *   *   *   *

IN THE SUMMER of 1870 the prison governor informed us that a parliamentary commission had been appointed to inquire into our treatment, and that we could have the help of counsel to prepare our cases. We immediately communicated with our friends; and when we learned that the commission was to be a secret one, and no counsel of ours would be allowed to appear, my companions pronounced the inquiry a sham, and decided to take no part in it. I decided on a different course and made up my mind to give evidence. I knew that the truth or falsehood of matters that affected me were some of the principal questions in dispute; and I had confidence in my ability to prove their truth. Were I to follow the others' example and refuse to give evidence it would be a victory for the government, for they would be able to assert that the reason I refused to present my case was that I was unable to substantiate my allegations.

I ultimately decided to employ my wife as counsel. The authorities consented to let her consult with me; but did not permit her to attend until the day the commission opened, though she had come to London and stayed on for a fortnight in order to appeal for the necessary visiting order. After she had returned to Clonakilty, the order arrived there; and some advisers put it into her head that it was wrong for me to take a course different from that taken by the other prisoners. In consequence, she grumbled about coming.

The following letters passed between us before she came; and, over the related sittings of the commission, we were put into a room together for consultation, with an officer looking on outside the glass-paneled door.

Strand House, Clonakilty,
7 July, 1870

My dear Rossa,

    The enclosed letters, if you are permitted to read them, will explain why I am not at Chatham. I can easily see how your disbelief in the honesty of the inquiry, combined with your anxiety to talk unreservedly with me, have induced you to grasp at the offer of 'interviews' held out to you so tardily, and to write, wishing me to return. I have not done so; will not do so; and — as Mr Butt remarked — 'wash my hands of the commission' and the false privileges the commission can grant.

While I can understand another man putting aside all considerations but the satisfaction of meeting his wife, I cannot understand it in you, who have, since I first knew you, held the public interest far in advance of mine or your own gratification.

Do not fear for me. To endure has become second nature. I want no compromises. 'All or nothing' have come to be my watch-words. So I will have all my husband or none of him; and will have all its promises from the Crown, or none of them. And as I cannot have the peaceful wedded life I hoped for once, why I can make up my mind to lead a strong single one. Don't, therefore, after so much endurance, abate or alter any of your principles or aspirations through consideration for me.

This letter must needs be a short one, as I wish to send it with as little delay as possible. I received yours from London yesterday. When I think of all the indignities I was put through in the capital of Great Britain by British officials, I feel as if I could curse — only I'm trying to be a saint.

With love from all at home and kindest regards and good wishes to General Halpin, McClure and your other fellow prisoners.

Your affectionate wife,
M.J.

Chatham Prison,
9 July , 1870

My dear Wife,

Have just received yours of the 7th. It is some ease of mind to hear from you, and a pleasure to learn that you are so strong. I am determined to pursue a certain course. That course is to give evidence before the commission; and to see if anything relevant to their inquiry is contained in a part statement I laid before them on Monday, the 4th. I didn't make this statement as a complaint. I simply stated matters that I experienced by virtue of prison discipline, and leave it to them to examine or not examine me as to the truth of what I stated.

After a conversation with those gentlemen, and my expressing a willingness to be examined, the decisions were: they would take the paper I gave them as a part statement; would not go into my examination until they came again on Tuesday the 19th; that every day till then I could have my wife's assistance in preparing my case (if my wife came); and that I could then give them the rest of my statement if I wrote any more.

I am really pleased, Mollis, that you are so strong; that that sickness of expectation and 'hope deferred' have left you and you have made up your mind for the worst, for it is only thus that you can act for the best. It seems you write under a mis-apprehension of the time for visiting me being past, and to be unaware that there is over a week yet. I would wish you to be final on this point; and it would be well if you would, by the car-driver, send a telegram to Bandon for the governor of the prison, saying whether you will or will not come. I shall expect you to do that.

'Don't, therefore, after so long endurance, abate or alter any of your principles or aspirations.' 'Tis funny — you to be writing these words to me, if you are acting in this matter on your own. So different from the threatening notice you sent me from America of 'not living with me if I neglected my family in future'; but I am glad that at last you are strong.

Ever fondly,
Rossa

Sunday, 5AM, 10 July

My dear Wife,

After having slept on your letter — or rather, having spent the night awake on it — I write another, more decisive note than the one I wrote last evening.

There is one condition on which I would tell you to stay in Clonakilty; and that is, that all the visiting friends of all the prisoners have agreed to not avail of the permission to visit until this commission has done its duty; and that no prisoner is to have a visit from anyone. If you have entered into such a compact, I will so far yield to the public opinion as to tell you to hold to it. If you have not, I will not want you to be swayed by advice other than mine; and ask you, with any authority you may concede to me as your 'dead husband', to come.

There are two other reasons for not coming which I would hold valid. They are — the absence of any desire on your part to see me or have a long, private conversation with me; and the absence of money necessary to defray the expense of coming.

There may, Mollis, be some 'husband pride' breaking out here, for I think I feel a little humiliation at being obliged to say to my companions when I meet them by and by, 'My wife wouldn't come.'

I am to go through this inquiry whether you come or not; your advice or assistance might not change my course; and that course I have determined on with a view to public more than personal interests. But I feel I could go through it with a lighter heart if you could cheerfully respond to my call.

If you are coming, telegraph from Bandon to the governor to tell me. If you are not, send the unwelcome message by the first car-driver who passes bound for Bandon. Attend to this, for I have several days work struck out for you.

I got from the authorities six of my 'suppressed' letters to you, and twenty sheets of 'memorials' to the Secretary for State, and have these for you to copy in large hand for the commission. I shall have to go at them myself if you do not come, and writing has become most unpleasant for me, as it painfully aggravates my spinal condition. Time is hastening on; therefore, telegraph.

Yours, dear Mollis, ever faithfully.

Rossa

During our 'interviews' for the commission we talked very little about the inquiry or about the case I was to make out. I had settled all that before my wife came; and we spent the hours together getting and giving an account of our lives and all that concerned us in life. Our six or seven days communion with each other came (swiftly) to an end, and stone walls and prison bars again divided us. I shall close this chapter with the following two letters, each of which, I believe, speaks eloquently for its writer's state of heart and mind.

178 Stamford Street, Waterloo Bridge,
London,
9 August , 1870

My dear Rossa,

I know it is very ungrateful of me to have kept you in suspense. I have no excuse to offer but one that makes my delinquency worse.

I reasoned and argued with my disinclination, but could get no answer from it but 'Leave me alone; I am miserable. Bury Chatham; fly from it, forget it, for all my wretchedness lies there.' Since I last saw you I have sat for hours and hours with locked hands, closed lips, and vacantly fixed eyes blank with the load of misery I seem to be carrying.

I am so changed, hardened, disenchanted of my life, so utterly dead of heart and bare of hope, that if the prisons poured forth their occupants tomorrow, I should be incapable of more than the general rejoicing, for I am dead while yet I live. Life is not what I had hoped; is cold, wretched reality. It is not good for me to see you or to write to you. What's the use of concealing that the farther in soul and body I'm away from Chatham the less unhappy I have been? Do not blame me. I cannot sit down to write to you without having my passive melancholy turn into active anguish. I am weak, cruel, ungenerous, if you will, anything you choose to call me. I do not defend myself.

It is a cruel thing to say, but I would to God you'd never seen me — that I had died at school, or gone into the grave with that young cousin of mine at whose wake and funeral I first saw you. Then I should have missed the pangs of earth, and been less unworthy of the bliss of heaven. Now the spirit and the flesh both suffer. The light of Heaven seems no more to shine on the darkness of my life. God Himself seems to have deserted me.

When I left Chatham for London, I did so in a state of great disquiet on my father's account; and on arriving in London lost no time driving to Paddington Station. I reached it; actually had bought my ticket; and was importuning the porter to leave some other work and take my baggage, when the bell rang, the engine screamed, there was a final banging of carriage-doors, and I had the mortification of hearing the train pull out of the station as the porter got halfway to it. No other train could be had in time to catch the Bristol boat. I telegraphed home to learn if Papa was so ill that I should go by that horrid Dublin route; but got no answer. Telegraphed again, and put up at the Great Western Hotel. Friday, Saturday, Sunday — no answer to my messages. Vexed, I telegraphed to Papa, to sister Isa, to Tim and to the party he boarded with in Cork; and on Monday evening had an answer from them that would have made me excessively angry, only it relieved my fears for Papa. He was ill, certainly, but it was not dangerous, and their anxiety to see me at home was their principal reason for alarming me. Though I pretended to Tim I was outraged at being alarmed, still I treasure this fact as proof of my family's affection, so clearly had they read my mind from the tone of my letters, and so promptly had their love for me suggested the readiest way to bring me home again!

I have had a letter from the Rossa and Kickham committee. It seems they are heavily in debt, and naturally turn to me to get assistance in the form of a few 'readings'. I could not refuse. To the men individually I would not have begrudged three times the labour I shall have. But I have some fears about associating my work with theirs in England. 'Twould be all right in Ireland, but I don't think it will serve me with

Irishmen in England who have little sympathy with petition failures. However, I'm pledged to them, and, sink or swim, will do my utmost.

I think my friends begin to feel it might be dangerous for them to show their faces here. I have only seen the visages of my 'old friends' – the detectives. So I am utterly alone and friendless, left to my sad thoughts. I went the evening before last with my landlady's niece to walk from Westminster to the end of the Embankment. The boats had stopped running, the river was quiet, and the moon was spreading a cloak of silver on the water. We leaned for a long time on the Embankment's low parapet. So softly the waves lapped against its granite, so gently the mild waters invited me to their breast, that I could not wonder that many a poor wretch, deceived by a love of the world, should be tempted to throw herself into so soothing a bosom as the Thames then unveiled. One could not help but think what a dreamless rest might be got by trusting one's weary body to such a soft and winning nurse!

One thing, Cariss, you may be sure of – I will never take the same amount of trouble for you or for any other man again. Human love is selfish, except in youth's first enthusiasm. It becomes a passion, living only as long as the object gives pleasure, and ceasing when the object thwarts the will, offends the vanity, or fails to minister to the self-love, pride, passion or power of the pretended lover. You often said you loved me, but I never put your love to proof; and never believed but that if I did put it to proof, I should find it wanting. I remember that I never showed the slightest inclination to interfere with your movements but a shadow, slight, yet perceptible to me, would come between us.

Give my most affectionate regards to each and all your prison friends. Don't forget to tell McClure I wrote to his family; and, in fact, have obeyed every direction with which I was entrusted by either. When I get news for them from any quarter, it will not be my fault if they are not apprised of it.

If you wish me to take advantage of the governor's permission to see you, tell him so, and I'm sure he'll be good enough to order his secretary to drop me a line. Tim will be here in a few days, and when I've had a conversation with him I may be less barren of gossip for you. But in any case, if you wish me to run down to Chatham, say so, and I shall go, even if you had no more desire than to find fault with this letter and with me.

Do not tear this letter in anger, for its words are held together by so slight a thread as a hair from the head of your affectionate wife,

Mollis

Chatham,
13 August, 1870

Mrs O'Donovan Rossa:

By Jove, Mollis, I don't know what to say to you! I should like to talk to you 'unter vier augen' as the Germans say (under four eyes) on those distinctions you draw between love and passion. The characteristics of the latter may hit me, you think, but I'm not going to give myself to you at such a valuation. And you are wrong in thinking that, because I might differ a little from you, I have little religion. I told you that I had a particular mental prayer — that if the Almighty interfered in the petty ways of this world, He would in His mercy send me my punishment here, and peace thereafter. This is a pretty hard prayer, in view of the possibilities of years of absence from you, and under the pains and penalties of this servitude.

I fell asleep last night at half-past ten, and didn't wake until half-past four. 'Twas the best sleep, I may say, I've had since I saw you. Can it be that a letter that you think would trouble me only calms me? 'Twas hard of you to leave me thinking so long that perhaps another blow was given you in your father's death.

Since I saw you, I dreamt twice that you were married and settled down in the north of Ireland. If I dream it a third time, I don't know what will happen to me. One thing in my dreams I like is that I always find myself faithful to you, and no seductions can woo me away from you.

You say you could curse fame. Ah, I could say it, too; but what we want is to be happy. And that is what no mortal ever was in this world. If you and I had the fruition of our desires today, new ills would be engendered. I would no sooner be outside the prison than other troubles would assail me; and the realization of yours, without feelings of a longing of the soul for something else, would be as impossible.

I do no wonder at your finding most relief when most distant from Chatham. The same thoughts occur to me, when, half-in-joke, half-earnest, I speak the word 'divorce', granting that Church, state, society, and you above all, would allow this. I don't think you would be happy with another husband while I lived. Your ills might be only imaginary; but they would be thorns nevertheless. Suffering is what the world will have from man and woman. Yours is intense; and if you would fly from it, the world would not be charitable.

I suppose I have lost your esteem by showing myself to you so clearly lately.

Fondly.

Rossa

With that letter I included another:

My love,

Here is an exact copy of the letter that went astray. The governor gave me the original, suppressed one, to rewrite it. This day week you paid me that visit, and I am most anxious since, and troubled, fearing that some other ills awaited you through your father's illness. You said you would write or telegraph, or be back in a week. The week is past, and — no news from you.

I have applied for permission to write to Mr Gladstone. If I am allowed to do so, I shall ask him for a copy of the report, and for permission for you to visit me while you are reading in England, say, once every two months. In France a wife can

visit a political prisoner upon showing her marriage certificate; and if, as you think, there may be a desire to make a
distinction between us and other convicts, this may be
granted. You can keep on writing, and be more commu-
nicative than formerly. Never think that anyone is to see your
letters but me, or, if you must think differently, think that
they are priests, who will not talk about our exchanges of confidence.

You left in a very depressed state of mind. All the
'ambition', 'pride', and 'individuality' of the first day were
gone. Cannot you recover them now that we are separated? I
shall have to do something to win the old place in your affec-
tions. But, must close. I do not believe a word of your saying
you would never take the same amount of trouble for me or
for any other man again.

You might send me Shawn's letter and those others you
promised; and write me once every two months. And make a
reply to this if it does not vex you terribly. I don't intend to
vex you, though your words, being held together 'by a hair of
your head' would, I suppose, convey that they are exceedingly
fragile. I thought to ask you for that curl that hung in your
forehead, but forgot. Send me that poem, if it is printed. And,
if you give readings, send scraps to the governor, telling about
them. Do these things, or get them done. If I do not get
them, let not the reason be that you didn't try!

Yours, my poor woman, ever fondly, and faithfully too.

Rossa

P.S. I mustn't call you 'Love' any more.

17. Material from the Proceedings of the Devon Commission

THE COMMISSIONERS APPOINTED to the inquiry were Lord Devon (chairman), George C. Broderick, Stephen E. DeVere, Dr Robert D. Lyons and Dr E. Headlam Greenhow. They commenced their hearings on 24 May 1870 and ended on 20 September. They had sixty-three sessions, eight of them in Chatham Prison. July 4 was their first day there, and during the three previous days, Halpin, McClure, Mulleda, O'Connell and I were kept from chapel and in solitary confinement, lest we avail of our ordinary intercourse to combine in making a case against the authorities.

I have their statements before me in a 'Blue Book' published by the Queen's printers (Eyre & Spottiswoode, London), and will include excerpts from some of them in this record to show that, though they were prisoners in the hands of a cold-blooded enemy, they were still men, trying even in their bonds to uphold the cause for which they had suffered. Halpin wrote:

Gentlemen,

From my knowledge of the capacity of some of the witnesses who should, and very likely will, be examined by you, to make false reports and lying statements about the class of prisoners whose treatment is to be inquired into, I have no hesitation in saying that such witnesses will not tell the truth except under oath and through a strict cross-examination.

I did not from the beginning believe that the government would appoint a commission to prove that its own public statements were untrue; or that it could afford an investigation that would unveil the facts and lay the official sores

253

open to public view; and I find that the actions of the state authorities, and of the commissioners since their appointment, justify this conclusion. The commission is to be secret, and act in the dark, refusing the representatives of the press admission, and denying counsel any right to act on the prisoners' behalf. Every artifice that cunning could suggest has been resorted to to keep us in the dark...

To comment on such acts would be a waste of time. The commissioners give me permission to write to my friends on the subject of the commission. Mr Bruce takes that permission away. The commissioners tell me I can have the assistance of a friend in making up a statement. Mr Bruce says I cannot. What a mockery, what a sham, is this white-washing commission, appointed by the Home Secretary to cover up his falsehoods and his frauds! The orders of the commission, as well as those of the Home Secretary, are plainly intended for the public eye. They are meant to deceive, to pretend to confer rights in public which are taken away in private. Perfidy has long been the characteristic of England's rulers, and it appears they have no intention of shaking it off.

John McClure, born in America, concluded:

I feel compelled to decline to take part in the upcoming proceedings in consequence of experiencing a want of confidence in the impartiality and completeness of the investigation. I may, I think with propriety, add here that a torturous, living death, with every circumstance especially adapted to render life miserable, has been an alternative which the public and my government were led to believe was a singular act of clemency when, in 1867, the government of England awarded penal servitude for life in exchange for an unnatural but speedy death.

I have to say that three years of this 'alternative' give me every reason to view that 'act of clemency' in a totally different light.

There has been a sad lack of that magnanimity toward a

fallen adversary which is so much admired in, and expected from, a generous and humane victor. To treat me as if I had been guilty of some degrading crime is hardly deserved...

Such a proceeding but degrades the power that can inflict on honourable men the infamous punishments allotted to the vile outcasts of society.

John Devoy said:

Five years bitter experience, to say nothing of the record of seven-hundred, have made me look with suspicion on everything emanating from the quarter in which your commission had its origin. In conclusion, I never asked for an inquiry because I believed that a complete and impartial one would not be granted; and that if friends of mine, or of the other prisoners, did ask, it was for a public one.

Henry Mulleda said:

After careful and deliberate consideration, I came to the conclusion that I could not do other than decline to make any statement. I am actuated solely by the conviction that in acting otherwise, I should be but aiding and abetting a delusion as I am convinced that nothing but a full, fair and public inquiry will ever succeed in eliciting the whole truth.

When I look over the proceedings of the commissioners at Portland Prison, I find that the actions taken by the prisoners there were similar to many of ours. All refused to have anything to do with them. Governor Clifton, examined by Lord Devon, was asked what each of the prisoners said when he offered them paper to make statements.

Devon: 'What did George Brown say?'
Clifton: 'This prisoner declined to take the paper I offered him, saying "I do not want to say anything; I want to have nothing to do with it'.'

Devon: 'Did Luby make any statement?'

Clifton: 'He asked if the Earl of Devon was the same nobleman who was on the Land Commission in Ireland. I told him, "I believe he is". The prisoner replied that Dan O'Connell had said at the time that it was like a jury of butchers trying a sheep.'

Devon: 'Did John O'Leary make any statement?'

Clifton: 'He declined to receive any paper, saying that the commissioners might have spared themselves the trouble, as he did not intend to make a statement.' .

Devon: 'Did Michael Sheehy make any statement?'

Clifton: 'The prisoner declined to receive any paper, and stated that while in British pens he would make no statement. He had been treated badly, and had plenty of complaints. "Dr Blaker knows the state of my health. If there are Irishmen coming over to sit on this commission, they are in the pay of the British government."'

Devon: 'Did Mortimer Shea, alias Moriarty, make any statement?'

Clifton: 'This prisoner declined to receive any paper, saying that he did not wish to have any connection with the commission.'

Devon: 'Did Edward St Clair make any statement?'

Clifton: 'This prisoner declined to receive any paper, saying that he did not wish to have any connection with the commission.'

Devon: 'Did John McCafferty say anything?'

Clifton: 'McCafferty declined to receive any paper, or to make any statement until he goes outside, when he will do it under oath. He further stated that he would not go before the commission unless by force.'

Devon: 'Did Patrick Walsh make any statement?'

Clifton: 'This prisoner declined to take any paper, and, when informed that he would not be sent out to work during the three days, said, "I wish they would stay away. If they are my countrymen, they are humbugs."'

Devon: 'At the time you asked those prisoners the questions

to which they gave the replies you have recorded, were they brought singly before you?'
Clifton: 'They were, my lord.'

The commissioners didn't seem to be at all satisfied with this state of things. Sending for John O'Leary, the chairman asks him:

Devon: 'Do you wish to make a statement to the commission?'
O'Leary: 'Yes. I wish to say that I asked for no ccommission; and when I heard some time ago that commissioners were appointed, I fully made up my mind to make no statement of grievances to any body of men who would be sent down. And as to anything about my treatment in prison, whatever I do say I intend to take my own time and place for saying. It would seem that what you want to know is, whether we have been subjected to any hardships except those incident to persons sentenced to penal servitude. I may complain that we have been treated no worse than murderers and thieves.'
Devon: 'Do you wish to make any statement on those points?'
O'Leary: 'No, not to you. Not that you should be under a delusion of my having more serious reason. Actually, you must take us to be an extraordinary humble-minded class of men, to think we would make no complaints.'

At the Invalid Prison in Woking, Denis Dowling Mulcahy has a long argument with the commissioners. He wants all the safeguards necessary to a fair and impartial inquiry, and failing to get them, refuses to go into his case.

Mulcahy: 'Did I understand your lordship to say that the report of Messrs. Pollock and Knox would not be allowed?'
Devon: 'It will not.'
Mulcahy: 'Well, my lord, I must say that I think that is a very important document, for if I gave evidence to them which they have suppressed, I should think it very requisite to understand that.'

Devon: 'That is no part of our inquiry.'

Mulcahy: 'But I have learned from my friends that that report has been made use of repeatedly by the Home Secretary. I wish to show that I have stated many matters to those commissioners that were not reproduced in their report; yet that report was used as evidence against us to prove that we were untruthful.'

Devon: 'We cannot go into that.'

Mulcahy: 'Very good, my lord.'

Devon: 'But you can go into anything you think is material in the absence of that report.'

Mulcahy: 'Yes, but if I had the report of Knox and Pollock I could show that I stated to them two or three very important facts with regard to the bread and water, and the hemoptysis, and being sent to Dartmoor, when it was known (as I can show from the very documents I have here now, which have come from the prison books and are the most meagre abstracts they could make) that while I suffered from hemoptysis I was sent to the quarries.'

Devon: 'I think I must tell you, Mulcahy, that you have received all the papers which, under the sanction of superior authority, it is decided are to be given you.'

Mulcahy: 'Very good, my lord. I consider them insufficient to prove the charges, and that the powers of the commission are too limited to enable me to substantiate my case.'

Mr William Pitt Butts, the governor of Chatham Prison, was recalled. He brought with him my letter to the commission, which Lord Devon read aloud:

The Secretary of State knows that since you were here I applied for a copy of the Knox and Pollock report; and he leaves my application unattended to. I have been shown by my wife an official statement emanating from that honourable gentleman, and I very reluctantly say that there is something wrong in every paragraph of it. He says that my letters to my wife were suppressed because they contained falsehoods. I present to you six of those letters; undertake to show you that they do not contain a single falsehood; and with all due respect ask you to invite the Home Secretary to be present.

Yours very obediently,

Jeremiah O'Donovan Rossa

P.S. I desire that all witnesses at the inquiry be examined under oath.

Devon: 'You stated just now that three letters written by prisoner Halpin to Mr Motley, to Mr J.F. O'Donnell, and to Mr Callan, were suppressed by order of the Secretary of State?'

Butts: 'They were, my lord.'

Devon: 'Are you in possession of the Secretary's letter announcing that they were to be suppressed?'

Butts: 'I am.'

Jeremiah O'Donovan Rossa was next called.

Devon: 'I should explain to you, Rossa, that we are a commission appointed by government, but entirely independent of government, for the purpose of inquiring into the treatment of yourself and other prisoners at present confined to prisons in England under the Treason Felony Act. I had better name the commissioners for you. This is Dr Greenhow; this, Mr DeVere; this is Dr Lyons; this is Mr Broderick; and I, Lord Devon, am the chairman. Our object is to receive in the fullest and freest way, from any of the prisoners into whose cases we shall inquire, any statement, orally or in writing, or both, you may wish to submit. This statement will be made to us in a private room, out of the hearing of any person connected with the prison; and whatever the statement may be, it will in no way prejudice the future position of the prisoner as regards the prison in which he is held. He will be none the worse for it in any way.

Do you wish to defer your examination until you have had opportunities to confer with your wife, or with friends?'

Rossa: 'Well, I have written something; and am prepared to give it to you. If you would look over it, I then would be prepared to answer any questions you put to me, and be ready, when you come again, to be examined further.'

Devon: 'We think it would be better not to enter on your examination now. If, after seeing your wife, you wish to make a supplementary statement, it can be put in an envelope and handed to the governor, who will hand it to us.'

Rossa: 'I have no objection, my lord, that he should get a copy to send to the director, or to the Secretary of State, or to any others you wish.'

Devon: 'Your examination being deferred to the 19th, is there anything you wish to state now before you withdraw?'

Rossa: 'Well, my lord, you said "anything I would say would not prejudice me in the future". But I do not know how you could — though you might be very much inclined to — protect me if the authorities desired to keep punishing me; for they can get thousands of excuses to say that a breach of discipline is involved; and I do not know how you would be able to learn of it or become aware of it.

I had a long statement for the commissioners. I will not reproduce it in full, as it would only be repeating many things I previously have asserted. One of the commission's objects was to ascertain if we were treated 'exceptionally'; and I laid particulars of such treatment before them, leaving them to judge if their examination of me was pertinent to their business.

Assuming you may want to elicit the whole truth, I have reason to fear you cannot succeed, and here is one of them: I was thirty-five days in this prison with my hands manacled behind my back. I have reason to believe that this putting me in irons was by order of the Board of Prison Directors. One way or another, the story gets into the world; and though the treatment was an exertion of prison 'discipline', the government deem it proper to deny it, and the Board of Directors hold an inquiry at this prison to prove that no such punishment took place. My letters are suppressed because I write of my treatment, and the British government defame me by saying I have told lies in them. I have asked you to call for those letters to question me on them, and I hope you will do so.

Mr Gladstone wrote vividly of the treatment of the Naples prisoners. But where is the man coming to see an English prison can speak to a prisoner and ask him for information as to his treatment? That man is not to be found. The visitor will find everything in apple-pie order; and, as Mr Gladstone saw in Naples, he will see excellent 'rules and regulations' posted everywhere. He will see a Bible in every cell, even in ones where the victim is chained and being starved. And if he comes on a Sunday he will see 1,500 men parading for chapel, each with a Bible and a prayer book exposed to view. What wonder if he says to himself, 'This is a paradise of saints!' He little knows the curses that are burning, the hell that is seething, under this phylactery face which 'discipline' makes her votaries assume, at the peril of losing their daily bread.

I do not see any rule authorizing 'discipline' to deprive a man of the use of the Bible for six months; yet this punishment was imposed on me. I do not see anything in the rules to warrant the authorities stripping me naked once a day for three or four months; yet 'discipline' does it. I also fail to see any rule that obliges me to bathe in water in which other men have bathed or washed; and this I had to do often.

When I applied to Director Gambier for a sufficiency of coarse bread, and remarked that England would not refuse that as a right to the state prisoner of any other country, he refused it, with the observation that 'England has no "state prisoners" nowadays.'

As to 'exceptional' treatment, how is it explained that I have been separated from the rest of the Irish prisoners and sent to Chatham, under the circumstances I state? That in Portland I was separated from the Irish prisoners and sent among a gang of English prisoners? That, while in Portland, the rest of the treason-felony prisoners working in mid-winter in a shed, I was placed outside the shed and prevented from having that little shelter the others had from the poison-laden blast? And how is it explained that when 'under report' the same day with some of my fellow prisoners on a charge of talking while at work, they got twenty-four hours on bread and water, while I got seventy-two, with fourteen days solitary confinement on penal-class diet?

The 'Blue Book' sets out the principal grounds for my assertions that I and my companions were abused, humiliated, tortured and half-starved in the course of our confinement. It records:

1. That he was repeatedly punished by being placed on bread and water and 'penal' diets; felt extreme hunger in consequence; and lost much weight and strength.

2. That he was repeatedly placed in absolutely dark or darkened cells, on several occasions without bed, blankets or rugs, and as a result suffered intensely from the cold.

3. That he several times wrote to his wife (under the one-letter-every-six-months rule) only to learn later that his letters had been suppressed because they contained accounts of his and his companions' ill treatment. The Portland governor told Rossa he 'couldn't be sending his love letters to his wife. It would lessen his punishment.' The same official told him, 'Twenty years ago, you would have been hanged.'

4. That he was handcuffed with his hands behind his back over a period of thirty-five days. (He conceded that this punishment was imposed because he threw a half-bucketful of water in the governor's face). Also, that he was kept in handcuffs overnight at Millbank.

5. That he was punished frequently for refusing to salute a prison governor, though on one occasion, such an official told him. 'I treat you with contempt.' And was subjected to personal violence because of such refusals or because he refused to comply with what he felt were unreasonable rules, including those of silence, imposed on the prisoners.

6. That he was deprived of spiritual comforts (attendance at Mass, Communion, or other religious services) for several months of his confinement.

7. That he was refused permission to send a brief note to his mother (to be enclosed in a letter he was sending to his wife). His mother was then over seventy-years-of-age and in bad health.

8. That he was often punished for 'refusing to work with thieves.'

Rossa freely admitted that he ignored or violated prison rules he considered to be arbitrary or unreasonable, or ones that were exclusively imposed on him.

A high point in his testimony was reached when Dr Lyons, possibly the commissioner most impressed with his testimony, volunteered to have Rossa's handcuffs placed on his hands behind his back, so he could have a more heightened sense of the prisoner's suffering.

Lyons asked Rossa to provide him with precise information as to:

a. The number of days he was on bread and water during the whole term of his imprisonment.

b. The number of days he was on 'penal' (punishment) diet.

c. The number of days he was in 'dark cell'.

d. The number of days he was in handcuffs.

Rossa provided the information in point:

a. Bread and water days – 123

b. 'Penal' diet – 231 days (in 'dark cell', of which

c. moreover, 28 were spent in 'absolutely dark cell').

d. Days in handcuffs – 35 consecutively; 37 in all.)

I will end my case by giving some extracts from the commissioners' findings:

> *From the report of the commissioners appointed to inquire into the treatment of treason-felony convicts in English prisons.*
> It appears that Medical Officers of convict prisons are not required to possess qualifications in both medicine and

surgery; and that in some instances, and at certain seasons, the medical charge of a large infirmary, and of 1,200 or 1,500 convicts out of hospital, devolves on a single officer having only one professional qualification.

In the public-works prison, and in parts of the invalid prison at Woking, the cells, being designed mainly for sleeping, are, we think, too small for health, unless further provision be made for ventilation. All the 'dark cells', but especially those at Millbank, appeared to us to be imperfectly ventilated, a defect which the entire exclusion of light renders the more injurious to health. The dark cells (e.g., Pentagon V, Millbank) from their restricted dimensions and defective ventilation, demand immediate attention.'

The arbitrary use of handcuffs as a measure of restraint, calls for notice. We have to report that there does not seem to us to be that uniformity in practice, or unanimity in the interpretation of powers entrusted to governors, which we should deem to be desirable on so important a subject...

We find a great concurrence of opinion that manacles may be imposed for a period of seventy-two hours or longer. Finally, the chairman, while admitting that the period of seventy-two hours cannot be exceeded without reference to a director, stated that, in his opinion, under a literal construction of this rule, provided the full period of the order is not exhausted by the continuous imposition of manacles for seventy-two hours day and night at any one time, a prisoner, if the governor sees fit, may be kept in manacles an indefinite time.

We are of opinion that, except for the immediate control of personal violence, and for a short period of time to be defined by the directors, manacles should not be imposed without the written order of a governor or deputy governor after a hearing on the case; and that the order should specify the manner in which the manacles are to be applied, whether in front or behind, and the period for which they are to be so continued.

The allegation is that, with the exception of nights and mealtimes, O'Donovan Rossa remained in handcuffs with his hands manacled behind him from June 17 to July 20.

We carefully examined, with reference to this allegation, the entries made at the time in the governor's journal, the chief warder's report book, and the 'separate cell' book. These entries substantially tally, and are conclusive on one point. They place beyond all possible doubt that Rossa had handcuffs on, either 'before' or 'behind', with the intervals already referred to, for thirty-four days.

At Pentonville and Dartmoor, the governors informed us that refractory prisoners are not to be kept in 'dark cell' for more than four hours, whereas in Chatham we found that a prisoner had been so confined for periods running from one to three days — very severe punishment. We also think that a prisoner in 'dark cell' should be allowed to retain his bed, blanket and rug while confined therein.

Punishment for offences by diminution of food, or alteration of the kind given, is common to all prisons we have visited. Bread and water diet, under which one pound of bread is allowed daily, is frequently employed for a period of one to three days by a governor's sentence. It may be extended to twenty-eight days by the sentence of a director, with 'penal class' diet every fourth day. 'Penal class' diet for six months may be imposed by a director, and may immediately succeed twenty-eight days on bread and water. We cannot but call attention to the very serious consequences that may result from the continuing of such punishments too long or repeating them too frequently.'

With regard to those in the infirmary, we think that arrangements should be made to facilitate attendance at religious service of all who are able to leave the sick ward; and, as regards those under punishment, we entertain grave doubts whether the reasons given for denial of such opportunities, viz., that attendance at chapel would be a temporary mitigation of the punishment enforced, should be allowed to outweigh the spiritual advantages which may accrue from such attendance.'

Certain allegations were made by two of the prisoners in

reference to circumstances attending their transmission from Ireland. It is alleged that due consideration of the inconveniences incidental to a sea voyage and a long journey was not shown by those in charge. Should it be found that such circumstances occurred as were detailed to us, provision should be made against their recurrence.

Searches: The rules which prescribe and enforce searching are, with slight variations as to the frequency of the practice, common to all convict prisons; and it did not appear to us that the treason-felony prisoners were subjected, in this respect, to any exceptional treatment, except at Pentonville, where some of them had to undergo weekly searches for a short period after their first arrival. It was stated strongly to us by all the prison officers we questioned on the subject, that the continuance of searching is necessary for the exclusion of prohibited articles, and for the personal safety of those who are charged with prisoner custody.

We therefore do not feel justified in suggesting any change, other than that the naked search of a prisoner should not take place in the presence of other prisoners, and should be conducted by selected officers.

As to some of the treason-felony prisoners, complaint was made that, at Pentonville, they were obliged at bedtime to put out their day-clothes and cell-furniture. It was explained to us that this measure, though exceptional, was enforced, not as an indignity, but as a precaution against escape, a course uniformly adopted in similar cases.

Deprivation of flannels: On arrival at Pentonville, the flannels supplied to the treason-felony convicts at Mountjoy were taken from them. We are of opinion that, as they arrived in mid-winter, and as some of them appear to be men of delicate constitution, and one was deformed and weak in frame, flannels in lieu of those they had worn up to that time, and which it was necessary to send back to Mountjoy, should have been given to them without waiting for the intervention of the Medical Officer.

Association: Another general complaint of the treason-felony prisoners was that whereas the offence of which they had been convicted was of a special character, implying, in their view, no moral degradation, they had been associated with other prisoners undergoing sentences for gross and heinous crimes. We state the facts: At Dartmoor, none of the prisoners except Mulcahy and Lennon have been so confined. Mulcahy was transferred to Dartmoor on February 8, 1867, and thence to Woking on May 8 of the same year. During that time, he was associated with ordinary prisoners. Lennon was transferred to Dartmoor on December 30, 1867, and is still there. He also is associated with other prisoners. At Chatham, except in the infirmary, the treason-felony prisoners, as a rule, have not been associated with other convicts, or been employed on the public works. Rossa was for some time the only treason-felony convict in this prison, and he was then worked 'in association'. On a subsequent occasion (June, 1868) he was compelled, as a measure of punishment, to labour with ordinary prisoners on the public works. After some days, he refused to continue such work, in consequence, he alleges, of 'the unpleasant life he led with them'. For this he was reported, and was awarded three days on bread and water.

Occupations: Several complaints were made by these prisoners of their having been obliged to perform certain tasks of a degrading character, e.g., to wash the clothes of other prisoners, and to clean out cells and even privies. It is perfectly true that those who were received at Portland, on their first arrival and for a few days pending the receipt of instructions from the central authority, were assigned to the washhouse; but subsequently they were placed on the public works as a separate party.

It is true that in the winter of 1866, during a storm of unusual severity, rain was driven in through the walls of Hall D of Portland Prison, and that the cells occupied by certain of the treason-felony convicts were partially flooded, and their beds and clothing became a good deal wetted.

In one instance only did the cxommission detect portions

of food unfit for human use in the supply sent in for the infirmary. This occurred at Chatham on July 4, 1870, when three pieces of mutton of greenish colour in part, and of a very bad smell, were pointed out by the commission.

Charges have been made which come under the head of medical treatment. They have reference chiefly to alleged want of proper attention on the part of the Medical Officers to the prisoners' calls for medical aid. We have already expressed our opinion on the systems of medical attendance and infirmary management; and shall have occasion to discuss the more important of the complaints on this score in a subsequent section of our Report.

In fact, the commission had occasion to discuss, and concede the validity of, complaints on these and related grounds in the cases of seven of the Irish 'politicals', including one who died subsequently in infirmary as a result of his alleged maltreatment. The concluding section of the commissioners' report states:

One especial question was forced on our attention in the course of our inquiries, though strictly it does not fall within the letter of our instructions. It is whether prisoners convicted of a crime so exceptional in its nature that it has been thought right to modify prison discipline in their cases might not with advantage be more completely separated from the general convict population. We cannot be insensible to the difficulty, not always unattended with danger, of allowing exceptional indulgences to a few individuals in the midst of a larger prison population. Bearing this in mind, we are led to the conclusion that the difficulties attendant on the location and treatment of political offenders may perhaps be most readily and effectually overcome by setting apart, from time to time, a detached portion of some convict prison for prisoners of this class; and we recommend this subject to the consideration of Her Majesty's government.

We remain, Sir,

Your obedient, humble servants,

Devon
George C. Broderick
Stephen E. de Vere
Robert D. Lyons
E. Headlam Greenhow
3 Parliament Street,
September 20, 1870

18. Release and Banishment

IF YOU HAVE read thus far (and more particularly perused the last chapter) you will see that I have been corroborated in virtually everything I have stated regarding my prison life. It was vexatious to be flatly contradicted by Dr Burns, and by Warders Good, Cranston and others, but I had been learning patience a long time, and my schooling stood to me. The commissioners behaved like gentlemen; but Dr Greenhow did not seem to like the points I was making, and looked as if he wished me to break down in my case. Mr Broderick was very deferential, and I conceived a particular liking for him. My four or five days acquaintance with Mr de Vere was rendering him quite familiar to me. And I had much sympathy for Dr Lyons when I saw his hands cuffed behind his bank, and the agonized look he gave when he asked me if mine were actually manacled in that manner for thirty-five days. He had just lunched; his flask was on the table; and when his hands were loosed he poured some whisky into a tumbler and offered it to me. I declined at first, but he pressed me, and as it was such a novelty to touch anything so Irish in that quarter, I made conversation with this friendly enemy. Lord Devon offered me a chair, but I felt too independent to sit in such company, and continued to give my evidence while standing.

The hearings of the commission having come to a close, I returned to my companions and my old trade of stocking-mending. We speculated on the developments that would probably follow when the report would be published, for I knew that the Home Secretary and Mr Gladstone would stand convicted as false witnesses. In the event, on the very day the commission's report was

271

published, the announcement was made of our upcoming release. They took from July to December to prepare the book, during which time I kept preparing to get out information to the public in case of foul play. All year, amnesty meetings were being held in Ireland and England, and petitions were gotten up to the Queen, or to her manager, Mr Gladstone. The one that came when events made it judicious for him to release some of us was presented by Mr McCarthy Downing, the member for Cork. The first to sign that petition was the Lord Mayor of Dublin and, through him, Gladstone conveyed the news that we were to be released on condition of leaving the country.

Downing Street,
16 December, 1870

Gentlemen,

I have to inform you that Her Majesty's government have carefully considered the cases of the convicts now undergoing sentences for treason and treason felony; and that they have recommended to the Crown the exercise toward them of the Royal clemency, insofar as it is compatible with the assured maintenance of tranquillity and order.

They will therefore be discharged upon the condition of not remaining in, nor returning to, the United Kingdom.

W.E. Gladstone.

Soon after this announcement the prison governor informed me that I had received a conditional pardon. My sentence was to be changed from perpetual imprisonment to banishment for twenty years; and unless I accepted those conditions the pardon could not be granted. I would leave the country; but would give no promise not to return. If I did come back before the twenty years were over, let the government take whatever course it deemed proper, but it should not be said that I had made a promise and had broken it. I got paper to give a reply, and here is that reply:

22 December, 1870

To the governor of Chatham Prison:

Sir,

I don't think I can make a fairer response to the official document you read for me today than to give you this paper which I withdrew from Mr McCarthy Downing; and to tell you that I will abide by its terms. Here they are:

22 March, 1869

Mr Downing,

You having asked me if I would leave this country or Ireland on condition of my being let out of prison, I reply that I would, with the understanding that if I am found in England or Ireland again without the permission of the British government, I render myself liable to be recommitted to prison.

My children are in Ireland, and I would wish to see them. If the authorities impose on me the obligation of going straight from the prison to the ship, I will do so; but if they can afford me a few week's citizenship in Ireland by my giving an assurance of carrying myself as privately and silently as possible, I will give them that assurance.

*   *   *   *   *   *

EVERY PRISONER WAS asked to where he would go, and I at first said Australia. My wife was willing to face any part of the world with me, and I was anxious to evade the Fenian factions in the United States. I knew enough of things, and of my own nature, to know that I could do very little in the way of following up my past life there; but I was now public property, and public opinion was to master me.

While my wife was assisting me she came to Chatham every morning, and went to London each evening. She met some of the men who were prominent in the Irish national movement, and one and all they declaimed against my going to the Antipodes. I would be going under the British flag; would be looked on as deserting the cause. No; I should go to America, where we would be able to unite the factions and do everything we were moved to do for 'the men at home'.

I changed my mind and made known my intention of going to New York. It is well known to my companions that we left prison resolved to take no action in Irish politics in America unless we were able to unite all in one party; and how we were cajoled and dragged into a course we had decided against is a story in itself.

Mr Fagan came to Chatham on 5 January, 1871, and brought with him the necessary papers. Saloon passages had been engaged for us, and we were each to be supplied with a suit of clothes and five sovereigns for pocket money. I was the first he sent for, and he presented the patent of pardon, asking me to sign acceptance of it. I wrote simply: 'I accept this patent of pardon.'

'Here, Mr Fagan; I suppose that will do.'

'Well, I don't know,' he answered. 'I think there is something else wanted — say, "without mental reservation".'

'Please write out what you think proper,' I told him, 'and if I don't see anything unacceptable in it, I will copy and sign it.'

The director wrote and I copied and signed the document, putting quotation marks around 'patent of pardon': 'I, Jer. O'Donovan Rossa, having seen and heard read the conditions of my release from prison as contained in the "patent of pardon", accept them unconditionally and without reserve.'

He then gave me possession of the parchment, with a round plaster of wax attached to it.

After receiving this, I asked Mr Fagan if he would give me all my suppressed letters. He could not do so, but there were some which were made up to be given me; the rest I could not have. He proposed to have them burned, and, as I could not get possession of them, I consented.

'Now,' said he, 'I have a sealed letter for you which I have never read, nor do I know what it contains. I am instructed to give it to you after you receive your pardon; and here it is.'

London, 20 December, 1870

Mr O'Donovan Rossa,

I have for some time past looked forward to congratulating you on your release and expressing good wishes for your future career. I do not feel I have the right, nor would it become me, to offer you advice, especially of a political nature. Though you and I are nearly of the same age, our experiences and views of life are very different, nor would it be reasonable to expect that you should regard Fenianism in the same light that I do. At the same time, I would venture to implore you, before connecting yourself with it again, either in the United States or elsewhere, to take counsel with your wisest and most disinterested friends, with your good wife, and, let me add, with your own best feelings and aspirations.

I will say no more, except that I shall always hear of you with friendly interest. Indeed, I should not have said what I have said, had I not formed a conviction (which I have freely avowed) that you are worthy of a happier destiny than has yet been yours.

I rely on your honour to regard this letter as confidential, and remain, though little known to you,

Your friend.

I must omit this friend's name; however, my reply went:

Chatham Prison, 5 January, 1871

Sir,

It is a poor thing to thank you in words, and I have no other way to thank you for your letter and very kind wishes for my welfare. Our experiences in life are, as you say, different, yet if we could speak our minds to each other, our views regarding Fenianism might not be as far apart as you think. I would expect your enlightened mind to regard me as it would the inhabitant of any other conquered country, and would allow you the right of the conqueror to maintain his conquest. But we cannot talk, and time or opportunity do not permit me to write thus, even if our acquaintance could warrant my communicating freely and candidly with you. I should wish to see Irishmen and Englishmen friends as well as neighbours. Nowadays, when mighty armies and weapons of destruction are before our eyes, and the possibility of their being used in the interests of tyranny so patent, I would much rather see, between the peoples of these islands, a strong bond of Union and Brotherhood such as would repel any thought of aggression, than see the ever-recurring efforts of the one to bind down the other. If English statesmen would turn their talents to our union, and not to our division, it would enlighten my exile.

I don't know how winds will drift me, but this you may be sure of, that no course will ever find me fostering ill-will between Englishmen and Irishmen; and if you, as a writer, make a similar endeavour to dissipate those prejudices which exist and seem to be by some influence cultivated between the two peoples, I will ever remember you with kindness.

I shall, as you desire, consider your letter a private one.

There is one matter of concern to me; I am leaving behind me, among our soldiers and the Manchester men, some whom I have influenced into the course which led to their imprisonment; and this cannot tend toward my rest. If I had time in the country, I intended to ask the Home Secretary if there were any conditions of release for these men. I thought that the government might altogether close this open sore of political prisoners in England. Could you do anything in the matter? If you could, I would ask you to meet me at the Cunard steamer in Queenstown on Sunday next.

P.S. A message has reached me from one of the prisoners, and here are his exact words: 'They have me nearly dead. I am now doing twenty days bread and water, and have no bed at night. My name is Dan Reddin; I am one of the Manchester men.' The man has repeatedly been under punishment. I am expected to make his case known when I get out of prison — and I honestly tell you, I have no desire to rush into print. I intend to speak to Mr Fagan today, with a view to his relaxing the discipline in this prisoner's case. Perhaps the most becoming way for me to do it is to lay this letter before him.

The 'Daniel Reddin' referred to was the young man who

became helplessly paralyzed in prison, and who tried to get an indictment against Dr Burns and other officials on account of the ill-treatment he received from them. The snow was thick on the ground at the time of my release; and he was obviously suffering acutely.

My correspondent did not meet me at Queenstown, but when I reached America I received a letter from him saying he was out of London when mine came. He wrote very kindly and promisingly. I would let you read it except it might betray who he was; and he had relied on my word of honour to regard that as confidential.

When I came to New York I was forced into public politics; and, as this was taking the course my correspondent would dissuade me from, I felt delicately about replying. I could not feel it manly to follow up the favours I expected from him in the release of the soldier prisoners; and, as this was the principal object of my letter to him, I did not reply to his. Could I have foreseen the little good I could do here for the cause of Irish independence, I would have taken a contrary course. I would rather look back now to the release of Johnny O'Brien or Sergeant McCarthy three years ago than to anything I have done, or seen done by Irishmen in America, to forward the cause of Irish revolution.

*   *   *   *   *

EVERYTHING HAVING BEEN made ready for our departure, we took a last look at our cells and descended to the courtyard. We made a request that Halpin be brought down so we could bid him adieu. He had refused to sign any conditions: he intended prosecuting the perjurers who swore against him as soon as he got out of prison, and signing a conditional paper would be signing away his right to do so. It was as painful a parting as you could imagine to see us in our broad-cloth bidding farewell to him in his convict grey.

We took our seats in coaches, two warders seating themselves with us; the deputy governor entered a gig; someone shouted 'All right!'; the prison gates swung on their hinges, and in a moment we were outside them; but though outside and on our way to freedom, yet were we prisoners still. In that land that affords a refuge to the political prisoners of all the world, there was no resting place for us — no freedom until we were placed beyond its boundaries.

We were driven to the railway station in Chatham, and, having been conducted into a carriage, saw the deputy governor enter the compartment next to ours, and the train started. Arriving in London, we were placed in coaches and driven to the station from whence the trains start for Liverpool. The deputy told us there was time for refreshments; if we liked, we could have some. We consented, and were conducted to a private room in the building. Here a table was already prepared for us. We had sandwiches, wine and ale. We ate, drank, and thanked the deputy, who, now that he wasn't a jailer, was a very amiable gentleman. He made himself as agreeable as possible, and telegraphed to have everything ready for him as he went along. Detectives were everywhere we made a stop or changed cars or coaches. It was deemed necessary to observe the greatest secrecy regarding our removal, lest any demonstrations should spring up along the way, and our escort did his best to hide us.

Having taken such a lunch as we had not enjoyed for five years and four months, we, with detectives behind and detectives before, were stealthily conducted to the train, and after a ride of several hours found ourselves in Liverpool. A crowd was at the station there, and Mulleda, who was well known by the Liverpool Irish, had lots of friends around him. Coaches were drawn up to receive us, and, as I stepped out to the platform, one man gave me his arm, and his kindness was imitated by another who saw I had another arm to spare. I thought that they were some of our friends, and we had a great laugh afterwards when we learned that they were detectives. Another hour's drive through Liverpool brought us to Merseyside, where a tugboat was waiting to convey us on board the steamship *Cuba*. She lay in the middle of the river, ready to sail the next morning. It was about ten when we got on board, and the deputy ordered a supper. We had a grand time of it. Ship's officers, convicts and jailers fraternized over the champagne. We retired to our berths about two in the morning, and the warders did duty over us by remaining up and keeping guard outside our doors.

At about nine o'clock, before the ship sailed, the deputy invited us into his room, and, laying five sovereigns before each one of us, said he had instructions to give us so much for pocket money. We took the English gold, and shook hands with the officer. He went back on the tugboat, and the *Cuba* steamed down the Mersey. But though the deputy had left us, his two deputies remained. We were prisoners still, and they had charge of us until we started for the Cove of Cork, where the ship was to take on the Irish mails.

Ireland once more! There she lay, with her hopes, and the high hopes of our youth, blasted. As we drew near to land, the jailers drew nearer to us, and we were reminded that we were not allowed to go ashore.

Twelve years before, I had lain in Cork's county jail, and this same harbour received the Neapolitan exiles who had broken loose from their jailers while at sea. Mr Gladstone championed them. He and all the English people were jubilant over their escape, and heartily welcomed their arrival in Ireland. Now, he is England's Prime Minister, and not only has he countenanced in his prisons the very treatment he vehemently condemned in the Neapolitan ones, but when we approach our native land on our way to banishment, he forbids us to set foot on its soil.

As soon as we cast anchor, police and detectives came on board to keep us to our quarters during the five or six hours we would be in harbour. The Cove pilot informed me that my wife had arrived in town the evening before, and I savoured the prospect of having her as a fellow passenger to America. Small boats came alongside, and in them I recognized two of my Portland companions, Pat Barry and Jerry O'Donovan, with several other of my old-country friends. None of them would be allowed on board, but as the mountain could not come to Mahomet, Mahomet went to the mountain; and, seeing Davey Riordan begging for leave and not being allowed to shake hands with me, I jumped over the side of the ship into their little boat. You'd think that this was the signal for an outbreak, such a commotion arose. Detectives ran here, jailers ran there, everyone ran somewhere; but after a handshake with my friends, I climbed back up the side of the ship and delivered myself into the hands of my keepers.

During the day, four or five crowded steamers from Cork came down river and kept hovering around our ship. The cheering was immense, and the enthusiasm showed us that the old cause was uppermost still in our people's hearts.

A committee presented clothes and money to us. They had an address for us also, but one of the conditions of allowing them to come on board was that this was not to be presented. My wife and my youngest child met me, and would accompany me to America.

*   *   *   *   *

APPROACHING NEW YORK, a pilot was taken on, and the newspapers he brought us showed us that, arrived in the New World, we would be in a very delicate situation. The Irish there were joyous at our release, and the politicians of the city were at their head. As our ship neared land, torches blazed and cannon boomed. 'Ship ahoy!' A government cutter. The ladder was let down; a portly gentleman stepped on board, and I was introduced to the Collector of the Port of New York. On behalf of the government of the United States he tendered me and my companions the welcome and hospitality of 'free America'. The government vessel was alongside to receive us, and accommodations had been engaged at Astor House.

I thanked him, but, as I was only one of five, desired the Collector to see the others with me. During our interview, some of the city fathers came on board from another craft, and, having met some of the other ex-prisoners, were tendering us a welcome and hospitality on behalf of the great city of New York. The city vessel was alongside also, and apartments had been engaged for us at the Metropolitan. The question of our reception had become a party fight! I found it impossible to get a word with one of my companions without half a dozen of the partisans from both sides bawling out, 'Rossa – this way,' and 'Rossa – that way!'

The Collector asked if he could have private words with me. I went with him to the captain's room, and he briefed me in somewhat this way: 'Mr O'Donovan, I'm an Irishman; not without some sympathy for your cause; and wish to see our people respected in their new home. I am pained at what you have witnessed here tonight. You have been years in prison; are banished from your native land. You turn your faces here, the national government has come to receive you; and a faction that for years has been degrading the character of our race steps in to create a disturbance. The Irish are glad of your release. But they have gotten into the hands of a party of thieves and swindlers who on every important occasion use them against the interests of the country; and, as you see tonight, to our common disgrace. Tammany Hall is not greater than the national government; and if you take a statesman-like view of the case, you and your friends will come on board the cutter with me.'

The door was burst in, and I was seized bodily and borne to the centre of the saloon section. Room was made for the five exiles to come together to receive an invitation of welcome from the municipal government. We were introduced to John Mitchel and Richard O'Gorman. And a scene developed that baffles description.

A college professor from the West who had sat at our table during the voyage whispered to me, 'Rossa, if I might offer an advice, it would be this: receive the invitation from the nation first. Let the government cutter receive you from the English ship, and let the national flag carry you to American soil; and when you are landed in the city, accept the other invitation if you wish.'

The increasing din, however, and the shouting and shoving forbade a quiet thought about anything. We saw acquaintances on both sides of the ship warmly contending. All of them were our friends, but the fight had waxed so warm that we saw we could not avoid making half of them our enemies if we accepted either of their invitations.

In the midst of the melée, Dr Carnochan, the health officer of the port, came and ordered the ship to be quarantined as there was a smallpox case on board, and no passengers could be allowed ashore till further orders. The health officer was from the Tammany side, and this was a vivid illustration of the party's tactics. If we accepted the national invitation, the health officer could not allow us to infect the city with smallpox; if we accepted the city's invitation, there mightn't be much danger from the contagion!

We asked time for consultation; were conceded it; decided we would go to a private hotel; and returned to the saloon and read the following reply to our would-be hosts:

To the members of the Several Receiving Deputations:
Gentlemen,

We thank you all for your invitations, and will try to accept all; but are only a few of many. Fellow prisoners are on the way, and we will take no public step until they arrive. You may look on us as representing the cause of Ireland, for the interest of which cause we desire that all the Irish should be united. It is painful to us to see so much disunion amongst yourselves. For that your reception affects us as individuals we care little compared with what we feel about its effect on Irish independence interests. And as you have not united cordially to receive us, we will not decide on anything until our brothers' arrival. We will remain on board tonight, and go to a hotel tomorrow.

Very respectfully,
Jer. O'Donovan Rossa
Charles U. O'Connell
John Devoy
John McClure
Henry S. Mulleda

If this did not please everyone or anyone, it calmed the elements, and the storm began to subside. The morning after our arrival we left the steamer and went to Sweeny's Hotel, telling the proprietor we would pay our own way, and requesting him not to receive money from anyone on that account. A sum of money 'for the exiles' had been subscribed prior to our arrival, which was in the hands of Mr O'Gorman. He presented us with fifteen thousand of it; and when we came to inquire about our hotel bill, found that it had been paid. Deputations, invitations, addresses and congratulations continued to pour in, and the hotel was besieged with visitors. Our hands became swollen and sore from handshaking. A most generous welcome, but we were heartily wishing that it would end.

We encountered many difficulties in our desire to steer clear of politics. Two phases of the mania were raging – the Irish and the American – and of the two, the former was the worst. Different sections of what was called the 'Fenian' element surrounded us, all calling loudly for 'union, union, union'. But when we turned our attention to their call, we found that the union each sect wanted was adhesion to itself. We were called upon by all to start something that would embrace all. If we did not do so, we were negligent. On leaving the prison we had decided not to become involved with the Fenian question here. But if we did not respond to the calls being made upon us, it would be said thereafter that we had shirked our duty. We started the Irish Confederation, with a platform broad enough to give standing room to every kind of Irish organization in the country; but the very men who called most loudly for action on our part were the first to set their faces against the success of our work. When they saw that they could not swallow us up, they raised the cry that the exiles were 'tyrannical' and 'wanted to control everything'; and this cry, in the interests of division and disorder, has continued to the present day.

When I saw that I could do no more in America than help to build another faction or party where so many existed, I gave up on the Confederation. I was disgusted with America's 'Irish politics', disgusted with hearing and seeing societies organizing to aid Irishmen in Ireland fight England, and not sending over one red cent. Worse than that – the men most energetic in calling for money to help 'the men at home' were cutting the throats of 'the men at home' by industriously circulating the lie that they were not fit to be entrusted with such funds.

This set me to thinking. I had stood as a freeman in an enslaved land. For this I had suffered six years imprisonment, and in prison had tried to keep my soul unshackled. Nursing a determination to retain my independence, I again found myself in a rebel's role.

In company one day, the conversation turned to the exiles'

reception; and, while admitting that the demonstrations were genuine, I asserted that, in the end, there was more of the American politician in them than of anything else. I also said that we Irish of New York are politicians before we are Irish. Not that this is wrong. The Irishman has done as much as any other man to make America. His sweat and blood are in its soil. And having no country of his own, he is bound more closely than other for-eigners to its institutions. So it is only natural he should take a keen interest in all that concerns the public where his lot is laid. But what I don't like to see here – and what I think I do see – is Irishmen kicking up their heels as if the country belonged to them.

In this company I speak of, Captain Tom Costello disputed what I had said about our people being more American than Irish, and I promised him I would test that out at the next election. Soon an opportunity presented itself. William Tweed represented the most Irish district of the city. His term of office had expired and he was up for re-election. I went to Collector Murphy and told him I would run against Tweed if he gave me support. He got me the nomination, and a thousand dollars; and I got seven thousand votes against Tweed's thirteen thousand. Tweed was thereafter charged with the robberies for which he is now doing ten years penal servitude. It was the Irish who elected him. I say it to show how much they are in the hands of those tricksters who use them to the shame and disgrace of our national reputation.

A cry was raised against me. I had gone against Tammany Hall, against the Irish; had done what no public Irishman had done before; was a renegade. A club of the Confederation in a southern city wrote saying they could not have confidence in contributing further money for Ireland while I was on the directorate. And I received several intimations that I had committed political suicide.

An Irishman, writing in *The Globe* of 6 November , 1871, said:

In a few years, O'Donovan Rossa has done more to bring about the disreputable state of Irish national sentiment than all the mishaps and blunders of ten years mismanagement of Fenian organizations. Is it not lamentable and pitiable that future efforts for Ireland's redemption by true men are marred and sullied by this man's stupidity?. Oh, Irish patriots and martyrs, how you and your great cause are blurred by the mercenary conduct of Rossa! His course in this matter has done more damage to Irish nationality, and more to destroy future confidence in so-called Irish patriots, than the treachery of all the perjured informers of hundreds of years! How absurd that a course of stubbornness on his part whilst in prison gained him a notoriety that, when free to act and perform, he had not the brains to guide his political conduct into a consistent and legitimate channel!. O'Donovan's work for Ireland is over and done, his political career passe; his grave is open, and will forever be closed on Tuesday next. What a name, what renown, what imperishable honours he and his country would have gained if England's bloody government had never pardoned him!

I opposed Tammany — the only party that ever gave representation to an Irishman. I was lost. 'My career was ended.' But I was satisfied, and the Irish here may be satisfied that while I live I will oppose Tammany while it disgraces the Irish character by the men she selects to represent us. John Mitchel is a consistent advocate on that side of the House for the last twenty years. Hostility to England's government of Ireland is the grand characteristic of the Irish spirit, and he is the grandest representative of that in America. Has Tammany taken him to represent the Irish people? No; he doesn't want such favours; they are not offered to him, but are given to men fit only to be the representatives of slaves; who, having Irish names and rowdy manners, degrade our character by presenting in their persons spurious examples of our manhood and intelligence.

I have had something to do with immigration since I came. I know that many are forced to leave the old land, but many more are deluded into coming. As an example: Con Callaghan comes to America, induced by letters written home by Mort Downing, who declared he was making a fortune. It becomes Con's turn to write home; and, as he was as good and industrious a man as Mort in the old land, he must stand equally well in reputation there; and he writes that he is making a fortune, too. Then, brother-in-law Johnny Shea must try his luck, and breaks up house and brings a large family to New York, assuming that his well-off friends here will help him. He takes his family bag-and-baggage to Con's or to Mort's, and finds them in a fourth-floor lodging. Johnny, in turn, must write home, and be as boastful as the others, so the deception continues. I have witnessed several cases of this kind within the past year, and have seen bitter looks of distress and disillusion when the friends subsequently met.

The Common Council of New York this week passed a resolution that no outsider coming to New York should be employed here while a six-month resident of the city was out of employment. Let this be taken to heart by my friends in Ireland who intend emigrating; and let them not be coming out here and going back disappointed, as so many have done this present year. There is plenty of room in this country for the oppressed peoples of all the world if they settle down on the land. But if they are not up to this or are otherwise unable, there is little here for them. My countrymen may hear and read about Irish immigrant-aid societies. But these are moneymaking concerns, and the newcomer arriving in New York impoverished or stricken by sickness finds himself miserable and pitiable, and no 'benevolent' society to lend him a dollar or a helping hand.

This is not as it should be. The Germans do better for their people; have organizations to help them out West. The Irish have only Tammany, and Tammany has governed these immigration departments for years to the enrichment of officeholders and the neglect of the immigrants' interests and those of the nation.

I have said that in running against Tweed I committed political suicide with the Irish; but I closed my career with an act that killed me entirely: I became a 'communard'. As the stories of such sudden deaths are somewhat tragic I will tell of mine.

While I was in prison in England, publicity regarding my treatment was the only protection I had for my life. There was a French exile in London named Gustave Flourens. He became interested in my case and translated an account of my treatment into French and German and had it published in the continental papers. This vexed England, and she conceded to the demand of public opinion the commission of inquiry that established the truth of our ill-treatment and led to our release.

When the French 'roubles broke out, Flourens went to France. After the war of the commune he was charged with having engaged in it, and he was shot. Rossell and others were also shot twelve months or more after the cessation of hostilities.

A commemoration was held in New York for these men, and, like many another, I went to view it. As I was standing on the corner of Fifth Street and the Bowery, General Ryan (lately murdered in Cuba), seeing me, came out of his carriage, and invited me inside. Weeks before, he had written me a letter offering himself and his sword should any fighting need to be done; and believing that he would fight in our cause and fight bravely – as bravely as, in the event, he died – I had respect for him.

Said he: 'Don't you disapprove of the shooting of those men in cold blood, now that that war is over?'

'I certainly do,' I said.

'Then is it afraid you are to take part in their commemoration on account of the cry of "mad dog" that has been raised against them? You know that that cry was raised against yourself.'

This nettled me. I bade 'good-day' to O'Feely Byron, who was with me. It was a cowardly thing to be afraid, when my conscience told me that my impulse was right. And with a 'Come on, then, General,' I went to my political grave.

ButI desire to take my leave with words of peace. My course in the old land has brought me the esteem of the people there. It is more than a reward for anything I have tried to do to uphold the Irish name. Anything I have done since I came to this country has been done in an effort to make my present and future life consistent with my past. I have made mistakes; will possibly make more. It is to enable my countrymen to judge justly of my conduct that I introduce this matter of the commune. Those who know me will need no explanation. Those who do not may read the following extract from one of Gustave Flourens' letters on my behalf:

The *Marseillaise* has already published a moving letter from this unfortunate victim of the English 'Liberals'. *The Irishman* has just published a second. This letter has been reproduced by the English *Standard*, which has accused us of inventing the first letter of the citizen Rossa.

I send you the translation of the letter published by *The Irishman*. All commentary is superfluous. At some steps from the splendid mansion from which the House of Lords governs England are to be witnessed atrocities that have no parallel even in the Neapolitan prisons of the Bourbons — the same prisons that so horrified Mr Gladstone.

I do not know Rossa, but I love him for his simplicity and the calmness and firmness with which he relates his frightful torture.

Gustave Flourens

The man who would run me down for going to that man's commemoration must indeed be very hard to please.

19. A Backward Glance, and a View Forward

TEN YEARS HAVE passed since I wrote the preceding chapter of this book; and that chapter showed that, in America, I had already gotten into trouble with the Irish people on account of my having become acquainted with General Ryan in connection with Irish revolutionary affairs. He has since fought and fallen, battling for the freedom of another oppressed people, in Cuba. But the unpopularity that visited me then from riding in the general's carriage at the 'communist' commemoration was as nothing to that which visits me now from my not being in the chariot that is to ride roughshod over landlordism and other agencies of English tyranny in Ireland without striking a blow. The lines of the Land League poet may be remembered:

Land for the landless

Land without striking a blow!

I'm sorry I cannot believe in getting liberty for Ireland so softly and sweetly; and sorry I forfeit the esteem of my people because of my firm adherence to the principle of all Irish patriots — that it is 'by the blows alone men strike in their strength that the chains of the tyrant can be broken'.

England now as ever is at her tyrant work in Ireland. Her Habeas Corpus Act is suspended for the fiftieth time in this century; her jails are filled with our people; her soldiers and police shoot down men, women and children; her janizaries break into newspaper offices, smash up type and machinery, and carry off to prison every one they catch on the premises.

And what remedy, what resistance? None; none save the appeals of the leaders in prison and out of prison to follow on with agitation on the line of 'passive resistance'; to 'keep the peace' and 'not to break the law'. It looks like emulating O'Connell, and cannot be better appraised than by a passage from John Mitchel's book, *The Last Conquest of Ireland*:

> The people believed in O'Connell's power, wisdom and truth. From his prison he sent weekly messages to the Repeal Association announcing that the independence of the country was never so certain; that he rejoiced to be imprisoned for Ireland; that above all he abjured the people to be peaceful and patient. Peaceful and patient they were! They kept the 'peace' as their 'Liberator' bade them; and the land was never as free from 'crime', lest they should 'give strength to the enemy'.

The leaders of the Land League in Ireland are in prison today. From their prisons they issue a manifesto to 'pay no rent' — a manifesto that Mitchel in '48 said would ensure a general resistance and rising of the Irish people against the enemy. But when no fight is meant now; when the leader says the man is a liar who says there is fight behind his movement, I can't see my way to the freedom of Ireland through that movement. Its treasurer has to take up his residence in Paris, and writes and telegraphs from there to America that the landlords of Ireland are 'completely under the feet of the tenantry'. But Irish papers and telegrams daily bring us news that evictions are taking place in every Irish county. If the Irish revolutionary element had preserved itself intact these few years past it would be prepared for the present crisis; for never in Irish history has the spirit of resistance to landlord law in Ireland been so general, and the uprising of one county, with a victory over the army of exterminators, been so likely to bring every county in Ireland to its feet.

Eleven years have passed since I left my last English prison. Since then I have endeavoured to continue with the previous purposes of my life. To further those aims, I have sought, since I came to America, admission to every society having an Irish name or an Irish object in view. I have been refused admission to some; have acquired membership in others; and am working today in the Council of the Fenian Brotherhood and in the Council of United Irishmen. And have been expelled from one Irish society, and been branded by that expulsion 'a traitor to Ireland', because I would not give up my association with the Brotherhood. And the society that expelled me claims to be the ultra-Irish revolutionary group in America!

With the history Irishmen have, or ought to have, by heart, it is surprising how easy it is to persuade them to expect redress of their grievances from the parliament of England — that parliament which has so often cajoled and deceived them, whose actual function it is to rivet the chains by which they are held in bondage. I don't know is it the innate slavery engendered in the Irish blood during seven-hundred years of subjection; I don't know what it is. But there it is — the people agitating for their rights, and sending good men to the London parliament to get them. It is, to my mind, the evasion and avoidance of what alone will ever get Irish rights from England — the fight and preparation for the fight.

All English statesmen and historians tell us it is fight alone will compel England to give up Ireland. The most able living one (James Anthony Froude) came to America seven or eight years ago, and told us England was never going to give up her hold of Ireland until she was beaten to her knees. I heard him say so. I believe him. But I also believe that the Irish people are able to beat England to her knees.

If Irishmen are to wage a successful war against England, they will have to fight England with her own weapons. Two years ago, England had a war in the Kaffir- and Zulu-lands; and, to bring the natives to their knees — with dynamite and other 'resources of civilization' as Gladstone calls them — blasted them in the very mountain caverns in which they had sought refuge. And two years ago, when Gladstone was out of office and in opposition to the Disraeli ministry, he said, speaking of Ireland, that an act of eviction was an act of war, tantamount to a sentence of death. Now, under his own ministry, those 'acts of war', those 'sentences of death', are executed in every Irish county.

A hundred years ago, America fought for independence against the oppressor of the nations, and, in the commencement of that fight, appealed to Ireland for assistance, and got it. In July 1775 the first Continental Congress met in Philadelphia, and issued to the Irish nation an appeal for assistance. Here are some of the words of that appeal:

> We are desirous of possessing the good opinion of the virtuous and humane. We are particularly desirous of furnishing you with the essence of our motives and objectives, the better to enable you to judge of our conduct and determine the merits of the controversy with accuracy and precision... You have ever been friendly to the rights of mankind, and we acknowledge with pleasure and gratitude that your nation has produced patriots who have nobly distinguished themselves in the cause of humanity in America.

And in that war of hers, America got from Irishmen the aid she asked; and in every war since, America got from Irishmen the aid she deserved; so much so that there is as much Irish blood fertilizing the tree of liberty in America today as there is of the blood of any other people.

Months ago, the newspapers of America contained telegrams to the effect that the English government had made a demand on the American government for the extradition of O'Donovan Rossa. A strange demand, considering that England paid my passage from an English convict prison to New York, having previously presented me with a parchment paper requiring that I not return to England, Ireland or Scotland during a period of twenty years. If Irishmen will turn their attention from 'agitation' to 'the resources of civilization', I'll be back to Ireland in spite of England before the twenty years are up.

The fight goes on as I write. Irishmen are learning that England has to be stricken to her knees before she will surrender anything she has once seized.

'If it was only a barren rock in the middle of the trackless ocean,' said Lord Palmerston forty years ago, 'that England got possession of by force, she will never surrender it without being confronted by force.'

I shall put on record here the policy of action that eventually will bring England to her knees. It has been acted upon by Irishmen during the past two years as far as means will permit; and is creating considerable alarm in England.

What Ireland Can Do

The policy and program of action laid down by a Catholic priest and adopted by the United Society of the Fenian Brotherhood, the Advanced Nationalists, and the United Irishmen.

The freedom of Ireland implies the reduction of England to a position much inferior to that which she had occupied for centuries. It very probably would entail the loss of her Asiatic and African possessions, and the total separation from her of all her colonies. England is preeminently the hypocrite, the robber, the perjurer, the murderer, the pirate of the universe; but her well-educated leaders have always been remarkable for their perspicacity, and for their devotion to the interests of a country that has shed enough blood to drown in one great sea all the English on this planet.

These reflections make it plain that England cannot consent to Ireland's freedom; and that violence alone must establish that freedom if it is to exist. These propositions I consider axiomatic.

Ignorance is impotence. There never was a nation better acquainted with this fact than England; and she has used it to make Ireland incapable of resistance. She has not only darkened the intellects of the Irish people by reducing them to a state of gross ignorance, but has thereby made it easy for impostors to delude their consciences. The Irishman's property is in slavery; his conscience, in the matter of his country, is in slavery. England thoroughly understands that emancipation of the Irish intellect and conscience would very promptly terminate that thralldom. Unable to keep the Irishman of the present day wholly illiterate, she represents the history of his own country as a farrago of nonsense and barbarity, and diverts him from inquiry into Irish matters to the study of her annals, which she teaches him to regard as the inspirers of noble thoughts and the prompters of glorious achievements.

No nation can become or remain free in which self-reliance is not a national characteristic. England has always laboured with extreme earnestness and persistence, and with some success, to eradicate this quality from the Irish character. She is daily repeating to the Irish people what she has been saying to them for centuries, that there is some radical imperfection in their character; and that by reason of it they are incapable of autonomy.

That there are dissensions among the Irish people is not remarkable; that they are not a thousand times as sharp and numerous is prodigious. For centuries, England has been sowing them with all the might of her sovereigns, her parliaments, her armies, her preachers, her orators, her writers and her dupes. She has omitted no crime, spared no money, wavered before no hardship, to attain success; yet England screams today for help against those whom she pretends to mock as incapable of anything but dissension.

The Germans slaughtered one another, with the aid of foreigners often, for thirty consecutive years; the French have horrified mankind with their internecine wars; other continental nations have drenched their soils with the blood of their countrymen. In these United States, immense consanguineous armies have shed rivers of blood, brothers not rarely meeting in deadly conflict. The surface of England herself was for centuries scarlet with the blood of civil war. Yet she tells us that these melancholy spectacles are not evidence of incompetence. The Irish have not spilled their proportion of blood in civil strife; nevertheless, England and her hirelings and dupes assure us that they are more given to bloody dissensions than their neighbours, hence are unfit for freedom. This monstrous lie, unremittingly inculcated, causes honest Irish hearts to question the wisdom of violent proceedings to recover Irish liberty. Its exposure would substitute courage for fear, resolution for indecision, and confidence for faintheartedness. Ireland, enlightened and virtuous, cannot be kept in slavery. God save her!

The clergyman who wrote that for the Society of United Irishmen is a parish priest officiating in the United States. An exemplary man of peace, he knows that Ireland can never free herself from England without war.

O'Connell, too, was a man of peace, but in his indignation would cry out that 'they who would be free, themselves must strike the blow.' And at a banquet in Cork City in 1843, in the presence of priests and people, he said:

> Suppose some penniless, shoeless Irishman who made his way across the Channel on the deck of a steamer, found himself in Manchester or St Giles, and collected a number of Irishmen about him, and one was to ask him, 'What news?'; to which he would reply, 'Your father was cut down by a dragoon; your mother was shot by a policeman; or your sister — I will not say what has befallen her'. Let this happen, and I will ask Peel: 'How many fires would blaze in the manufactories of England?'

Those very outrages occurred in Ireland this year. A policeman drove his bayonet through the body of Ellen MacDonough in Belmullet. The manufactories of England did not blaze then to any great extent. I hope they will soon, and keep blazing till England is convinced she will lose more than she can gain by holding Ireland.

As this book will live longer than I shall, I include in it some articles from the *United Irishman* of the week in which I am writing, so that men of the future may judge how the battle of Ireland was going in the year 1882.

Jawbreakers

'Twas a coal torpedo at first; and an infernal machine secondly, that blew up the *Doterel*. Then, 'twas nothing but spontaneous combustion that blew her up, and no one was to blame. But the ghost of the *Doterel* is still haunting the minds of the English ministers, and cannot be laid while the vengeance of the 'Irish skirmishers' lives. The inquiry into the destruction of the *Doterel* seems not yet to be ended; and all the jawbreakers in the dictionary of modern science are brought into use to account for what smashed her jaws.

One telegram yesterday says 'xerotine siccatine' did it; and the *Tribune* this morning says:

The statement of the survivors of the British sloop of war *Doterel* (blown up in the Straits of Magellan in April last), which the commander in chief at Portsmouth has forwarded to the Admiralty, shows that heuotine siccative, similar to that which exploded on the flagship *Triumph* on the Pacific station recently, was the cause of the disaster.

A *Sun* reporter asked Mr Rossa what this 'siccatine' or 'siccative' was. Rossa took out a large envelope marked 'For Skirmishers', and read a letter in which the writer said, 'The medicine will act in five minutes or six hours, as desired.'

'This siccatine,' said Rossa, 'can be put in a bottle; and is safe unless the bottle is cracked. Then, it explodes and burns. The Skirmishers in England and Ireland have other materials besides bombs and torpedoes. The English knew that this explosive was used, and sought to hide the fact. This siccatine is a terrible thing – worse than this.' And Rossa showed us a small iron bomb.

Well, we are in a position to prove that xerotine siccatine was not the cause of the disaster; and if England will appoint a commission, and get permission from President Arthur to have that commission sit in New York, we'll summon evidence to show that it was not xerotine siccatine struck the blow – provided England pays all the expenses. The Irish people will yet make her pay dearly for the tyrant game she is playing in Ireland, and sicken her with something bitterer still than 'siccatine'.

The London *Herald* reported a similar story on 15 January, 1882:

Referring to the explosion of an infernal machine on board the steamship *Oxenholme*, the *Daily News* New York correspondent has telegraphed the following:

O'Donovan Rossa says he is not surprised to hear this. Irishmen in England and Ireland are determined to blow up anything English at every opportunity. He has no doubt that the machines were put on board at Liverpool with intent to destroy the vessel, but he has no direct knowledge, because he cannot tell when the men in Ireland intend to strike. 'We send them money,' he adds, 'and means to work with; and they use them as they think best. We will continue to use the machines till England does Ireland justice. This is only one instance. The *Doterel* was another. I know that the *Doterel* was blown up by an infernal machine.'

Its sister paper, the New York *Herald*, responded:

It will be observed from one of our cabled dispatches that the American correspondent of the *Daily News* is striving to propagate the impression in Great Britain that that Irish knave, O'Donovan Rossa, is a person of large influence in the United States. But it is safe to affirm that there are not a dozen decent persons in the country who would ever know of the blatherskite's bluster, but for the undue prominence which this correspondent and fellows of his sort have given it. No respectable part of the community cares what Rossa says. And the man himself is undeserving even of notoriety until, like Guiteau, he meets his fate some day at the end of a hangman's rope. That such will be his fate if he does not accomplish a cowardly evasion of justice, we cannot doubt; and we think he deserves it as richly as Guiteau does. But while no decent persons here care what Rossa says, they do care that reputable British newspapers like the *Daily News* should permit their American correspondents to cable such trash to them.

What rigmarole the New York/English organ-grinder flings! But this abuse by a prostitute doesn't trouble us. The English press of America used to say a hundred years ago that George Washington was a scoundrel deserving of the hangman's rope; and England employed Hessians and Indians to get his scalp. We see now that Gladstone is disposed to introduce in this session of parliament a measure of 'home rule' that 'will astonish the natives'. We thoroughly understand this game. It is not Gladstone's home rule we want, but none of Gladstone's rule. And we'll have that before five years if the Irishmen now wasting their energies on parliamentary agitation only turn a little of their attention and assistance to the skirmishing work. 'Tis of that that Gladstone is afraid!

On 27 January, 1882, the customs authorities seized two tons of the *United Irishman* on its arrival at Folkestone. The work that England fears most is the work Irishmen should study and practice most. England dreads secret organizations, dreads that the Irish people may carry the war into England. I believe in the efficacy of both to make England do justice to Ireland. I believe with John Mitchel that for all Ireland's wrongs, her artificial famines, packed juries, perjured judges and grinding landlords, there is but one remedy – the edge of the sword.

And with Mitchel's teaching before our eyes, and O'Connell's failure, we are back in the rut of 'moral force' and 'parliamentary agitation'. And here are the men who are 'gone with a vengeance' – the men who, it was prophesied, would return with a vengeance – expending their energies to reason England out of Ireland, show her up to the world as a monster of injustice, and make her so ashamed of herself that she will come to her knees and cry *'Peccavi!'* As well reason with a tiger that has his fangs in the body of his prey.

The most painful thing to me in finishing this chapter is to see by the papers that evictions are still taking place in every Irish county. England wants to exterminate us; and while we submit to the process peacefully and without retaliation, the land is dead, no matter how loud the agitation in it. Mitchel, after describing an eviction, says in his *Last Conquest*:

> It is but fair to tell that sometimes an ejecting landlord or agent was shot by desperate, houseless men. What wonder? There were not half enough of them shot. If the people had

not been too gentle, forgiving and submissive, their island could never have become a horror and a scandal to the earth.

Things must change; the people must change. My faith is strong. It is possible I will write another book if I live long enough. As secretary of the Fenian Brotherhood I have present possession of its papers, and the Council will give me permission to use them. Outside of Mr Stephens, I know as much about the movement in England as any other man living. Publisher Kennedy has made me an offer for the book, and I'll write it.

Appendix A

CONFLICTING TESTIMONY ON THE MANACLING OF O'DONOVAN ROSSA; FROM REPORTAGE IN *THE IRISHMAN* OF 12 JUNE, 1869.

The Treatment of O'Donovan Rossa

Reply of the government and prison officials to Sir John Gray's question in the House of Commons:

Last Friday week, Sir John Gray asked the Secretary for Home Affairs the following question, notice of which he had given two days previously:

> Whether the Secretary's attention had been directed to the statement to the effect that the prison authorities so secured the hands of one of the political prisoners by manacles behind his back that he could neither dress nor undress, or raise food to his mouth; and continued this cruelty for thirty-five days. And, if the statement was true, was the circumstance reported to the Home Office; and was there an objection to placing the report before the House, with a statement as to whether the officer guilty of this cruelty was reprimanded or otherwise dealt with, and how?

Mr Bruce, Home Secretary, replied (in part):

> I am obliged to my honourable friend for making this inquiry, for it is clear that the statement, if true, ought to be explained; if not true, ought to be contradicted. The facts ... are these. On June 17 he was reported for throwing the contents of his cell pot in the governor's face, when under punishment in the 'separate cells'. The prisoner, having committed these acts of violence, and being a very powerful man — so powerful it required three or four warders to master him — was for a while manacled with his hands

behind his back. But, so far from being kept in this condition for thirty-five days, he was only so for a part of a day.

Rossa's review of page 59 of the report of Lord Devon and his brother commissioners focused on a letter from Chatham Prison dated 4 June , 1869, viz:

Wm. Fagan, Esq.

Sir,

With reference to your telegram requesting to know how many days Reg. No. 9549 (O'Donovan Rossa) was placed in handcuffs after his assault on me, I have the honour to inform you that he was placed in them on the morning of June 17th and kept in them each successive day (as a measure of precaution to prevent his repeating a similar act when visited by myself or an officer of the prison) till the 20th of July; the handcuffs being invariably removed each day at 7:45 PM, and not being replaced till the following morning.

T. F. Powell, Governor.

Rossa comments:

'There is no doubt but that this information was required for the Home Secretary, and that he had it in his possession the same evening he made his statement in the House... But, should any of my jury hesitate, I will not yet press for Mr Bruce's conviction. I will give the Secretary three additional weeks to get the information from the Board of Prison Directors, and will direct the jury's attention to another session in the Commons on the evening of 29 June. I quote from *The Irishman* of July 3rd:

George Henry Moore (a member of the House), having reason to doubt the truth of the reply given to Sir John Gray, introduced the subject a second time. 'I have been furnished with a formal deposition corroborating the original statements in all their essential particulars. It has been sent to me by Messrs. Merriman, solicitors of this city, who state in their letter that they have taken it down from the deponent's own lips, and here it is:

'Joseph Kay, of 16 Cross Street, Palace Road, Hackney, late assistant-warder from 5 April, 1865, to 5 November, 1868, states that the prisoner Rossa, in the months of June and July 1868 was handcuffed for about six weeks...with his hands behind him, from 10 minutes past 5AM till 7:30PM, his hands being removed to in front of him, though still handcuffed, while he took his meals. The first meal, the breakfast, occupied from 5:30 till 6AM; dinner from 12:15 till 1:15PM; supper. 6:15 till 6:45PM; and at 7:30 the handcuffs were removed on his going to bed. During the whole of these six weeks he was confined in a separate cell, with the handcuffs on him behind his back, except when partaking of his meals.

'This statement is quite inconsistent with the contradiction stated by the Secretary to the House. I trust that the Minister will cause such inquiry to be made into the matter as will elicit the truth.'

To which, Secretary Bruce answered that two or three days ago, the honourable member gave notice that he intended to controvert the statements made on this subject in the House. He (the Secretary) applied to the honourable member for the name of his informant, but he declined to give it.

Mr Moore interjected: 'I had no permission to give the name.'

Secretary Bruce continued that he gathered from the statement of the honourable member that his informant was a warder who had been dismissed; but, if his name had been supplied, he could have made inquiries as to the reasons for his dismissal and whether his testimony could safely be received. At this Mr Moore declared, 'I know nothing about it.' Nevertheless, the Secretary presumed he must have left the establishment in November, as the circumstances of which he spoke occurred between June and November, 1868.

It certainly would have been more satisfactory if the honourable member had given him an opportunity of inquiring into the character of his witness, he said. He believed in preference the testimony of the governor and deputy governor.

Appendix B

ROSSA'S 'PATENT OF PARDON'

Chatham Prison, 5 January, 1871

VICTORIA, by the grace of God, of the United Kingdom of Great Britain and Ireland, Queen Defender of the Faith and so forth, to all to whom these presents shall come – Greeting!

Whereas at a Special Commission of Oyer and Terminer and General Jail Delivery, holden at Dublin in and for the County and City of Dublin on the eighteenth day of December in the year of Our Lord, one thousand eight hundred and sixty-five, Jeremiah O'Donovan Rossa, late of Skibbereen in the County of Cork, was in a lawful manner indicted, tried, and found guilty of certain felonies, and was duly sentenced to be kept in penal servitude for the term of his natural life; and whereas, in consideration of circumstances humbly represented to us on behalf of said Jeremiah O'Donovan Rossa, we have thought fit, on the conditions hereinafter contained and expressed, to extend our Royal mercy unto the said O'Donovan Rossa. Know ye, therefore, that on the conditions hereinafter contained and expressed, we of our special grace, certain knowledge, and mere motion by and with the advice and consent of our right trusty and well beloved cousin and councillor, John Poyntz, Earl Spencer, KG, our Lieutenant General and General Governor of that part of our United Kingdom called Ireland; and according to the tenor and effect of our letter under our royal signature, bearing date at our court at St James' the thirty-first day of December in the thirty-fourth year of our reign, and now enrolled in the Record and Writ Office of our High Court of Chancery in Ireland aforesaid, have pardoned, remit and release, the same Jeremiah O'Donovan Rossa, or by whatever other names or additions of name, office, art, mystery or place the said O'Donovan Rossa is known, called or named, from the felonies of which he stands convicted as aforesaid, and all the singular convictions and attainders thereupon; and, save as hereinafter mentioned, all pains, penalties and forfeitures thereby by him incurred as aforesaid, or incident to or consequent upon the said felonies or any of them, or the commission thereof, or the judgment had thereupon as aforesaid; and our firm peace to him for the same.

We, on the conditions hereinafter contained and expressed, do give and grant by these presents, forbidding that the said Jeremiah O'Donovan Rossa, by the justices, sheriffs, escheators, bailiffs, coroners, or other officers or ministers, or our heirs or successors on the occasion aforesaid, may be molested, disturbed, or in any way aggrieved for the same, so that on the conditions hereinafter contained and expressed, he, the said Jeremiah O'Donovan Rossa, may stand in open court, if any person against him shall be willing to speak on the occasion aforesaid. And our further will is, and by these presents, for us and our heirs and successors, we do grant, that these our letters patent, or the enrollment thereof, shall in all things be firm, good, valid, sufficient and effectual in the law, and shall be as well to the said justices and sheriffs, escheators, bailiffs and coroners, as to all the other officers and successors, a sufficient warrant and discharge in that behalf.

Provided always, and it is hereby declared, that these our letters patent be enrolled in the Record and Writ Office of our High Court of Chancery in Ireland aforesaid, within the space of six calendar months next ensuing the date of these presents. And further, that the said Jeremiah O'Donovan Rossa shall forthwith depart out of the United Kingdom of Great Britain and Ireland, and shall remain out of the said United Kingdom for the space of twenty years from the date of these presents. And further, that the said O'Donovan Rossa shall not, during the said space of twenty years exercise, or attempt to exercise, within the said United Kingdom, any capacity, right, access or privilege, of which he was or has been deprived, or which was or has been lost, forfeited or extinguished or suspended by the felonies aforesaid, or any of them, or by reason of his having committed the same felonies, or any of them, or been convicted of, or adjudged guilty of, or sentenced or attained for, such felonies or any of them.

In witness whereof, we have caused these our letters to be made patent. Witness, John Poyntz, Earl Spencer, our Lieutenant General and General Governor of Ireland, at Dublin, the third day of January in the thirty-fourth year of our reign.

Enrolled in the Record and Writ Office of Her Majesty's High Court of Chancery in Ireland, on the third day of January, one thousand eight hundred and seventy-one.

M. J. Brady, A.C.R. & W. (Attest)
Ralph Cusack, Clerk of the Crown and Hanaper

Appendix C

Bourke, General T.F. Born in County Tipperary. He went to the US as a boy. Fought on the Confederate side in the Civil War. Returned to Ireland for the projected Fenian rising. Captured, he was sentenced to death. Sentence was commuted. After his release he became a well-known speaker at Fenian gatherings in America.

Burke, Colonel Ricard O'Sullivan. Born in County Cork. He organized Fenian groups in the US army during the American Civil War. Organized the rescue of Colonel Tom Kelly and Captain Tim Deasy in Manchester, in course of which a British police-sergeant was killed, and in consequence of which 'the noble hearted three' (Allen, Larkin and O'Brien) were hanged. Many were killed in the attempt to rescue him from Clerkenwell Prison. On his return to the US he continued his Fenian activities.

Costello, Augustine. Irish-born officer in the US army. He came to Ireland with arms on the *Erin's Hope*, in 1865. Was captured, and sentenced to fifteen years penal servitude.

Davis, Thomas. Poet, and a founding organizer and principal writer for *The Nation* .

Devoy, John. As a young man, he joined the French Foreign Legion. Was in charge of recruiting and organizing Fenian militants in British army units in Ireland. After his release (with Rossa) from Chatham Prison, he went to America and devoted the remainder of his life to the Irish cause. Was active in endeavours to obtain arms and assistance from the German High Command in the World War I period. Described by Padraig Pearse as 'the greatest of the Fenians'.

Downing, Colonel P.J. One of three brothers who were friends of Rossa and other leading Fenians in Cork and Kerry. He served in Thomas Meagher's 'Irish Brigade' in the American Civil War.

Duffy, Charles Gavan. With Davis, was joint founder and editor of *The Nation*. One of the leading spirits of the Young Ireland movement. Was tried and acquitted four times for his part in the 1848 rising. Subsequently became Prime Minister of Victoria, Australia.

Duffy, Edward ('Ned'). Native of West Roscommon. Organizer for, and aide of, 'Head Fenian Centre' James Stephens. Died, assertedly of ill-treatment, in Millbank Prison.

Emmet, Robert. Leader of the 1803 rising. Hanged publicly in Dublin after his famous speech from the dock, ending, 'When my country takes her place among the nations of the earth, then, and not till then, let my epitaph be written.'

Fitzgerald, Lord Edward. One of the best-loved leaders of the United Irishmen in 1798. Son of the Duke of Leinster, he became a convert to Wolfe Tone's Irish Republicanism. Died of a wound he received resisting capture.

Halpin, Colonel William. Served in the US army. Was a member of the military council of the Irish Republican Brotherhood. Came on a mission to Ireland ahead of the *Erin's Hope* expedition. Was still serving his sentence when Rossa and others of 'the Cuba Five' were released.

Keogh, Judge William. Born in County Galway. Developed much popularity as a champion in parliament of Irish and Catholic rights. In a turn-around sensation in 1852, he accepted the post of Solicitor-General in return for his support for the British government in Ireland. Became the most hated figure in that land because of his harsh attitudes toward, and sentences of, Fenian defendants. He began to show signs of mental instability after a financial scandal involving him and a close associate, John Sadlier. Committed suicide.

Kickham, Charles. Poet, novelist, and lifelong Fenian. His health was ruined from his prison experiences. He was a fellow inmate with Rossa in Pentonville and Portland; and Chairman of the supreme council of the Irish Republican Brotherhood at the time of his death in 1882. His hearing and sight had been severely impaired by a childhood accident with gunpowder.

Luby, Thomas Clarke. Son of a Church of Ireland clergyman. Was involved in the 1848 rising. Founder-member of the Irish Republican Brotherhood, for which he formulated the membership oath. Journalist and author. After his release he settled in the USA., continuing his Fenian activities. Supported O'Donovan Rossa's 'Skirmisher' efforts.

McCafferty, Captain John. Born in Ohio of Irish parents. In course of a colourful career as a guerrilla officer in the Confederate army, he became a Fenian. Came to Ireland for what he hoped would be a Fenian rising, but was arrested. Was released on condition that he go back to the US. He returned to Ireland, however, when a subsequent rising became imminent. Organized the raid on the Chester Castle armoury. His death sentence was commuted to servitude for life. Was released and deported in 1871. Once proposed a plan (which was rejected) to kidnap the Prince of Wales and hold him hostage until remaining Fenian prisoners would be released.

McCarthy, Sergeant Charles. Decorated twice for bravery during the Indian Mutiny. Sentenced to life servitude for having sworn soldiers into the Fenian movement. Was released after twelve years, his health broken. Two days later, at a breakfast meeting with Charles Stewart Parnell, he died suddenly. At the inquest, the jury returned a verdict of death from heart disease aggravated by his prison treatment.

McClure, Captain John. Born near New York of Irish parents. Served in the American Civil War. Had a leading part in the 1867 Fenian Rising, and was captured after a running battle at Kilclooney Wood. Sentenced to life imprisonment. Was released with Rossa in 1871.

Mitchel, John. Son of a Presbyterian minister from County Derry. Preached revolution in the columns of the United Irishman, which he had founded. Transported to Van Diemen's Land, he subsequently escaped, and got to the USA. He wrote Jail Journal, a classic of prison literature.

Mulleda, Henry S. Functioned as Ricard O'Sullivan Burke's assistant in arms purchases. Was involved in an attempted rising by Drogheda Fenians which failed because of the non-arrival of expected arms. Received a seven-year sentence.

O'Brien, William Smith. A Protestant landlord of County Clare and a member of parliament. Converted to nationalism, and was a leader of the 1848 Rising. Sentenced to penal servitude for life. Served five years in Van Diemen's Land.

O'Connell, Charles Underwood. Born in County Offaly. Served in the American Civil War. Became a Fenian, and was arrested upon landing at Cobh in 1865 with papers entrusted to him by James Stephens. Sentenced to ten years penal servitude.

O'Connor, James. Wicklow-born journalist. member of the staff of the Irish People . Sentenced to ten years. Was an IRB envoy to the USA in 1870. He took a prominent part in subsequent land agitation, and was imprisoned again in 1881. A member of parliament for many years.

O'Leary, John. One of the 'towering figures' of Fenianism, and a veteran of the '48 Rising. Associated with Rossa *et al* in the publication of the *Irish People*. Upon release from prison he lived for some years in Paris. As president of the supreme council of the IRB, he refused compromises with constitutionalism. A man of impressive literary capacity, he influenced many younger writers.

O'Leary, Patrick ('Pagan'). Born in County Cork. Went to the USA where he abandoned theological studies to fight in the Mexican War. A head wound was said to have been the cause of his later eccentric behaviour. He abandoned his Christian name, and insisted on being called 'Pagan'. He returned to Ireland as a recruiting officer for the IRB and was said to have recruited 'thousands of soldiers' into that organization (many of them serving in the British army). Was arrested in the act of administering the IRB oath to a soldier on the Bridge of Athlone, and drew seven years servitude.

O'Mahony, John. Scholar and revolutionary. Veteran of the '48 Rising, and a founder of the Fenian movement. Principally active in the American branch of the movement, and during the Civil War raised a Fenian regiment in the Northern army.

St Clair, Edward Pillsworth. Born in an English army barracks, son of an Irish troop-sergeant. Became a Fenian in London. Served with Garibaldi in Italy. Was a Fenian organizer in the British army. Sentenced to ten years penal servitude, he was released in 1871, and went to the U.S.

Stephens, James. 'The greatest power (for a time) in Fenianism,' the other of comparable stature, perhaps, being O'Mahony. Unquestionably, he had extraordinary talent for organization and conspiracy, and was regarded as important enough to be spirited out of Richmond Prison (Dublin) following the general round-up of Fenian eminents in 1865. Subsequently, however, he was accused of vacillating and failing to measure up to his leadership responsibilities. He left for France at the end of January, 1867, and spent the rest of his career there.

Tone, Theobald Wolfe. Co-founder of the Society of United Irishmen in 1791. A man of broad views and nationalist theory, he could well be regarded as the leading spirit of modern Irish republicanism. Died in prison from a deep wound in the neck – attributable, his son was convinced, to foul play by his military captors. Two days before, he had been sentenced to be hanged for his part in the '98 Rising.

Warren, Colonel John. A native of County Cork, he had taken out US citizenship. He was arrested after landing in the *Erin's Hope.* Demanded to be tried as a citizen of that country, but when his demand was refused, abandoned his defence, and was sentenced to fifteen years. Eventually, he was released on a writ of error.

CAGE ELEVEN
GERRY ADAMS

Gerry Adams was interned without trial on the Maidstone prison ship and in Long Kesh during the 1970s. Twice sentenced for attempting to escape from internment, he served most of his time as a sentenced prisoner in Cage Eleven of Long Kesh.

Cage Eleven is his own account – sometimes passionate, often humourous – of life in Long Kesh, of the 'screws', of the daily techniques of getting by and, above all, of his fellow prisoners.

The *Sunday Press* (Dublin) found it 'wry, humourous, passionate and self-mocking... It will never win the Booker prize but when the work of most of the participants in literature's yearly orgy of hype and hysteria has been consigned to history, Adams's slim volume will still be alive and well.' In England the *New Worker* wrote that 'Fortunately for the reader Gerry Adams, unlike many politicians, is a very good writer;' while the *Socialist Worker* described it is 'immensely readable... shows the tragedy of British rule in Ireland.'

Since 1983 Gerry Adams has been MP for West Belfast and President of Sinn Féin. He is also author of *Falls Memories*, *The Politics of Irish Freedom* and *A Pathway to Peace*.

Paperback £4.95
ISBN 0 86322 114 9

SECOND CLASS TAXI
SYLVESTER STEIN

'The first satirical novel written about apartheid... a great book.'
Cape Argus

'Both comical and sad... well worth reading for a lighter look at the whole situation.' *Anti-Apartheid News*

'Very funny... a delight to read.' *Rand Daily Mail*
'The first and one of the best satirical novels about the daftness and the pain of apartheid... clothed in a robust Dickension humour that stretches from savagery to affection.' *Guardian*

'The satire is quite outstandingly brilliant.' *News Letter*

'In face of all the strong feelings about apartheid, it is a daring experiment to try to be funny about it, but this book succeeds.'
Glasgow Herald

'You will remember this book when many more serious ones on the subject are forgotten.' Elizabeth Bowen, *The Tatler*

Paperback £4.95
ISBN 0 86322 117 3

A GOLDEN TREASURY OF IRISH POETRY A.D. 600 to 1200

EDITED AND WITH TRANSLATIONS BY
DAVID GREENE & FRANK O'CONNOR

These poems we have edited for the general reader only, and consulted only our own pleasure in the poetry when deciding which poems to include and which verses to omit.

In this collection from the greatest period of Irish poetry Frank O'Connor and David Greene edited a large selection of poems of the period with imaginative scholarship, providing prose translations of each poem.

'Mr. O'Connor is a translator in the class of Rossetti, Pound or Waley.' *Times Literary Supplement.*

Paperback £9.95
ISBN 0 86322 113 0

WEST OF WEST
BRIAN LALOR

'*The eye he turns on this beautiful and much-loved area is always perceptive, often very witty, sometimes a little jaundiced, but always true to the essential spirit of the place and its people.*' CORK EXAMINER

The beautiful landscape of West Cork in the south of Ireland has attracted many artists and writers from Holland, Germany, the United States, England, and other countries – people who have settled in the area and created a vibrant artistic community.

One of those who came to live in West Cork was Brian Lalor. Born in the east of the same county, he had studied in England and Greece and had become an archaeologist specializing in ancient buildings on French, British, American and Israeli excavations.

This fascinating account of the fourteen years he spent in West Cork is paralleled by more than ninety etchings of the locality.

Paperback £9.95
ISBN 0 86322 109 2